Headline
Diplomacy

Headline Diplomacy

How News Coverage Affects Foreign Policy

Philip Seib

Praeger Series in Political Communication

PRAEGER

Westport, Connecticut
London

Library of Congress Cataloging-in-Publication Data

Seib, Philip M., [date]
    Headline diplomacy : how news coverage affects foreign policy /
    Philip Seib.
        p.   cm.—(Praeger series in political communication, ISSN
    1062–5623)
    Includes bibliographical references and index.
    ISBN 0–275–95374–2 (hardcover : alk. paper).—ISBN 0–275–95375–0
    (pbk. : alk. paper)
    1. Foreign news—United States. 2. Press and politics—United
    States. 3. United States—Foreign relations—1945–1989. 4. United
    States—Foreign relations—1989– I. Title. II. Series.
    PN4888.F69S45   1997
    070.4′332′0973—dc20   96–21520

British Library Cataloguing in Publication Data is available.

Library of Congress Catalog Card Number: 96–21520
ISBN: 0–275–95374–2
    0–275–95375–0 (pbk.)
ISSN: 1062–5623

First published in 1997

Praeger Publishers, 88 Post Road West, Westport, CT 06881
An imprint of Greenwood Publishing Group, Inc.

Printed in the United States of America

∞™

The paper used in this book complies with the
Permanent Paper Standard issued by the National
Information Standards Organization (Z39.48–1984).

P

Copyright Acknowledgments

The author and publisher gratefully acknowledge permission for use of the following material:

Excerpts from *Big Story*, by Peter Braestrup. Novato, California: Presidio, 1994. Used by permission of
the publisher.

Excerpts from "Real-Time Television Coverage of Armed Conflicts and Diplomatic Crises," by Nik
Gowing. Working Paper 94–1, Joan Shorenstein Barone Center, John F. Kennedy School of Government,
Harvard University, June, 1994. Used by permission.

Excerpts from "A Television Plan for the Next War," by Lawrence Grossman. *Nieman Reports*, Summer
1991. Used by permission of the Nieman Foundation.

Excerpts from *Somalia, Rwanda, and Beyond: The Role of the International Media in Wars and
Humanitarian Crises*, Edward R. Girardet, ed. *Crosslines* Special Report 1. Dublin: *Crosslines Global
Report* and the Italian Academy for Advanced Studies at Columbia University, 1995. Used by permission.

for Christine

Contents

Series Foreword

Those of us from the discipline of communication studies have long believed that communication is prior to all other fields of inquiry. In several other forums I have argued that the essence of politics is "talk" or human interaction.[1] Such interaction may be formal or informal, verbal or nonverbal, public or private, but it is always persuasive, forcing us consciously or subconsciously to interpret, to evaluate, and to act. Communication is the vehicle for human action.

From this perspective, it is not surprising that Aristotle recognized the natural kinship of politics and communication in his writings *Politics* and *Rhetoric*. In the former, he established that humans are "political beings [who] alone of the animals [are] furnished with the faculty of language."[2] And in the latter, he begins his systematic analysis of discourse by proclaiming that "rhetorical study, in its strict sense, is concerned with the modes of persuasion."[3] Thus, it was recognized over 2,300 years ago that politics and communication go hand in hand because they are essential parts of human nature.

Back in 1981, Dan Nimmo and Keith Sanders proclaimed that political communication was an emerging field.[4] Although its origin, as noted, dates back centuries, a "self-consciously cross-disciplinary" focus began in the late 1950s. Thousands of books and articles later, colleges and universities offer a variety of graduate and undergraduate coursework in the area in such diverse departments as communication, mass communication, journalism, political science, and sociology.[5] In Nimmo and Sanders' early assessment, the "key areas of inquiry" included rhetorical analysis, propaganda analysis, attitude change studies, voting studies, government and the news media, functional and systems analyses, technological changes, media technologies, campaign techniques, and research techniques.[6] In a survey of the state of the field in 1983, the same authors and Lynda Kaid found additional, more specific areas of concerns such as the presidency, political polls, public opinion, debates, and advertising to name a few.[7] Since the first study, they also noted a shift away from the rather strict behavioral approach.

A decade later, Dan Nimmo and David Swanson argued that "political communication has developed some identity as a more or less distinct domain of scholarly work."[8] The scope and concerns of the area have further expanded to include critical theories and cultural studies. While there is no precise definition, method, or disciplinary home of the area of inquiry, its primary domain is the role, processes, and effects of communication within the context of politics broadly defined.

In 1985, the editors of *Political Communication Yearbook: 1984* noted that "more things are happening in the study, teaching, and practice of political communication than can be captured within the space limitations of the relatively few publications available."[9] In addition, they argued that backgrounds of "those involved in the field [are] so varied and pluralist in outlook and approach, . . . it [is] a mistake to adhere slavishly to any set format in shaping the content."[10] And more recently, Nimmo and Swanson called for "ways of overcoming the unhappy consequences of fragmentation within a framework that respects, encourages, and benefits from diverse scholarly commitments, agendas, and approaches."[11]

In agreement with these assessments of the area and with gentle encouragement, Praeger established the Praeger Series in Political Communication. The series is open to all qualitative and quantitative methodologies as well as contemporary and historical studies. The key to characterizing the studies in the series is the focus on communication variables or activities within a political context or dimension. As of this writing, nearly forty volumes have been published, and there are numerous impressive works forthcoming. Scholars from the disciplines of communication, history, journalism, political science, and sociology have participated in the series.

I am, without shame or modesty, a fan of the series. The joy of serving as its editor is in participating in the dialogue of the field of political communication and in reading the contributors' works. I invite you to join me.

                                                              Robert E. Denton, Jr.

NOTES

1. See Robert E. Denton, Jr., *The Symbolic Dimensions of the American Presidency* (Prospect Heights, Ill.: Waveland Press, 1982); Robert E. Denton, Jr., and Gary Woodward, *Political Communication in America* (New York: Praeger, 1985; 2nd ed., 1990); Robert E. Denton, Jr., and Dan Han, *Presidential Communication* (New York: Praeger, 1986); and Robert E. Denton, Jr., *The Primetime Presidency of Ronald Reagan* (New York: Praeger, 1988).

2. Aristotle, *The Politics of Aristotle*, trans. Ernest Barker (New York: Oxford University Press, 1970), p. 5.

3. Aristotle, *Rhetoric*, trans. Rhys Roberts (New York: The Modern Library, 1954), p. 22.

4. Dan Nimmo and Keith Sanders, "Introduction: The Emergence of Political Communication as a Field," in *Handbook of Political Communication,* eds. Dan Nimmo and Keith Sanders (Beverly Hills, Calif.: Sage, 1981), pp. 11–36.

5. Ibid., p. 15.

6. Ibid., pp. 17–27.

7. Keith Sanders, Lynda Kaid, and Dan Nimmo, eds., *Political Communication Yearbook: 1984* (Carbondale: Southern Illinois University, 1985), pp. 283–308.

8. Dan Nimmo and David Swanson, "The Field of Political Communications: Beyond the Voter Persuasion Paradigm," in *New Directions in Political Communication*, ed. David Swanson and Dan Nimmo (Beverly Hills, Calif.: Sage 1990), p. 8.

9. Sanders, Kaid, and Nimmo, *Political Communication Yearbook: 1984*, p. xiv.

10. Ibid.

11. Nimmo and Swanson, "The Field of Political Communication," p. 11.

Preface

A student who examines the influence of news coverage on American foreign policy will learn a lot about the give-and-take of democracy. With foreign affairs, as with the other topics of their coverage, journalists investigate and report—usually accurately, but sometimes not—and their work helps shape public attitudes about whatever policy or event seems important at the moment. Those who govern are expected to anticipate public opinion as they make policy, adjusting their efforts to respond to the public's will.

That is the theory. In practice, things often happen differently. Those who govern may try to keep the press from scrutinizing their work; they may feel that diplomacy should not be conducted in public view or be shaped by public opinion. Policymakers jealously assert their prerogatives, citing complexities of the world that neither press nor public can fully understand. This outlook can become paternalistic to the point of being antidemocratic, and it sharpens the adversarial relationships between journalists and those they cover.

A starting point in this unsettled process is to define foreign policy. Walter Lippmann wrote that foreign policy consists of "bringing into balance, with a comfortable surplus of power in reserve, the nation's commitments and the nation's power. The constant preoccupation of the true statesman is to achieve and maintain this balance. Having determined the foreign commitments which are vitally necessary to his people, he will never rest until he has mustered the force to cover them."[1]

Deciding what foreign commitments are "vitally necessary" has long been a subject of contention. In 1795, George Washington wrote: "My policy has been, and will continue to be . . . to be upon friendly terms with, but independent of, all the nations of the earth. To share in the broils of none. To fulfill our own engagements. To supply the wants, and be the carriers for them all . . . and that nothing short of self-respect, and that justice which is essential to a national character, ought to involve us in war."[2]

This relatively isolationist outlook remains popular in some circles today, but America's power has carried it beyond the role that Washington envisioned. In his examination of American diplomacy during the first half of the twentieth century, diplomat and historian George F. Kennan wrote, "By 1900 we were generally aware that our power had world-wide significance and that we could be affected by events far afield; from that time on our interests were constantly involved in important ways with such events."[3]

Kennan went on to ask important questions about the foundation of American foreign policy: "By what concepts were our statesmen animated in their efforts to meet these new problems? What assumptions had they made concerning the basic purposes of this country in the field of foreign policy? What was it they felt they were trying to achieve? And were these concepts . . . appropriate and effective ones? Did they reflect some deeper understanding of the relationship of American democracy to its world environment?"[4]

Those are the kinds of questions that frequently go unaddressed as policy is being shaped. As a result, problems develop. Here is where the press plays an important role: If those who make policy do not raise those questions, then journalists—as the public's surrogates—should do so.

James Reston of the *New York Times* wrote that the exercise of American power throughout the world should be accompanied not by a compliant press, but by "a relentless barrage of facts and criticism, as noisy but also as accurate as artillery fire." The job of journalists, he continued, "is not to serve as cheerleaders for our side in the present world struggle but to help the largest possible number of people to see the realities of the changing and convulsive world in which American policy must operate. It also means a redefinition of 'news,' with more attention to the *causes* rather than merely the *effects* of international strife."[5]

Headline Diplomacy was written to explore relationship of the government, press, and public as it pertains to foreign policy. This book owes much to Lippmann, Kennan, Reston, and others, whose writings over the years have stimulated analysis of many of the topics addressed here. By building a discussion of issues on a foundation of cases, most of them relatively recent, this volume may provide the next generation of those who make and cover foreign policy with some ideas about how to do their jobs.

The list of the cases included in this book is by no means comprehensive. It is a sampling designed to provide context for teaching, discussion, and further research. Press coverage of Israeli-Palestinian relations, the rival courtships of the press by Nicaragua's Sandinistas and contras during the 1980s, and the coverage of terrorism are among the many topics not considered here that are nonetheless worth studying to gain a better understanding of the connections between news coverage and policy-making.

Just how much influence the press really wields is the subject of an ongoing debate that often is not illuminating because the parties to the discussion have prerogatives and pride at stake. As a prelude to considering modern cases, chapter 1 offers the story of one of the most overt press efforts to shape the nation's foreign policy: the bellicose coverage that helped to push the United States into the Spanish-American War.

A century has passed since William Randolph Hearst and his colleagues embarked on their crusade, which in retrospect seems somewhat comic in its shrillness. But their bludgeoning worked; they got their war. Their success did not prove to be a lasting precedent for press power, but it is interesting evidence of what news organizations can do when their leaders abandon all restraint and have a clearly defined goal (and when policymakers let themselves be pushed).

Chapter 2 jumps forward to 1968 and another war, this one in Southeast Asia. News coverage of the Vietnam War has spurred extensive debate about its adequacy and its political impact. Lyndon Johnson was in the unfortunate position of being the first president to have to deal extensively with a "living-room war," compliments of television. (Although Edward R. Murrow had used radio in 1940 to bring the sounds of the London blitz into American homes, television had unprecedented impact.)

The Tet offensive that was conducted by the communist forces in early 1968 illustrated the intensity of pressure the news media can bring to bear on the policy process. Some historians believe that most journalists got the story wrong by calling the attacks a victory for the communists, even though they sustained massive losses and could not hold the territory they had seized. Nevertheless, the news coverage punctured the inflated expectations that the Johnson administration had created, and it defined the Tet offensive as a failure of U.S. policy. Soon thereafter, Johnson announced that he would not seek reelection.

Not all news coverage of war is so devastating to policymakers. As a counterpoint to the Tet reporting, this chapter also presents a brief look at the coverage accompanying the end of the Persian Gulf War in 1991. The accolades that George Bush collected from journalists hailing his war policy may have been based on simplistic judgments, but they stand in notable contrast to the treatment that Johnson's efforts received.

In addition to making judgments about the failure or success of foreign policy, the news media prod policymakers with the substance and tone of their coverage. Chapter 3 examines several cases, principally the 444-day Iran hostage crisis that bedeviled President Jimmy Carter. Also discussed are pressures on George Bush to assist the Kurds at the end of the Gulf War, on Bill Clinton to intervene in the former Yugoslavia, and on both Bush and Clinton to define a policy about Somalia.

A common thread running through these cases is how sensational news coverage undercuts policymakers' caution. Dramatic television pictures of brutalized civilians can create pressures to act that transcend concerns about the absence of a compelling national interest. Presidents are susceptible to such pressures. Sometimes the resulting policy works out well, but sometimes the crisis at hand merely worsens.

As chapter 4 illustrates, presidents and other policymakers are less likely to be pushed by news coverage if they have anticipated it and have taken the initiative to control, rather than be controlled by, the news media. A good example of this assertiveness was the Bush administration's handling of the press during the Gulf War. Clearly, people on Bush's team had learned much from the coverage of the Vietnam War and had taken steps not to let their chief end up as Lyndon Johnson had. Their tight control of the news media worked, but, had the war lasted longer and gone badly they might have found that their press policy itself was a political issue.

Bush was not the only world leader to have learned much from Vietnam War news coverage. During the 1982 Falklands War, British Prime Minister Margaret Thatcher was determined not to be undermined by the news media. She used censorship and public criticism of news organizations to control and distract journalists. Her strategy and Bush's efforts may prove to be the basic plan used (with some refinements) to manage the press during future wars.

Policymakers' relations with the news media may be colored by their efforts to manipulate coverage, sometimes to protect legitimate national interests, sometimes for less savory reasons. Most journalists acquiesce, at least for a while, because they recognize that some matters—such as national security—take precedence over the day-to-day demands of the news business.

As chapter 5 points out, however, some journalists become uncomfortable when their relationship with policymakers is too cozy. Protecting the public's right to know is so important that a retreat from aggressive reporting should happen only in extraordinary situations.

Two cases from John Kennedy's presidency illustrate these difficulties. During the run-up to the 1961 Bay of Pigs invasion, the press was perhaps too cautious in its reporting about what turned out to be a foreign policy disaster. But the following year, during the Cuban missile crisis, news organizations' restraint was probably wise. Of course, the stakes were very different in the two instances; the Bay of Pigs invasion was a limited, conventional attack, while the missile crisis involved the risk of nuclear war.

As with military action, when intelligence operations are at issue, policymakers urge journalists to proceed carefully or, better yet, not to proceed at all. Espionage requires secrecy, and journalism demands openness. The two jobs are fundamentally incompatible.

Further manipulation may occur when government officials leak information to serve their own purposes. The situation is worse when they use disinformation, as when they release "news" that they, but not reporters, know to be untrue. News professionals have to be constantly alert or they will find themselves being misled by sources who care a lot about their own agendas but very little about the public's need to be accurately informed.

Chapter 6 addresses the responsibility of the news media to call the public's attention to events that policymakers might prefer to ignore. The Ethiopian famine of 1984 was covered by the American media as something of an afterthought; news executives had apparently assumed that "just another starving Africans story" would be of little interest to their audiences. They were wrong. The public responded with an outpouring of donations; popular imagination was further captured by fund-raising efforts such as "Live Aid" concerts and the song "We Are the World"; and the Reagan administration dramatically increased its food shipments to Ethiopia.

In this case, the process worked well. The press covered the story, the public responded, and policymakers reacted. But in many other instances, that flow of news and action never becomes more than an ineffectual trickle.

Part of the news media's job is to tell the public not only what it wants to know, but also what it needs to know. That means sounding the alarm when vicious conflicts such as the 1994 Rwandan War are raging. Maybe the United States does not have an appropriate role in every such case, but even decisions by the public and government *not* to act should be based on good, timely reporting.

News organizations are more likely to find interested audiences for such stories if the public's knowledge of foreign affairs is steadily cultivated. This means not just providing information but also showing how that information is relevant to the lives of news consumers. If you are an American assembly-line worker and your job depends on overseas sales, you probably will be interested in news reports about international econom- ics, as long as those stories avoid overemphasizing abstract economic principles and focus instead on how you will be affected. Stories like that will build a constituency for foreign news.

In addition, the audience for stories about foreign affairs is growing because the technological reach of the news media is expanding. Chapter 7 examines the appeal and dangers of live coverage. Real-time news has changed the schedule of diplomacy, removing the luxury of time from the foreign policy process, especially during crises. Coverage of the rise of the Berlin Wall in 1961 and of its toppling in 1989 illustrates how pressures on policymakers differ depending on how quickly the news media get infor- mation to the public.

The Gulf War was the first war to be covered live, which changed the way policymakers did their jobs and altered even more drastically the role and responsibilities of journalists. Live coverage may have affected the outcome of the 1991 coup in the Soviet Union, and it enhanced the drama and political effects of the Tiananmen Square protests in China in 1989.

In these instances, television technology was very impressive, but tele- vision journalism less so. For reporters, "going live" often means abandon- ing editorial judgment and serving as a conveyer belt that passes along whatever is dumped on it. Checking accuracy and considering the potential impact of information may get shortchanged in the rush to be fast and be first. Real-time coverage requires real-time ethics.

Politics is changing at least as fast as journalism's technology is. Chapter 8 looks at the new world order, or disorder, with which journalists must come to grips. The Soviet Union's collapse has altered almost every facet of American foreign policy and has redefined the context of foreign affairs journalism. During the next few years, the journalistic agenda must be reshaped to give cohesion to coverage, especially to reporting about such tragedies as the implosion of the former Yugoslavia.

Chapter 9 considers current and prospective relationships between those who make foreign policy and those who cover it. Americans' attitudes about their nation's role in the world are changing, as are their judgments about what news stories are important to them. Despite isolationism's return to vogue, news organizations remain responsible for letting their audiences know what is going on in the rest of the world and why these events are important.

With the increasing reach of cable and satellite television, plus the expanding use of computer networks as information channels, more individuals and organizations will be news audiences and news sources. Additional voices can enhance the diversity of news, but the growing volume of information flowing to news consumers requires new efforts to ensure journalistic accuracy and balance.

The role of policymakers also is affected by this diversity. The diminution of the threat of global nuclear war has not removed nations' quest for power. A politician with dreams of "Greater Serbia," a cleric bent on launching a holy war, a separatist group with an affinity for terrorism, a head of state determined to choke off the world's oil supply . . . all these can still cause much turmoil and agony. Their efforts must be countered and covered.

The extent of the news media's influence over American foreign policy often depends on the caliber of political leadership. When a president clearly and forcefully defines a general world view, as well as specific goals and strategies, the impact of news coverage on policymaking is minimized. On the other hand, when an administration's foreign policy is ill-defined or unrealistic, news coverage has greater impact. Moreover, in the latter situation the public is likely to rely more heavily on the news media's version of events as they occur.

The relationship between policymakers and the press is not a competition. As is pointed out in the final pages of chapter 9, effective policy-making and enlightened journalism complement each other. Both parties to this relationship—and the public—will benefit from watchful coexistence.

For their valuable help while I was writing this book, I thank my research assistant Victoria Snee, Joe Clark, Violet O'Hara, Bob Moos, Tom Tunks, and the many diplomats, journalists, and scholars whose books and articles are listed in the bibliography. This is a fascinating field for research and writing, and I hope it will receive wider academic and journalistic attention.

Of all the sources for this book, the greatest inspiration came from the work of George F. Kennan, a wise man and fine writer.

Chapter One

Prelude: Mr. Hearst's War

Much of the news media's influence on foreign policy-making is indirect. Journalists shine their searchlight on events. Sometimes this captures the attention of the public and politicians; sometimes it is ignored.

News reports may speed up decision making or make a small matter suddenly loom large. Only rarely does coverage in itself substantively change the course of policy. Political leaders usually keep their balance, no matter how dramatic the tilt of reporting. Events themselves, not the coverage of them, determine policy.

But if news organizations set aside their commitment to accuracy and objectivity, amplify their voices to a sustained roar, and pursue a policy goal with single-minded fervor, they may create a superficial "reality" that captivates the public. The resulting public opinion can overwhelm all but the most resolute politicians. This does not happen often, but when it does, it offers convincing evidence of the influence of news media on the making and implementing of policy.

A century ago, some of America's most aggressive news organizations displayed their clout in this way. Coupled with the lassitude of some political leaders, the press's assertiveness helped produce the Spanish-American War.

FUELING A CRISIS

Cuba in the 1890s was a troubled outpost of Spain's decaying empire. Autocratic colonialism met with increasing resistance on the island; insurrection broke out in early 1895. Spain initially responded harshly and then moderated its position, eventually promising autonomy. But leaders of Cuba's revolutionary junta demanded independence.

Ninety miles from the Florida Keys, Cuba was closely watched by the United States. Intervention had its appeal. In an April 1895 article, "Are Americans Spoiling for War?" *Literary Digest* cited a revival of belief in manifest destiny, sympathy for Cubans' desire for freedom, and the prospect of war profits as reasons for the United States to contemplate taking action against Spain.[1]

Other publications also were stirring the waters. In an editorial in September 1895, the *Chicago Tribune* attacked Spanish tactics in Cuba, describing a "carnival of slaughter" and "wholesale butchery of old and young women, children, and even infants."[2] The same month, the *Tribune* polled American governors about the situation in Cuba and announced that "with hardly an exception the governors believe that the government of the United States should not stand idly by to see a gallant people overthrown and the few liberties remaining to them utterly annihilated by one of the most tyrannical nations on earth."[3]

Such exhortations did not move President Grover Cleveland. The president consistently proclaimed U.S. neutrality, repeatedly criticized zealous Cuban sympathizers in the United States, offered American mediation that would preserve Spanish sovereignty in Cuba, and sought a Supreme Court decision to limit American-based filibustering expeditions that were exacerbating Cuba's turmoil.[4] When Congress in early 1896 passed a concurrent resolution recognizing that a state of war existed within Cuba, Cleveland ignored the measure.[5]

In the 1896 presidential election, Republicans returned to power as William McKinley defeated William Jennings Bryan. McKinley's victory coincided with the rise of publisher William Randolph Hearst, who was in the process of turning the *New York Journal* into one of America's most sensational and successful newspapers. Hearst had declared his own war— against his rival Joseph Pulitzer's *New York World*. This contest was a no-holds-barred fight for readers; inconveniences such as accuracy and responsibility were cast aside.

In his quest for greater circulation, Hearst wanted a continuing story that would grab readers and hold them. What could be better than a war? Even before McKinley took office in March 1897, the *Journal* was demanding war with Spain. According to Hearst's biographer W. A. Swanberg, the *Journal* "conceived war as a class issue—something demanded by the justice-loving masses and opposed only by bloated Wall-Streeters who feared that war would upset the market."6

McKinley, however, would not be easily stampeded. While a member of Congress and governor of Ohio, he had paid careful attention to public opinion as he shaped policy. Pragmatic rather than dogmatic, he took seriously his responsibility to represent what his constituents wanted.7 In addition, he was a neophyte in foreign affairs. Throughout his pre-presidential career, he had concentrated almost exclusively on domestic matters. During his first years in the White House, he lacked a solid team of foreign policy advisers, and some analysts contend that he never developed a sustained, comprehensive foreign policy.8

In his inaugural address, delivered March 5, 1897, McKinley seemed to be following Cleveland's lead: "We have cherished the policy of non-interference with the affairs of foreign governments. . . . It will be our aim to pursue a firm and dignified foreign policy which shall be just and impartial, ever-watchful of our national honor and always insisting upon the enforcement of the lawful rights of American citizens. We want no wars of conquest. We must avoid the temptation of territorial aggression. . . . War should never be entered upon until every agency of peace has failed; peace is preferable to war in almost every contingency."

This did not sit well with the *Journal*, which called McKinley's speech "vague and sapless."9 But McKinley remained committed to moderation. When an apparently more progressive government came to power in Spain in the fall of 1897, seemingly disposed to improve the situation in Cuba, McKinley was willing to give it time. In his message to Congress in December 1897, McKinley asked that any action on Cuba be delayed for a year to give Spain a chance to implement its promised reforms. He said of this new regime, "I shall not impugn its sincerity, nor should impatience be suffered to embarrass it in the task it has undertaken."10

The president's course was undermined by press reports from Cuba. Dressing up fact with much exaggeration, papers such as the *Journal* and the *World* published a litany of horrors designed to drown out moderate voices. In his book *American Diplomacy*, George Kennan wrote: "American public opinion was deeply shocked by the tales of violence and misery from the island. Our sensibilities were not yet jaded by the immense horrors and cruelties of the twentieth century. The sufferings of the Cuban people shocked our sensibilities, aroused our indignation."11

The Cubans seeking independence understood the importance of American public opinion in their efforts to get the United States to intervene on their behalf. Revolutionary leader José Martí had been a journalist and helped orchestrate a propaganda campaign.[12] But the Cubans did not need to do much on their own. They were receiving plenty of help from U.S. news organizations. Here is a passage from a typical *New York World* editorial, published in November 1897: "The situation on the island is intolerable. Humanity itself revolts against it, and when humanity and diplomacy meet face to face in American affairs diplomacy gets the worst of it every time. If Spain will not put a stop to murder in Cuba, the United States must."[13]

Such editorials were backed up by reporting from the likes of famed correspondent Richard Harding Davis. Writing for the *Journal*, Davis provided stories such as "The Death of Rodriguez," about a rebel who had been captured and publicly executed by firing squad. This is an excerpt: "As . . . I looked back, the figure of the young Cuban, who was no longer a part of the world of Santa Clara, was asleep in the wet grass, with his motionless arms still tightly bound behind him . . . and the blood from his breast sinking into the soil he had tried to free."[14]

Hearst's *Journal* found no shortage of incidents. When two *Journal* reporters were briefly detained in Havana by Spanish officials, the *Journal* growled, "No surer road is open for the popularity of the new president [McKinley] than the abandonment of the new cold-blooded indifference to Cuba to which Cleveland has committed our government."[15]

This story was nothing compared to the tale of Evangelina Cisneros, the teenage niece of the Cuban revolutionary president. She had been sentenced to twenty years in prison for rebellious activity. The *Journal* not only described her plight in lurid detail, but it also organized letter-writing and petition campaigns directed at the Spanish queen regent, asking for the release of Cisneros.

After the initial spate of stories, little was heard about Cisneros for a few weeks. Then came even more sensational news: She had escaped from her Havana prison. And better yet, the jailbreak had been engineered by none other than a *Journal* correspondent, Karl Decker. Smuggled out of Cuba by Decker, Cisneros sailed to New York, where she was cheered at a Madison Square Garden rally. She then traveled to Washington, where she was received by President McKinley.[16] By the time Hearst finally grew tired of the Cisneros story, the *Journal* had devoted 375 news columns to her saga.[17]

A story with more political substance was also broken by the *Journal*. The Cuban revolutionaries intercepted a letter from Spain's minister in Washington, Enrique Dupuy de Lome, in which he described President McKinley as "weak and catering to the rabble; a low politician who desires . . . to stand well with the jingoes of his party."[18] The *Journal* published the text of the letter in February 1898, under the banner headline, "The Worst Insult To The United States In Its History." The *Journal* ran the five-page facsimile of the minister's handwritten letter, with the translation printed seven columns wide.[19] Dupuy de Lome resigned before the U.S. Department of State could demand his recall.

Throughout these events, Hearst's purpose remained constant: to see the United States go to war with Spain. His intent was made clear in an exchange of telegrams with Frederic Remington, the famous artist dispatched to Cuba by Hearst in December 1896, to record scenes of Spanish brutality, Cuban misery, and the fighting that Hearst was certain would come. Finding no action, Remington wired Hearst: "Everything is quiet. There is no trouble. There will be no war. I wish to return." Hearst responded: "Please remain. You furnish the pictures and I'll furnish the war."[20] (This incident was first related by *Journal* correspondent James Creelman in his 1901 reminiscences. No copies of the telegrams exist; some speculate that the story is apocryphal.) In any event, Remington did not remain. After a week, he completed some pictures and returned to New York. But the war, as promised, soon was furnished.

"REMEMBER THE *MAINE*"

Although difficult to measure precisely, the impact of press coverage of the Cuban situation was being felt. As Marcus Wilkerson has observed in *Public Opinion and the Spanish-American War*: "The influence of the press in stirring up opposition to Spain can best be arrived at through a study of the activities of the public and Congress in behalf of the Cubans as reported by the press." These activities included congressional debates, mass meetings and the raising of money in support of the rebels, enlistments in the Cuban (rebel) army, and petitions asking for American intervention. "Assuming that the press was the main source of information about Cuba, these activities were evidently the direct or indirect result of newspaper propaganda. The influence of the press on Congress is shown in the frequent references to newspaper accounts of atrocities" made by members during debate, such as one senator reading into the *Congressional Record* a *New York Journal* story about "horrors" in Cuba.[21]

The president remained cautious. In his book about McKinley's foreign policy, John Dobson has noted: "McKinley's desire to do the will of the people led to certain difficulties. The people's desires were not always obvious, especially when the yellow press and hostile politicians raised a clamor. Consequently, the president sometimes took considerable time to arrive at a final decision."[22]

McKinley's caution was soon put to a test it did not meet.

On January 25, 1898, the American battleship *Maine* arrived in Havana harbor on a "courtesy" visit. The Spanish commander sent a case of fine sherry to the *Maine's* captain and officers. All was civility in Havana, while, at home, the *Journal* headlined its story about the *Maine's* arrival with "Our Flag In Havana At Last." The paper urged that American vessels occupy all Cuban ports and force the withdrawal of the Spanish troops.[23]

On February 15, the *Maine's* forward magazines exploded, ripping the ship apart and killing 266 seamen. When Hearst heard the news, he called the editor who was preparing the next morning's edition of the *Journal* and told him: "There is not any other big news. Please spread the story all over the page. This means war."[24]

In the days following the explosion, American and Spanish investigations were launched to determine the cause. Was it sabotage or an accident? The *Maine's* captain, Charles Sigsbee, urged that "public opinion be suspended" until the inquiries were completed.

But public opinion was being subjected to a barrage of sensational invective against the Spanish. The *Journal* ran an average of more than eight pages per day about the *Maine* and the prospects for war. According to historian Swanberg, the *Journal* and other papers were "whipping public fury to a point where all these official efforts were rendered useless, a trivial shadow play unheard behind the din of the headlines."[25]

A sampling from a week's worth of *Journal* headlines shows what Swanberg meant:

February 16: "Cruiser *Maine* Blown Up In Havana Harbor."

February 17: "The Warship *Maine* Was Split In Two By An Enemy's Infernal Machine." Accompanying this headline was a seven-column drawing of the *Maine* anchored over mines, with wires leading from the mines to a Spanish fort on shore, from which the evil Spaniards had presumably detonated the charge. No evidence of this was ever found.

February 18: "The Whole Country Thrills With The War Fever."

February 23: "The *Maine* Was Destroyed By Treachery."

With all this going on, Hearst recruited three U.S. senators and two members of the House of Representatives to travel to Cuba on a Hearst yacht, at Hearst expense, to investigate conditions there and write reports for the *Journal*. The paper also appealed to readers to write to their congressmen demanding war. By February 26, the *Journal* claimed to have forwarded more than 15,000 of these letters to Washington.[26] Two weeks later came this pronouncement: "The *Journal* can stake its reputation as a war prophet on this assertion: There will be a war with Spain as certain as the sun shines unless Spain abases herself in the dust and voluntarily consents to the freedom of Cuba."[27]

The *Journal* was doing what it could to make sure the McKinley administration and Congress would fulfill this prophecy. Hearst used a special train to rush the many "extras" published by the *Journal* to Washington.[28] Still prophesying, the *Journal* in early April predicted that McKinley would send a message to Congress calling for intervention in Cuba. When he failed to do so, the paper accused him of having "deliberately tricked Congress and the people" and urged Congress to act on its own.[29]

To increase pressure on McKinley, the *Journal* ran stories such as interviews with the mothers of sailors killed on the *Maine*. One of them asked: "How would President McKinley have felt, I wonder, if he had a son on the *Maine* murdered as was my little boy? Would he then forget the crime and let it go unpunished while the body of his child was lying as food for the sharks in the Spanish harbor of Havana?"[30]

Hearst's intensity through the *Maine* crisis pitted him against the cautious diplomacy of the president. Two powerful men—one elected, one not—battled over the direction of American policy. Examining Hearst's motives, Swanberg has written:

Hearst was sincerely devoted to the Cuban cause and at the same time felt that American interests demanded the expulsion of Spain from the hemisphere. But he had no scruples against linking these defensible aims with a ruthless and vulgar drive for circulation, so that in the view of people of taste he had no unselfish impulses at all. . . . Hearst's coverage of the 'Maine' disaster still stands as the orgasmic acme of ruthless, truthless newspaper jingoism. As always, when he wanted anything he wanted it with passionate intensity. The 'Maine' represented the fulfillment not of one want but two—war with Spain and more circulation to beat Pulitzer. He fought for these ends with such abandonment of honesty and incitement of hatred that the stigma of it never left him even though he still had fifty-three years to live.[31]

Hearst was by no means alone in fueling war fervor. His archrival Joseph Pulitzer promptly sent a boat to Cuba carrying his reporters. Within a week, Pulitzer's *New York World* had sold 5 million copies.[32] The *World* reported that "Buffalo Bill" Cody had declared that 30,000 Indian fighters could chase the Spanish out of Cuba (this came after the *Journal* had reported that

600 Sioux Indians were ready to scalp Spaniards in Cuba). The *Journal* also cited an offer from bandit Frank James—Jesse's brother—to lead a company of cowboys into action.[33]

Each day, at the head of the *World's* editorial column, Pulitzer ran this statement about those who were killed on the *Maine*: "They died that Cuba might be free." In addition, the *World* daily ran the number of days since the explosion, implicitly criticizing the administration for its inaction.[34] (Perhaps McKinley grew as annoyed by this as Jimmy Carter did in 1980 when CBS anchorman Walter Cronkite intoned his daily reminder about how many days Americans had been held captive in Iran.)

Newspapers elsewhere in the country soon adopted Hearst's tone, some for philosophical reasons, others out of competitive necessity. The *Boston Herald*, for example, gave prominent display to sensational Cuba stories, in part because both the *Journal* and the *World* were rushing their early editions to Boston. The *Chicago Tribune* joined the ranks of those prodding McKinley, as in this April 1 editorial: "Again the President has asked Congress and the people to wait, pending a reply from Spain to his pacific propositions. It would be interesting to know what he hopes to accomplish by this desperate defiance of the popular will and this persistent fighting for time, and why he is making such strenuous efforts to protract and leave unsettled matters which should have been settled long ago."[35]

Not all news organizations fell into line behind Hearst, however. In a February 19 editorial about coverage of the *Maine* in the *Journal* and the *World*, the *New York Evening Post* wrote, "Nothing so disgraceful as the behavior . . . of these newspapers this week has ever been known in the history of American journalism."[36] The following month, the *Post* again attacked the sensational papers: "During the present war crisis, their lying with the view of promoting the outbreak of a war has excited the disgust and reprobation of all the intelligent portion of the nation."[37]

Writing in *The Atlantic Monthly*, E. L. Godkin noted: "Newspapers are made to sell; and for this purpose there is nothing better than war. War means daily sensation and excitement. On this almost any kind of newspaper may live and make money."[38]

In addition to criticizing the sensational coverage, some newspapers published information about the long record of fires in ships' coal bunkers and the kinds of accidents these fires produced.[39] Others invoked political logic: Blowing up the *Maine* would have been an incredibly stupid thing for Spain to do. The Madrid government clearly had been trying to avoid war with the United States. Far more likely suspects would be the Cuban rebels. They were worried about Spain's increasingly moderate diplomacy and were afraid of being shut out in a big-power deal. They desperately needed the United States to wage war on Spain.[40]

The insistent shrillness of the sensational press created an unsettling background for diplomacy. Soon after the *Maine* exploded, McKinley had said: "I don't propose to be swept off my feet by the catastrophe. My duty is plain. We must learn the truth and endeavor, if possible, to fix the responsibility. The country can afford to withhold its judgment and not strike an avenging blow until the truth is known. The Administration will go on preparing for war, but still hoping to avert it."[41]

In Madrid, the Spanish government was trying to mitigate effects of the *Maine* crisis. It welcomed investigation and agreed to submit the question of responsibility for the explosion to international arbitration—an offer the United States never accepted.[42] The U.S. minister to Spain, Stewart Woodford, negotiating with the Madrid government, told McKinley: "They cannot go further in open concessions to us without being overthrown by their own people here in Spain. . . . They want peace if they can keep peace and save the dynasty. They prefer the chances of war, with the certain loss of Cuba, to the overthrow of the dynasty."[43]

McKinley understood the extent to which the press was stirring up public opinion. He was an avid newspaper reader himself; he regularly saw five or six of the New York dailies, one or two from Chicago, and a half-dozen other large city papers, plus his hometown newspaper, the Canton, Ohio, *Repository*. His relationship with reporters was generally good, and he was accessible to them, as he was to other visitors to the White House, which was open to the public from ten until two daily.[44] After the *Maine* explosion, he instructed White House staff members to share telegrams from Havana with reporters, hoping to calm the newspapers.[45]

But he recognized that nothing would pacify Hearst, as well as other war-hungry journalists and politicians, except a declaration of war. Swanberg has summed up McKinley's position this way: "McKinley knew that the majority of the American people, misled by their newspapers, wanted war. He knew that many legislators, influenced by their angry constituents, wanted war. And he knew that his administration and the Republican Party would suffer unpopularity and loss of confidence if it made a stand for peace. Mr. McKinley bowed to Mr. Hearst. He went over to the war party. Without taking any stand, he submitted the whole problem to Congress in a message given on April 11. He dramatized his own abandonment of peace by burying the all-important Spanish concessions in the last two paragraphs of his speech."[46]

After almost two weeks of debate, Congress agreed, on April 24, on a bill declaring that a state of war existed between the United States and Spain. Hearst responded with a backhanded compliment in an editorial: "McKinley, the man of diplomacy, was a cinder in the eye of the American people. But McKinley, the man of action, begins well. He has signed the war resolution of Congress and sent his ultimatum to Spain."[47]

While McKinley was contending with the press and deciding how to deal with Congress, he was also being pressured by fellow politicians. Notable among them was Assistant Secretary of the Navy Theodore Roosevelt. When he first heard of the *Maine* explosion, Roosevelt wrote: "I would give anything if President McKinley would order the fleet to Havana tomorrow. The 'Maine' was sunk by an act of dirty treachery on the part of the Spaniards." McKinley, of course, would not take such drastic action. Roosevelt told friends that the president "has no more backbone than a chocolate eclair."[48]

Roosevelt and his allies exerted on McKinley a pressure similar to Hearst's, but more carefully considered. In June 1897, Roosevelt had given a speech reflecting a renewed commitment to the Monroe Doctrine: "If a foreign power . . . should determine to assert its position in those lands wherein we feel that our influence should be supreme, there is but one way in which we can effectively interfere. Diplomacy is utterly useless where there is no force behind it; the diplomat is the servant, not the master, of the soldier."[49]

Roosevelt articulated an aggressive nationalism that McKinley knew had a considerable following, and not just among certain newspaper publishers. Looking back on these times, Roosevelt wrote in his autobiography (published in 1913) about Cuba: "It was our duty, even more from the standpoint of national honor than from the standpoint of national interest, to stop the devastation and destruction. Because of these considerations, I favored war; and today, when in retrospect it is easier to see things clearly, there are few humane and honorable men who do not believe that the war was both just and necessary."[50]

McKinley also faced a restless Congress, where pro-war sentiment was magnified and inflamed by press coverage. The *Journal* ran interviews with pro-war congressmen under the headline "Armed Intervention At Once."[51] And, after delivery of the official report about the *Maine* from the court of inquiry—which found that the explosion had been caused by a mine—every member of Congress had "two or three newspapers in his district printed in red ink shouting for blood."[52]

Not everyone was swept away by the Hearst tide. When Hearst asked Grover Cleveland to aid his fund-raising efforts for a memorial to those who had died on the *Maine,* the former president replied, "I decline to allow my sorrow for those who had died on the 'Maine' to be perverted to an advertising scheme for the *New York Journal.*"[53]

Hearst remained undaunted. With Congress's declaration of war, he had won. His self-congratulation found its way onto the front page of the *Journal*: "How Do You Like The *Journal's* War?"

LESSONS: WAR, PEACE, AND THE PRESS

As the war neared its close with American victory certain, Hearst reveled in the impending triumph and looked ahead to even greater glory. A *Journal* headline read, "We're Ready To Whip Germany—She Cannot Bully Us."[54]

The war ended on August 12, 1898, less than four months after it had begun. In a signed *Journal* editorial on September 25, Hearst smugly described the role of the press: "The force of the newspaper is the greatest force in civilization. Under the republican government, newspapers form and express public opinion. They suggest and control legislation. They declare wars. They punish criminals, especially the powerful. They reward with approving publicity the good deeds of citizens everywhere. The newspapers control the nation because they REPRESENT THE PEOPLE."[55]

For good or ill, the power that Hearst described had been at work in bringing about what he considered to be "his" war. As Charles Brown has observed, the press was certainly influential, "but whether it was the newspapers' war or the *New York Journal*'s war, or publisher Hearst's war, as has been often said, is dubious. But it is also immaterial, for the press—the newspapers and the correspondents—acted as if it were."[56]

The Spanish-American War was a "popular" conflict, in the sense that it was, at least in large part, a creature of public opinion. George Kennan wrote that this war "occurred against a backdrop of public and governmental thinking in this country which was not marked by any great awareness of the global framework of our security."[57]

The decision to go to war, wrote Kennan, was:

attributable to the state of American opinion, to the fact that it was a year of congressional elections, to the unabashed and really fantastic warmongering of a section of the American press, and to the political pressures which were freely and bluntly exerted on the President from various political quarters. . . . There was not much of solemn and careful deliberation, not much prudent and orderly measuring of the national interest. When it came to the employment of our armed forces, popular moods, political pressures, and inner-governmental intrigue were decisive. McKinley did not want war. But when the bitter realities were upon him, there is no indication that either he or his Secretary of State felt in duty bound to oppose the resort to war if this was advantageous to them from the standpoint of domestic politics.[58]

As Kennan has noted, McKinley took the most politically expedient course. He followed—rather than led—public opinion. He certainly is not unique among politicians for doing so. When considering the shaping of that public opinion, a key question remains: Would there have been a war if the press had not acted as it did?

Although not all news organizations were the shrill war boosters that Hearst's *Journal* and some other publications were, the loudest seem to have had the greatest political impact. As early as 1895, Americans were receiving frequent news reports portraying Cuba as a martyr and Spain as a demon. The subtext beneath the often melodramatic stories about conditions in Cuba was one of more substantive geopolitics: Spain's intrusion into America's sphere of influence and its threat to American commercial interests.

Also involved was the opportunity for a nascent superpower to flex its muscles. In the Pacific theater of the war, the U.S. Navy defeated the Spanish fleet at Manila Bay. The United States seized the Philippine Islands (eventually paying Spain $20 million for them) and went on to annex Hawaii. Some politicians had the same plan for Cuba. This was blocked by the Teller Amendment, which emerged from the Senate's war debate and disclaimed any U.S. intention to take Cuba rather than to assure its independence.

Another factor: America had the wealth to finance its ambitions. When McKinley asked for a $50 million appropriation for the military, Congress passed the measure within three days. Woodford, the U.S. minister to Spain, reported that the vote "has not excited the Spaniards—it has simply stunned them. To appropriate fifty millions out of money in the treasury, without borrowing a cent, demonstrates wealth and power. Even Spain can see this."[59] Underlying the jingoistic rhetoric coming from Hearst and pro-war politicians was a recognition of this clout and a desire to use it.

Given McKinley's predisposition toward peace and the Spanish government's willingness to compromise, this war seems to have been far from inevitable. If the press had not been so vitriolic or if McKinley had been more assertive, public opinion might have merely simmered rather than boiled over. The Spanish-American War might well have been averted.

The continuum of news coverage affecting public opinion and then affecting governmental action remained intact as America moved into the new century. Even without Hearst-like flamboyance, the tone and substance of the news would continue to influence, if not define, American foreign policy.

Chapter Two

Defining Failure and Success

In foreign policy, success and failure often depend on the eye of the beholder. The government might pronounce a trade agreement or battlefield maneuver to be a triumph; a skeptical public may consider the same event a defeat.

The news media play a crucial role in defining "success" and "failure," at least insofar as the public is concerned. Journalists slice—sometimes too swiftly and neatly—through complexity, presenting an event in the starkest terms, devoid of rough edges and nuance.

Policymakers find this enormously frustrating. They claim, often correctly, that snap news judgments pull incidents out of context and impose the news media's frantic pace on events that are, by their nature, slow-moving and that may change considerably as time passes. It is as if someone puts a pot of water on the stove to boil, and several seconds later, the attempt is declared a failure because no bubbles are yet seen. The gradually rising temperature will bring the water to a boil in a few minutes—a success—But once the failure has been declared (perhaps by journalist reporting "live from the kitchen"), who will care about the eventual outcome?

Journalists have de facto power to set standards that policy makers must meet. The outcome of a treaty negotiation, the size of a trade deficit, the number of casualties inflicted or incurred in a war—these and other foreign policy matters are subject to news media judgments expressed in the substance and tone of coverage.

The public, particularly if it already has doubts about a policy, may accept the news media's criteria. Even if it turns out that the news reports were incomplete, misleading, or just plain wrong, public opinion may have solidified by then past the point of being able to be changed.

For those who govern, this is a nightmare that sometimes becomes real.

TET (1968)

At the end of January 1968, as the Vietnam War defied the efforts of peacemakers and warmakers alike to bring it to a conclusion, the Tet holiday (the lunar new year) was expected to provide at least a lull in the bloodshed. All sides had pledged to observe a truce for thirty-six hours. But early on the morning of January 30, the White House received word of attacks by communist forces on Danang, Nhatrang, Kontum, and other cities north of Saigon. That afternoon, the president learned that Saigon itself was under fire and that Vietcong soldiers had penetrated the American embassy. Overall, approximately 70,000 communist troops attacked more than 100 cities and towns.

First Reports

About fifteen minutes after the fighting began in Saigon, the Associated Press (AP) bureau in that city flashed word to the world about the attack.[1] This marked the beginning of a new level of reporting from Vietnam: bloodier, firsthand accounts of combat from the press corps—the 248 Americans and 379 from other countries (including 119 Vietnamese) who were accredited as war correspondents.[2] As Professor Kathleen Turner has noted in her study of how the war was reported, "the fighting was suddenly, inescapably, terrifyingly close to the Saigon-based news teams. The proximity of the battle guaranteed extensive coverage by media institutions: it was dramatic, it was easily accessible, and it was for many the first extended view of the enemy."[3]

The closeness to television cameras magnified the impact that coverage of the fighting had on Americans at home. CBS correspondent Morley Safer said: "The camera can describe in excruciating, harrowing detail what war is all about. The cry of pain, the shattered face—it's all there on film, and out it goes into millions of American homes during the dinner hour. It is true that on its own every piece of war film takes on a certain antiwar character, simply because it does not glamorize or romanticize. In battle, men do not die with a clean shot through the heart; they are blown to pieces. Television tells it that way."[4]

During the next weeks, the news got no better. President Johnson's newly confirmed Secretary of Defense, Clark Clifford, chronicled some of the events:

February 18: The Pentagon reported the highest one-week American casualty toll of the war, 543 killed, 2,547 wounded. We noted a new and disturbing trend: for the first time in the war, American casualties were significantly higher, proportionately, than those of the ARVN [Army of the Republic of [South] Vietnam].

February 23: The Selective Service announced it would draft an additional 48,000 men, the second-largest call-up of the Vietnam War.

February 25: [U.S. forces commander General William] Westmoreland told the Associated Press that additional troops would be needed in the war zone.[5]

As Americans received this news, they were also getting an unusually bloody dose of television reporting. Although a study of television news stories that aired between 1968 and 1973 has found that only 3 percent contained combat footage and 2 percent showed any dead or wounded, the level of violence in the televised stories was considerably higher during the 1968 Tet period (January 31–March 31).[6] A viewer watching network news five times a week "would have seen film of civilian casualties 3.9 times a week . . . more than four times the overall average of 0.85 times a week. Film of military casualties jumped from 2.4 to 6.8 times a week."[7]

Other disconcerting messages were being relayed to the public by the press. AP reporter Peter Arnett quoted an American major speaking of the battle for Bentre: "It became necessary to destroy the town to save it."[8] As Herbert Schandler has noted: "This widely repeated sentence seemed to sum up the irony and the contradictions in the use of American power in Vietnam and caused many to question the purpose of our being there. If we had to destroy our friends in order to save them, was the effort really worthwhile, either for us or for our friends?"[9]

If news coverage of Tet seemed harsh and negative to Johnson administration officials, they had themselves to blame, at least in part. As was noted in a 1985 study of press-military relations:

Since the administration lacked a coherent strategy and clear-cut objectives (other than not losing) but claimed "progress," its spokesmen could not define for either the military or the public what ultimate "success" would require. . . . [Journalists] widely assumed that there *was* a coherent strategy, and that "progress" (in killing enemy troops, pacifying the countryside, strengthening the South Vietnamese ally) was intended to further this strategy. Newsmen in Saigon concentrated on the agenda set by the White House. They sought to check in piecemeal fashion the claims of "progress" made by official spokesmen—and often disputed privately in conversations with trusted reporters by U.S. military commanders and advisers to the South Vietnamese in the field."[10]

This same study noted that, although journalists followed the White House lead in their reporting, their judgment was tempered by considerable skepticism about the administration's pronouncements. "Thanks to years of official optimism (notably from Defense Secretary [Robert] McNamara) that proved unfounded, newsmen in Saigon were inclined to discount *all* optimistic assessments by official spokesmen, even as they dutifully reported them."[11]

In all this, as Daniel Hallin has observed: "The journalists were inescapably a part of the political process they were reporting. If they said Tet was a political defeat for the Administration, they were helping to make it so; if they resisted the journalistic instinct to put Tet in that context, they were helping the Administration out. Most of them followed that journalistic instinct."[12]

Events large and small seemed to be undermining the administration. On a day when the White House hoped that upbeat comments by General Westmoreland at a press conference would dominate the news, the public's attention was instead riveted on an event photographed by the AP's Eddie Adams and filmed by an NBC crew. South Vietnamese Brigadier General Nguyen Ngoc Loan had summarily executed a captured Vietcong soldier on a Saigon street. Adams's photo captured the split-second of the bullet's impact.

This and the NBC film of the incident brought home the horrific nature of events in Vietnam. This was not John Wayne leading the good guys on a charge against a fierce enemy. In these images, the supposed good guys were executing prisoners. This unpleasant reality further jarred Americans, generating still more doubts about what we were doing and why we were doing it. Even Westmoreland later wrote, "The photograph and the film shocked the world, an isolated incident of cruelty in a broadly cruel war, but a psychological blow against the South Vietnamese nonetheless."[13]

Within a few days of the Tet offensive's beginning, both NBC and CBS aired television specials about the fighting. *Time* and *Newsweek* ran cover stories, complete with bloody photos. Editorials and opinion columns voiced doubts about the American role in Vietnam.

For example, Walter Lippmann, in his *Newsweek* column, wrote: "The war has taken a bad turn. Quite unexpectedly, we are faced with a question which has always been dismissed as unthinkable and absurd. Are we being 'defeated' in Vietnam? The very fact that the question is being asked is causing a shock of which the force is just being felt, of which the consequences are as yet incalculable."[14]

These concerns were raised not just by the "elite Eastern media." Even heartland voices were speaking out, as in this editorial from the Salina, Kansas, *Journal*: "It is hard for a proud nation such as this to admit defeat and error. But if we are a moral, honorable nation with a sense of duty and destiny, we cannot go on killing and destroying to perpetuate an error and deepen it."[15]

Press Criticism Intensifies

Similar to the Salina *Journal*'s message but reaching millions more people was a commentary delivered on February 27 at the conclusion of a CBS News special, "Report from Vietnam by Walter Cronkite." After a half-hour of reporting done while he was in Vietnam, Cronkite presented his final analysis from his New York anchor desk:

Who won and who lost in the great Tet offensive? I'm not sure. The Vietcong did not win by a knockout, but neither did we. The referees of history may make it a draw. . . . To say that we are mired in stalemate seems the only realistic, yet unsatisfactory conclusion. On the off chance that military and political analysts are right, in the next months we must test the enemy's intentions in case this is indeed his last big gasp before negotiations. But it is increasingly clear to this reporter that the only rational way out then will be to negotiate, not as victors but as an honorable people who lived up to their pledge to defend democracy, and did the best they could."[16]

Less than two weeks later, another news story dealt a major blow to the administration's efforts to convince the public that Tet had not been a massive setback and that the American commitment to the war should not be diminished. The bombshell was a front-page *New York Times* story on March 10, headlined "Westmoreland Requests 206,000 More Men, Stirring Debate in Administration."

This article had double-barreled impact. First the need to commit so many more troops to Vietnam was likely to generate even more public doubts about U.S. war policy; second, the "debate in Administration" seemed evidence of disarray in the ranks and was certain to erode further the public's confidence in policymakers' competence. Hedrick Smith, one of the authors of the *Times* story, noted that "for once, the press had let the public know about the government's plans while there was still time for the political system to react effectively. That had not happened often in this war."[17]

The same day, senior NBC correspondent Frank McGee concluded a network special with these words about the prospect of massive reinforcements: "All that would be changed would be the capacity for destruction. . . . Laying aside all other arguments, the time is at hand when we must decide whether it is futile to destroy Vietnam in order to save it."[18]

The comments of McGee, like those of Cronkite, were part of a Tet-inspired spurt of on-air opinion pieces. Daniel Hallin has noted that "the percent of television stories in which journalists editorialized or made commentaries on the news jumped from a pre-Tet average of 5.9% to 20% during the two months following the Tet attacks, and then fell back to 9.8% after Tet."[19]

From the White House's perspective, the news coverage remained negative. *Newsweek*'s March 18 cover story was "The Agony of Khe Sanh," with color photos and a gloomy text about the siege of this U.S. base located just south of the border with North Vietnam. The magazine also included an editorial that said, in part: "The time has come for a searching reappraisal of the U.S. role. *Newsweek*'s editors recognize they do not have all the answers, but they believe that a responsible journal must at least explore alternatives to the Vietnam cul de sac."[20]

Not all the news coverage was negative toward the administration's war policy. Washington Post columnist Joseph Alsop wrote: "As the captured documents continue to pour in . . . it becomes clearer and clearer that the Tet-period attacks on the cities were a major disaster for [North Vietnamese military commander] General Giap, if measured in terms of his planned goals. . . . The President will be feckless, foolish, and derelict in his duty (and he will also be acting against his own practical, long-range interests) if he fails to call up the reserves in order to insure negotiations on our terms."[21]

But even within administration ranks, such messages were not universally applauded. Undersecretary of the Air Force Townsend Hoopes (a leading Pentagon proponent of de-escalation) said of Alsop's work, "If it did nothing else, this kind of fustian trumpeting provided some comic relief during a bad month."[22]

Impact on Public Opinion

The incremental impact of news coverage on public opinion is always hard to measure, but post-Tet opinion poll results offer some indication of changes in Americans' appraisal of the war effort. A Gallup poll in early February found the number of self-described hawks had jumped up to 61 percent after Tet, while the percentage of people approving of Lyndon Johnson's handling of the war had dropped to 35 percent.[23] Neither hawks nor doves were happy with Johnson. By mid-March, a dramatic change had occurred: For the first time, self-professed doves in the public at large outnumbered hawks. Gallup data suggested that between early February and the middle of March, nearly one person in five switched from hawk to dove.[24]

Moreover, a Gallup survey conducted during the last week in February found a drastic shift from the previous November. Of the February respondents, 23 percent said that the United States and its allies were losing ground in Vietnam, up from 8 percent in November, while 33 percent said the United States was making progress, down from 50 percent in November.[25] Another poll, released during the second week of March, found that 49 percent of Americans thought that sending troops to Vietnam was a mistake—the highest figure ever. Only 41 percent approved.[26]

News coverage played a part in this shift by making clear what American military policy was and what it was not. Peter Braestrup, who had been the *Washington Post*'s Saigon bureau chief, later wrote: "Conventional military victory had been ruled out by the Administration. The goal, variously ornamented, was to weaken the foe sufficiently by attrition to permit the survival of a noncommunist South Vietnam and block communist expansion in Southeast Asia. It was not an inspiring vision. . . . 'Progress,' despite all the public rhetoric, was accurately portrayed by the media as slow and uneven."[27]

If this was the administration approach, Cronkite's prediction of a stalemate as the best possible outcome seemed valid, and sending 206,000 more soldiers simply to achieve stalemate seemed excessive. The White House, not surprisingly, challenged this reasoning. Johnson adviser Walt Rostow said the *New York Times* story about the additional troops "churned up the whole eastern establishment and created a false issue. It caused an unnecessary crisis and distorted things. It overrode the hopeful news and had quite substantial effects on public opinion. It gave a false picture of the situation."[28]

In his memoirs, published in 1971, the president himself said of this situation: "There was a great deal of emotional and exaggerated reporting of the Tet offensive in our press and on television. The media seemed to be in competition as to who could provide the most lurid and depressing accounts. Columnists unsympathetic to American involvement in Southeast Asia jumped on the bandwagon. Some senatorial critics and numerous opponents of America's war effort added their voices to the chorus of defeatism. The American people and even a number of officials in government, subjected to this daily barrage of bleakness and near panic, began to think that we must have suffered a defeat."[29]

But perhaps the "lurid and depressing accounts" were accurate. The public seemed to think so. As David Halberstam observed in *The Best and the Brightest*: "Day after day American newspapermen, and more important, television cameramen, could reflect [the Vietcong's] ability, above all their failure to collapse according to American timetables. The credibility of the American strategy of attrition died during the Tet offensive. . . . The Tet offensive had stripped Johnson naked on the war, his credibility and that of his administration were destroyed."[30]

Despite protests from the president and from aides such as Rostow, even within the administration there were those who understood the domestic political consequences of Tet. Clark Clifford, who had just been confirmed by the Senate as Robert McNamara's successor as Secretary of Defense, had a better grip on reality than did many of his colleagues. He later wrote: "The most serious casualty at Tet was the loss of the public's confidence in its leaders. Tet hurt the Administration where it needed support most, with Congress and the American public—not because of the reporting, but because of the event itself, and what it said about the credibility of America's leaders. Public confidence in General Westmoreland, high until Tet, was shattered, never to be rebuilt; for the rest of the American government, including President Johnson, it was severely damaged."[31]

Even top presidential aides were faced with choosing between the White House version of reality and the news media's version. Harry McPherson, a Johnson special counsel and speechwriter, said: "I would go in two or three mornings a week and study the cable book and talk to Rostow and ask him what had happened the day before, and would get from him what almost seemed hallucinatory from the point of view of what I had seen on network television the night before."[32]

News coverage had stirred and reinforced McPherson's doubts: "Like millions of other people who had been looking at television the night before, I had the feeling that the country had just about had it, that they would simply not take any more." McPherson noted that even

people like me—people who had some responsibility for expressing the presidential point of view—could be so affected by the media as everyone else was, while downstairs, within fifty yards of my desk, was that enormous panoply of intelligence-gathering devices—tickers, radios, messages coming in from the field. I assume the reason . . . [I] was more persuaded by what I saw on the tube and in the newspapers was that like everyone else who had been deeply involved in explaining the policies of the war and trying to understand them and render some judgment, I was fed up with the 'light at the end of the tunnel' stuff. I was fed up with the optimism that seemed to flow without stopping from Saigon."[33]

Impact on the President

Lyndon Johnson also seemed to swing between aggressive defense of his policies and uncertainty about his course. In his analysis of the news coverage of Tet, Peter Braestrup has noted the president's defensiveness and said that he seemed psychologically defeated.[34] Braestrup has also written that, "in contrast to John F. Kennedy during the 1962 Cuban missile crisis, or to Franklin D. Roosevelt after Pearl Harbor, [Johnson] started by setting a hesitant tone—which did not go unnoticed in the media. Initially the President sought to repeat his 1967 public-relations strategy, dominating the media with reassuring statements about Vietnam by subordinates."[35]

Johnson began with a press conference on February 2. He later wrote of this: "I announced that Tet had been a military failure for the enemy. However, I added: 'Their second objective, obviously . . . is a psychological victory.' "[36] He then dispatched his deputies to the talk shows: Secretary of Defense Robert McNamara and Secretary of State Dean Rusk to "Meet the Press" on NBC; Undersecretary of State Nicholas Katzenbach to "Face the Nation" on CBS; White House aide Walt Rostow to "Issues and Answers" on ABC.[37] The president also enlisted General Westmoreland, telling him to speak to the press at least once a day to "convey your confidence in our capability to blunt these enemy moves, and to reassure the public here that you have the situation under control."[38] The overall strategy was clear: recapture the airwaves, provide enough administration voices to drown out the naysayers, and use the news media to defeat the news media.

But a public relations effort is unlikely to succeed if its fundamental message is unacceptable to the public. Johnson either did not understand or chose to ignore this fact. Soon afterward, Townsend Hoopes, Undersecretary of the Air Force during Tet, wrote, "While pressure rose on every side for a reexamination of America's prospects and strategy, [Johnson] and his closest advisers gave the unmistakable impression that all the big questions had been long since resolved—and that the answer was to plunge on-ward."[39]

Hoopes also wrote:

"the scale, virulence, and tenacity of the Tet offensive had all but severed the remaining strands of the Administration's credibility. The President was speaking out forcefully, but his words and their tone struck his listeners as more shrill than reassuring; in them one detected a profound inner discomfort and unease, a thrashing about in uncertainty. In a Dallas speech on February 27, he said: "There will be blood, sweat, and tears shed. The weak will drop from the lines, their feet sore and their voices loud. Persevere in Vietnam we will and we must. There, too, today we stand at the turning point. The enemy of freedom has chosen to make this year the decisive one. He is striking in a desperate and vicious effort to shape the final outcome of his purposes."[40]

The same day as the president's Dallas speech, CBS aired Cronkite's Vietnam special, which concluded with his call to end the war through negotiation. Austin Ranney has described the impact of Cronkite's message:

On hearing Cronkite's verdict, the President turned to his aides and said, "It's all over." . . . As Johnson's aide Bill Moyers put it later, "We always knew . . . that Cronkite had more authority with the American people than anyone else. It was Johnson's instinct that Cronkite was it." So if Walter Cronkite thought the war was hopeless, the American people would think so too, and the only thing left was to wind it down. . . . As David Halberstam wrote, "It was the first time in history a war had been declared over by an anchorman." That is surely an overstatement; yet the authority of Walter Cronkite, added to the authority of Clark Clifford and other trusted presidential advisers urging Johnson to wind down the war, may well have tipped the balance.[41]

Johnson told his press secretary, George Christian, that Cronkite would change the minds of "middle-of-the-road folks who have supported the war all along."[42] And Christian later recalled that "shock waves rolled through the government" when Cronkite delivered his assessment.[43]

Nevertheless, Johnson proceeded aggressively, to the dismay of some advisers. Clark Clifford told a Johnson biographer:

In the middle of March, the President made two speeches. And they were really hard-nosed speeches, stern, facing up to the commitment we had made, very determined speeches—in effect they were something of a restatement of our intention to seek and achieve military victory in Vietnam. I was deeply concerned about them. By the time the two speeches were made, I had the strongest feeling that we ought to be moving in the other direction. I recall making the statement that what the President should do was make a speech about peace. I now knew . . . that if we were going after military victory we were headed down a road that had no end."[44]

In March, Johnson did scale down the plans for additional troops to be sent to Vietnam. A principal reason for this, he later wrote, was that "domestic public opinion continued to be discouraged as a result of the Tet offensive and the way events in Vietnam had been presented to the American people in newspapers and on television."[45]

Johnson kept stressing that "the way events in Vietnam had been presented"—not the events themselves—had caused his problems. He convened a special group of senior foreign policy and military experts, dubbed "the Wise Men," to be briefed on the state of affairs in Vietnam and to offer suggestions about what to do next. When a majority of this group told him the war should be ended, Johnson was astounded.[46] He did not believe that the facts warranted such defeatism. In his memoirs, he wrote: "I decided that the briefings had been much less important in shaping the views of these outside advisers than was the general mood of depression and frustration that had swept over so many people as a result of the Tet offensive. . . . If they [the Wise Men] had been so deeply influenced by the reports of the Tet offensive, what must the average citizen in the country be thinking? . . . I remained convinced that the blow to morale was more of our own doing than anything the enemy had accomplished with its army. We were defeating ourselves."[47]

On March 31, two months after the Tet offensive had begun, the president delivered a televised speech to the nation, reporting that he had ordered a limited bombing halt and new efforts to shift more of the war's burden to the South Vietnamese. In his conclusion he said, "I shall not seek, and I will not accept, the nomination of my party for another term as your president."

Appraising the News Media's Role

As he announced the end of his political career, Johnson was mindful of the press corps and the pressure he had felt from their recent coverage. In his memoirs he wrote: "Perhaps now that I was not a candidate commentators in the press and television might regard issues and efforts more objectively, instead of concentrating on criticism and cynical speculation."[48]

The following day, Johnson spoke to the National Association of Broadcasters and reflected on the impact of television's coverage of the Vietnam fighting: "As I sat in my office last evening, waiting to speak, I thought of the many times each week when television brings the war into the American home. No one can say exactly what effect those vivid scenes would have on American opinion. Historians must only guess at the effect that television would have had during earlier conflicts on the future of this nation: during the Korean War, for example, at that time when our forces were pushed back there to Pusan; or World War II, the Battle of the Bulge, or when our men were slugging it out in Europe."[49]

Playing this game of historical speculation offers intriguing scenarios. As Johnson suggested, suppose that televisions had been in virtually every American home during World War II, and suppose that there had been extensive coverage of the Battle of the Bulge—the German counterattack in late 1944 and early 1945. Would vivid scenes of heavy American casualties have undermined American resolve to demand unconditional surrender from Germany and pushed President Roosevelt into accepting softer peace terms?

Whatever the answer in this hypothetical situation, Johnson's point is worth considering. The nature of coverage influences public perception of events, which in turn influences the public's political attitudes and in turn influences the policymakers. Johnson presumably would have argued that this process is fine so long as the original depiction of events is accurate, which he believed was not the case during the Tet offensive. If coverage is skewed, the end result is that governing becomes much more difficult, because policy makers find themselves pressured to conform to the news media's version of events rather than to the truth. Johnson's premise was based, of course, on his belief that the press did its job badly during Tet.

The Chairman of the Joint Chiefs of Staff, General Earle Wheeler, agreed with Johnson, saying that Tet was a military defeat for the communists that became "a propaganda victory for the North Vietnamese here in the United States, [which] I attribute primarily to the press coverage at that time and to the dissident groups here in the United States."[50] But even Johnson's persistently hawkish national security adviser, Walt Rostow, hedged on this. Although he claimed that "the massive uninhibited reporting of the complex war was generally undistinguished and often biased," he also admitted that the administration's military and political leaders were not effective in presenting a "clear and persuasive" picture of what was going on in Vietnam.[51]

A notion popular in the White House was that news coverage was negative to the point of being unpatriotic and exerted a malign influence on public opinion. But this idea may have rested on a shaky foundation. As Don Oberdorfer has noted in his book about Tet: "One reason the press was not 'on the team' was because the country was not 'on the team.' To a substantial degree, the newsmen represented and reflected American society, and like the rest, they had no deep commitment to or enthusiasm for the war. As reporters learned more about Vietnam, they become more pessimistic, with inevitable impact on the public. The view of the public, in turn, influenced the mood of the press."[52]

A principal critic of the reporting about Tet—particularly of the coverage's implicit or explicit theme that the offensive was a major communist military victory—is Peter Braestrup, the *Washington Post*'s Saigon bureau chief during Tet. In *Big Story*, his detailed book about coverage of the offensive, Braestrup has made a case that the news reports were inaccurate: "Rarely has contemporary crisis-journalism turned out, in retrospect, to have veered so widely from reality. Essentially, the dominant themes of the words and film from Vietnam (rebroadcast in commentary, editorials, and much political rhetoric at home) added up to a portrait of defeat for the allies. Historians, on the contrary, have concluded that the Tet offensive resulted in a severe military-political setback for Hanoi in the South. To have portrayed such a setback for one side as a defeat for the other—in a major crisis abroad—cannot be counted as a triumph for American journalism."[53]

Compounding the problem of inaccuracy, according to Braestrup, was the failure to correct errors: "The record was not set straight. The hasty assumptions and judgments of February and early March were simply allowed to stand. . . . As is usually the case in crisis, most space and 'play' went to the Tet story early, when the least solid information was available. There was no institutional system within the media for keeping track of what the public had been told, no internal priority on updating initial impressions. As usual, the few catch-up or corrective stories were buried on the back pages. This practice in turn gave Saigon correspondents little incentive to produce such stories."[54]

As the Tet crisis faded, news organizations were inclined to abandon the story, at least as a primary topic for updated coverage. Braestrup has noted: "The result was that the media tended to leave the shock and confusion of early February, as then perceived, 'fixed' as the final impression of Tet, and thus as a framework for news judgment and public debate at home. At Tet, the press shouted that the patient was dying, then weeks later began to whisper that he somehow seemed to be recovering—whispers generally not heard amid the clamorous domestic reaction to the initial shouts."[55]

But even if this criticism of the news media is valid, even if their stories conveyed the wrong impression about the realities of the Tet offensive, how much political impact did this coverage have? The answer is complex; the coverage may not have been determinative in itself, but it was influential. Furthermore different analysts read the poll numbers differently. Although the Gallup survey found a substantial switch from hawks to doves by mid-March 1968, Braestrup has downplayed this. According to him: "There is no evidence of a direct relationship between the dominant media themes in early 1968 and changes in American mass public opinion vis-à-vis the Vietnam War itself. Indeed, public support for the war effort remained remarkably steady in February-March 1968, even as LBJ's popularity hit a new low, as measured by the pollsters. But we can observe unmistakable reflections of strong media themes . . . in the Congressional rhetoric and in the discussion by the politically active and media-sensitive elites outside Washington."[56]

Braestrup's criticisms have merit, particularly if the hard military facts about Tet are separated from the amorphous politics of 1968. The communist forces suffered enormous losses, they could not hold the territory they had overrun in their attacks, and their offensive failed to stimulate the popular uprising in the South that they had hoped would fatally destabilize the South Vietnamese government. But war is not just combat, and the news coverage of Tet reflected this. The American and South Vietnamese defeat may have been more political than military, but it was still a defeat.

Perhaps the most temperate judgment about all these matters came from Clark Clifford. In his memoirs (published in 1991), the former Secretary of Defense wrote:

Supporters of the war would later single out inaccurate reporting by the press during the Tet offensive as a major reason for the turnaround in American public opinion just when, they said, we were in a position to win in the field. This view is misinformed: the press made errors in reporting, as it does in every war, but the bulk of the reporting from the war zone reflected the official position. Contrary to right-wing revisionism, reporters and the antiwar movement did not defeat America in Vietnam. Our policy failed because it was based on false premises and false promises. Had the results in Vietnam approached, even remotely, what Washington and Saigon had publicly predicted for many years, the American people would have continued to support their government.[57]

COUNTERPOINT: CONCLUDING THE GULF WAR (1991)

Not all presidents find it necessary to fulminate against the news media. As the Persian Gulf War came to its quick end, President George Bush saw his high approval ratings being fortified by press coverage that was often adoring. This gave him leeway to proceed as he chose in devising combat strategy and in shaping the peace terms that he would impose on Saddam

Hussein. Later on, he might be second-guessed by journalists, but, when he most needed public support, he was being proclaimed a success by the press.

Here are some examples:

From *Newsweek*: "There were so many chances to blow it. He could have dithered when the Iraqis first invaded. He could have led the country into an anguishing new hostage crisis. He could have allowed Saddam Hussein to slip away through a messy compromise. But at each turn, George Bush remained steadfast. . . . The chattering classes may have doubted Bush, but the public believed in his leadership skills over the last six months, and they were rewarded."[58]

From *U.S. News & World Report*: "Journalists aren't supposed to deliver valentines to men in power. . . . But once in a while the rules are broken, and surely that moment has arrived for the 41st president of the United States. George Bush is turning the Persian Gulf crisis into a triumph of American leadership. . . . The prospects for peace and justice are rising again. And most of the credit belongs to one man."[59]

From *Fortune*: "He was not looking for this kind of 'defining moment' to mark his presidency. But now that war has arrived, future historians are sure to agree on one thing: The world's response to the conflict sparked by Saddam Hussein's brutal conquest of Kuwait bears the stamp of one man—George Herbert Walker Bush."[60]

Not many months would pass before the tone of Bush's coverage turned distinctly sour, but, when he most needed the public support that would leave him a free hand in the war, much of the news coverage of his efforts was soft (and in some cases, as above, squishy).

The political exigencies of George Bush's war were nothing when compared to those Lyndon Johnson had to face in Vietnam. But a small point is worth making: Just as news coverage can offset official pronouncements and do much to define a policy as failed, so too can it be a vital asset in proclaiming a policy to be a success. As the public shapes its opinion about the policy question of the moment, it pays attention to the tone of news coverage, at least for a while.

Chapter 3

Pushing the President

For a president, the ideal pace for making foreign policy is the pace he can set himself. He may wish to rely on just a few close advisers and work in secrecy (as in the Richard Nixon–Henry Kissinger partnership). More commonly, he may want to involve various members of his administration, test the political waters, consult members of Congress and various sages, coordinate actions with foreign allies, and generally make cautious—perhaps even stately—progress toward blunder-free policy.

Often, however, the luxury of time is denied; the pace of events dictates the president's pace, particularly during periods of crisis. News coverage can accelerate the tempo by heightening public interest. Depending on which aspects of the story the press emphasizes, coverage can also influence public opinion in ways that increase political pressure on the president to act in a specific fashion, such as more aggressively or more compassionately. The chief executive may soon realize that the ideal of nicely insulated policy formulation has evaporated. Instead, his every move is anticipated and then critiqued almost instantly.

Maybe this is fair; maybe not. Regardless, the president can find himself being shoved along a path at a speed and in a direction that he may not like. The news media can be an important catalyst in this.

IRAN HOSTAGE CRISIS (1979–1981)

On December 31, 1977, President Jimmy Carter dined with the Shah of Iran and Empress Farah in royal splendor in Tehran. Toasting his hosts,

Carter said, "Iran, because of the great leadership of the Shah, is an island of stability in one of the more troubled areas of the world."[1] Less than two years later, the shah had been driven into exile, the American embassy in Tehran had been overrun by followers of the shah's fundamentalist successors, and the embassy staff had been taken hostage.

Carter was not alone in overestimating both the shah's staying power and Iran's stability. Nevertheless, the embassy takeover on November 4, 1979, was singularly Carter's calamity, disrupting his presidency and helping to end his tenure after one term.

In the short run, the crisis worked to Carter's political advantage. His approval rating in the opinion polls jumped from 30 percent to 61 percent the month after the hostage-taking.[2] Part of this was the result of news coverage, especially on television. As Haynes Johnson of the *Washington Post* wrote:

Americans awoke in the morning to see the menacing figure of the ayatollah breathing hatred and preaching holy war against "pagans" and "heathens." They went to bed at night after seeing mobs of Iranian demonstrators marching before the occupied U.S. Embassy, waving their fists, shouting defiant slogans, burning the American flag and effigies of Uncle Sam and Jimmy Carter. Morning after morning, evening after evening, the TV networks showed those same scenes. Through TV, the Iranian crisis became institutionalized and a part of American daily life. . . . The political impact was immense. Attacks on Carter personally by Iranian leaders, prominently reported via TV to Americans at home, gave the President a stature he had failed to achieve in three years in office. Carter became the personification of the nation, the symbol of American resolve, the rallying point for Americans at home to respond to insults from abroad."[3]

The dramatic power of the confrontation was not lost on television news executives. ABC led the way, getting into Tehran first and then, four days into the crisis, launching its late-night report, "The Crisis in Iran: America Held Hostage." This program, which aired at 11:30 P.M. eastern time and later changed its name to "Nightline," reached 12 million viewers each night, according to ABC. The overall audience during this time period increased by about 4 million viewers during the first weeks of the crisis.[4]

The intensity of coverage and of public opinion rose together. "News telecasts, national as well as local, ended with shots of the American flag and the tolling of the Liberty Bell. The result was to make the Iranian story the focus of unprecedented national attention. As the networks continued to highlight the hostage story, the country became unified in opposition to Iran as it had rarely been on a single issue in the past generation. The

networks discovered something else—their Iranian broadcasts were attract-
ing enormous new audiences. Iranian coverage, and competition for new
angles of it, intensified."[5]

For a while, Carter fared well in the news coverage. The extensive and
widely watched reports depicted him as working to secure the hostages'
release while being abused by the demonized Iranians. But this scrutiny
carried a price; results were expected promptly. Middle East expert Barry
Rubin has written that raised public expectations "encouraged an accelera-
tion of diplomatic initiatives that might have been more effective through
calmer, quieter, and slower procedures."[6]

Carter administration officials later admitted that the heavy network
coverage "effectively eliminated the option of taking a low-key approach
to the crisis."[7] Top Carter aide Hamilton Jordan has written that "Monday-
morning quarterbacks" said that Carter "should have put the problem on the
back burner. But that was never possible. From the very first day the hostage
crisis dominated the news. . . . We never had a chance to 'control' the news,
as many critics contended, and put the hostages on the 'back burner.' "[8]

Once born, the news monster had to be fed with frequent status reports
that showed progress toward the goal of the hostages' return. Television
does not do well in covering a static situation. It likes to show the story
advancing, quantifiably if possible, with wartime body counts, election year
polling updates, and the like. Usually, coverage withers when the flow of
information dwindles, but, in this case, public interest was perceived to be
so high that reducing coverage was not considered an option.

Although news favorable to Carter might not have been consistently
available, other information was. By mid-December 1979, Iranian leaders
were making their case directly to American television audiences while U.S.
diplomats found themselves unable to make headway in serious negota-
tions.[9] Iranians also intensified the crisis by making activity at the Tehran
embassy a perpetual media event. Whenever the television cameras appeared, the chanting, fist-shaking demonstrators would swing into action.
Seeing this on their television screens at home, many Americans assumed
that Iran was a boiling anti-American cauldron. In fact, less than two blocks
from the embassy, life of downtown Tehran was proceeding normally;
people walked through shops and went about their business. Some critics
of the American coverage have charged that the networks used their
sensational footage without establishing the broader context in which the
activity at the embassy was taking place.[10]

NBC, as part of a deal to secure an interview with one of the American
hostages, gave an Iranian militant five minutes of air time without including

an American rebuttal. NBC correspondent Ford Rowan then resigned, charging that the network had allowed itself to be used as a propaganda tool by the Iranians.[11] Rowan said that his decision to quit was also due to the network's failure "to include U.S. government reaction during prime time when the hostage was interviewed."[12]

The president of NBC News, William J. Small, dismissed the charges that the network had been manipulated, but he conceded that the militant's unedited statement had been aired as part of the arrangement to get the interview with the hostage.[13] Bill Leonard, president of CBS News, said his network had refused to deal with the militants because "they were asking us to be a conduit rather than a journalistic organization."[14]

The administration certainly was aware that news coverage kept the political stakes high. Secretary of State Cyrus Vance said television "magnified the pressures to the extent that it kept [the crisis] on the front burner day after day in Iran and in the United States."[15]

As the first days and weeks passed, the public anger that had initially translated into support for Carter soon became impatience directed at the president. The volume and tenor of the media's coverage fueled this. Deputy Secretary of State Warren Christopher said: "Whatever influence ordinary coverage would have had on the crisis was magnified because the coverage was so intense. It was also magnified by the phenomenon of television, with its capacity to display news graphically, or bring it alive into the American home. . . . Coverage that reinforced a national sense of outrage and frustration put heavy pressure on the government to act swiftly and visibly."[16]

Carter may have exacerbated his problems by taking such a personal and high-profile role in efforts to free the hostages and by maintaining a palpable crisis atmosphere. Carter adopted a "Rose Garden strategy" for his presidential campaign, saying that events in Iran required his constant presence at the White House. He also kept calling crisis meetings of the National Security Council—more than 100 during the first six months.[17] The television coverage matched Carter's emphasis. During those six months, the three networks "devoted nearly a third of their weeknight news time to it."[18] For forty-three days, Iran was the lead story on all three networks, often consuming two-thirds of the day's newscast. Even the Russian invasion of Afghanistan could not bump the Iran story from its dominant position.[19]

Just as Vietnam had been the "living-room war," these events became the "living-room crisis." Writing in The *New Yorker* in January 1980, media critic Michael Arlen stated: "Day after day, night after night, the networks have brought us the news from the streets of Tehran, even when there was no news, or when what there was of it had been more or less produced by the host nation for the purposes of worldwide television coverage."[20]

Also in January 1980, CBS introduced an element of ritual to the coverage. Anchorman Walter Cronkite began signing off at the end of each edition of the "CBS Evening News" with, "And that's the way it is, [whatever the date], the —th day of the hostages' captivity." As the number grew larger, this nightly pronouncement became an implicit indictment of Carter's inability to bring the hostages home. Coming from Cronkite, "the most trusted man in America," the incremental political damage to Carter presumably was significant. Although the White House never complained to CBS about this repeated commentary, Carter, after leaving office, told Cronkite, "That announcement of yours every day didn't help."[21] Cronkite's nightly reminder and ABC's "America Held Hostage" program ensured that Carter would be unable to enjoy the political and diplomatic benefits of temporarily moving his handling of the matter beyond the sight of press and public.

Also working against Carter were fundamental differences in the mechanics of diplomacy and journalism. Quiet diplomacy is incompatible with intense, intrusive news coverage. Further, as Steven Weisman of the *New York Times* observed: "State Department aides are interested in keeping Iran's positions ambiguous or fluid, so that either they or other diplomats could negotiate. Journalists, on the other hand, tend to ask questions with the aim of eliminating ambiguities, which might make bargaining more difficult."[22]

A complicating factor for the administration was the prospect of a rigorous primary campaign during the coming months against Senator Edward Kennedy, who was challenging Carter for the Democratic presidential nomination. Showing the traditional deference to a president during an international crisis, Kennedy initially refrained from criticizing Carter's handling of the affair, but he could afford such apparent nobility because the news coverage was making his point for more effectively than he could have made it himself. Although he eventually attacked Carter's charitable attitude toward the shah, Kennedy knew that his cause was being well-served by news reports that fueled public impatience. Kennedy wanted voters to believe that Carter could not handle the presidency. Carter's lack of progress on a hostage release reinforced Kennedy's accusations of ineptitude.

The drip–drip–drip of Cronkite's daily count heightened the political worries of Carter's team. James Reston wrote in the *New York Times*, "It seems slightly mad, but it happens to be true, that those characters in the White House really felt some pressure from Uncle Walter's announcing every night the number of days of captivity of the hostages."[23]

Carter's annoyance was not caused by Cronkite alone. In early January, syndicated columnist Jack Anderson wrote, "It may not be fashionable to criticize President Carter while he is struggling so earnestly to cope with the Iranian crisis"—but, fashionable or not, Anderson went on to do it. He cited (without naming his sources) the "growing alarm in the backrooms of Washington" about Carter's "caution and indecision." More specifically, Anderson raised the specter of Middle East oil fields falling under the control of the Soviet Union, and he claimed that "Ayatollah Khomeini has said tauntingly that Carter lacks 'the guts' to take military action against Iran."[24]

The reaction by Carter loyalists to such columns or news stories was predictable: urge the boss to display his "toughness," whatever that might mean. Soon thereafter, in late April 1980, the United States launched a rescue mission. It failed, never reaching Tehran. Eight American servicemen were killed at a staging area in the Iranian desert in an accident involving the mission's aircraft. In a 1987 interview, former Vice President Walter Mondale said that the pressure from news coverage on Carter to launch a military rescue attempt was "tremendous." The impatience of Congress, said Mondale, had also grown, partly because of the flood of news reports, and was yet another factor pushing Carter toward a rescue effort.[25]

Jimmy Carter did not see the hostages freed while he was president. They were released on January 20, 1981, inauguration day, shortly after Carter's successor, Ronald Reagan, had taken the oath of office.

Carter was forced to deal with television-influenced diplomacy despite not fully understanding how potent that influence was and what forces were shaping it. *New York Times* correspondent Steven Weisman has written: "Television's coverage of the crisis was at least as much a product of the nation's obsession as it was an instigator; the network news shows all experienced surges in their ratings when the hostage situation came to a boil. But it is also true that when the camera crews were kicked out of Iran, American interest waned."[26]

In addition to their effect on public opinion, the news media became de facto diplomatic media. In his study of America's relationship with Iran, Barry Rubin has written: "As the air filled with leads designed to support or justify the strategies of various factions, departments, and individuals in Washington, the contents of articles and television stories on Iran took on dual meaning. The media-political relationship was by no means new in

Washington, but never before had it become so central to the policy making process. Given the absence of direct communication between Washington and Tehran, the media filled the task usually performed by embassies and back-channel exchanges."27

So many players, so many agendas, so much information . . . but how much real news? Those who want to make the case that the media were an uncontrollable bull in diplomacy's china shop can argue that the press—wittingly or not—was being used as a substitute for traditional governmental mechanisms. *Washington Post* ombudsman Bill Green raised important questions about this possibility soon after the hostages were released: "Has the American press become captive to its own capabilities; that is, do its splendid technologies influence the substance of what is conveyed? And did the Iranians take full advantage of that technology for their own purposes? If that is true, has the coverage of the Iranian obscenity set a precedent for other countries that might be tempted to have their own day in the American spotlight?"28

For Jimmy Carter, the long-lasting news coverage of the hostage crisis had a final, perhaps politically fatal, sting. Election Day 1980 was November 4, the anniversary of the embassy's being seized. In his diary for November 3, Carter wrote that his pollster was finding "a massive slippage as people realized that the hostages were not coming home. The anniversary date of their having been captured absolutely filled the news media. . . . This apparently opened up a flood of related concerns that we were impotent [and reminded them of other negatives]."29 Six months later, Carter reiterated this thought, telling historian Theodore H. White that one of the principal reasons he had lost was "the way television had celebrated the anniversary on that last weekend" of the campaign.30

In considering the Iran hostage situation as a precedent for other presidents' policy-making, a number of questions deserve consideration:

Was the relationship between Carter and the news media during the hostage crisis a precedent or an aberration in the grand chronology of president-press relations? When he was elected in 1976, Carter benefited from voters' anger about governmental lying and secrecy about Vietnam and Watergate. These governmental misdeeds also spurred journalists to become more aggressive, intent on fully covering crises before they became scandals. Coming so soon after the culmination of the Vietnam and Watergate stories, the hostage affair was certain to attract extraordinary press and public scrutiny. Although the news media's assertiveness has never receded to the pre-1970s level, the Iran crisis may have received louder and longer press attention at least partly because of when it happened.

Would news coverage have been less overwhelming, and thus put less pressure on the administration, if Carter had been more discreet in his response to the crisis? Perhaps the full-blown coverage would have continued anyway, forcing the president to fashion an equally intense response. But maybe the mutual escalation by news organizations and the White House could have been halted (or at least significantly slowed) if Carter had responded more temperately.

Did public opinion drive news coverage, or vice versa? Any answer to this question is largely speculative, but viewers' interest in television newscasts did diminish when the Iranians cut off the flow of pictures. It is reasonable to assume that, absent news reports or other stimuli, public opinion may be less volatile. The lesson here for future presidents interested in reducing public anger about an event such as the Iran hostage situation is to encourage toned-down reporting, especially by television news. If news organizations are reluctant to do this, a president should perhaps take his case to the public, arguing that excessive coverage is inflaming a delicate situation that he is trying to handle. That tactic might work, at least for a while. As is illustrated in Chapter 4, the executive branch *can* influence news coverage substantially if such an effort is carefully planned.

PROTECTING THE KURDS (1991)

President Carter may not have known exactly what he wanted to do to get the hostages out of Iran, but he clearly felt pressured by news coverage and public opinion to do *something*. President George Bush, on the other hand, knew precisely what he did *not* want to do during the final stages of the 1991 Gulf War: He had no interest in becoming embroiled in Saddam Hussein's ongoing battle with the Kurds living in northern Iraq. But news reports, particularly those with vivid television pictures, were a major factor in Bush's decision to change his policy.

At the conclusion of the Gulf War, American policy was to disengage as expeditiously as possible, even if that meant letting Saddam Hussein have a free hand in dealing with his internal opponents who had been urged by President Bush to rise up and drive Saddam from power. Soon after the liberation of Kuwait, Bush said, "American lives are too precious for us to be sucked into a civil war."[31] White House officials dismissed initial news coverage (mostly in the print media) of the Kurds as being too inconsequential to change public opinion or administration policy.[32]

Saddam did not need much encouragement to renew his efforts to decimate the Kurds in the north and Shiites in the south. The Shiites were mostly beyond the reach of news coverage, as were the Kurds who made their way into Iran. But journalists did have access to the Kurds who surged to the Iraq-Turkey border. Reports of their brutalization by Saddam and their plight as they sought refuge in the mountains were enough to help move British Prime Minister John Major from Bush-like nonchalance to calling for the creation of a protected haven for the Kurds.

As ABC's Deborah Amos later said, "The politics of that uprising [by the Kurds] was not understood very well by the viewing public, but the pictures were clear enough."[33] Veteran correspondent Daniel Schorr wrote that "the issue, as perceived by the public, was changing from military intervention in support of a revolution to compassionate intercession for the victims of Saddam Hussein's genocidal methods."[34] Press coverage matched this shift in mood. *Newsweek* ran a cover photo of a little Kurdish girl with the headline, " 'Why Won't He Help Us?': Bush's Dilemma." Newscasts carried wrenching images of the cold and hungry Kurds. The public's interest had been captured now, and politicians began paying attention.

The process picked up speed. On April 3, Bush said: "I feel frustrated any time innocent civilians are being slaughtered. But the United States and these other countries with us in the coalition did not go there to settle all the internal affairs of Iraq." The same day, however, the administration called on Saddam to stop the attacks and pledged economic aid, by way of Turkey, to the Kurds.[35] On April 5, the administration announced that the U.S. Air Force would drop supplies to the Kurds. (Part of this effort turned out badly; some of the supplies were dropped *on* the Kurds, killing a number of them.) After seeing the more extensive European coverage of the Kurds' situation, Secretary of State James Baker made a quick visit to a Kurdish encampment just inside Turkey on April 8. What he saw there led him to recommend an immediate, large-scale relief operation run by the U.S. military.[36]

Despite the belated supplies and protection for the Kurds, the perceived weakness of the administration's policy was affecting political opinion. It was seen as a reason for the dip in Bush's approval rating from 92 to 80 percent in a *Newsweek* poll.[37] As Daniel Schorr observed, "Within a two-week period, the President had been forced, under the impact of what Americans and Europeans were seeing on television, to reconsider his hasty withdrawal of troops from Iraq."[38] British journalist Nik Gowing has noted, "After all the vigorous controls during the Gulf War, television's new, highly mobile satellite technology had overcome the power of politicians . . . to control it."[39] Similarly, Deborah Amos wrote: "Public reaction was swift and strong, and governments were scrambling to fashion a policy to stop that slaughter and stop the pictures on the evening news. . . . It was a moment when the power of television journalism was at its height."[40] And on "60 Minutes" (CBS), Lesley Stahl said, "There's no way to ignore a million cold

and hungry people when they're in your living-room night after night."[41]
Bush himself underscored all this when he said at an April 16 news
conference, "No one can see the pictures or hear the accounts of this human
suffering—men, women, and, most painfully of all, innocent children—and
not be deeply moved."[42]

Television wields its influence even in its choice of format for a story.
When CNN broadcast Bush's news conference at which he announced that
camps would be set up for the Kurds, the screen was divided, with the
President in the lower right and a larger picture in the upper left of the
refugees. "Bush seemed to be responding to pressure from above."[43]

Schorr has attributed the change in policy to a change in public opinion
that was driven partly by news coverage: "The polls that had shown
Americans overwhelmingly wanting troops home in a hurry were now
showing that Americans did not want to abandon the Kurds, even if that
meant using U.S. forces to protect them. It is rare in American history that
television, which is most often manipulated to support a policy, creates an
unofficial plebescite that forces a change in policy."[44]

The "plebescite" was a manifestation of moral outrage about the treatment of the Kurds. But building policy on news-fueled outrage may create
problems. Deborah Amos has said of this, "The problem of deploying troops
for reasons of outrage rather than national security is that the commitment
is not very deep and that you might be willing to kill for such a policy but
not be killed."[45]

Along the same lines, *New York Times* television critic Walter Goodman
acknowledged television's impact on policy but noted that "the existence
of the Kurds was certified only when it was threatened within camera
range." He also wrote, "A picture that arouses sympathy does not necessarily enhance understanding," and he asked, "Should American policy be
driven by scenes that happen to be accessible to cameras and make the most
impact on the screen?"[46]

That question gets to the heart of the relationship between news coverage
and policy-making, and it raises other questions about the setting of foreign
policy priorities: Why help the Kurds but not the Shiites? Why intervene in
Somalia but not in the Sudan? Why does American policy about Bosnia
fluctuate while the killing is constant?

THE BOSNIA CONUNDRUM (1993–1994)

If a government has a carefully constructed policy to which it is firmly
committed, even the most incendiary television footage is unlikely to

produce more than a brief flurry of public relations damage control from officials. As the coverage and related public attention subside, those who govern continue along the policy route they have mapped for themselves.

The reverse is also true. The impact of news coverage on those responsible for policy-making is greatest when a policy is inchoate or otherwise soft. That was the case with the U.S. position about Bosnia when the Markale market in Sarajevo was hit by a mortar round in February 1994.

A single 120–millimeter shell landed in the midst of a crowd of Saturday shoppers. In itself, the carnage was unexceptional in that bloodied country, but televison news crews were able to get to the scene quickly and take pictures of severed bodies and other aspects of the gruesome chaos. After seeing this coverage, President Bill Clinton threatened to order air strikes against the Serbs, the presumed culprits, unless the shelling of Sarajevo stopped and the Serbs' heavy weaponry was withdrawn or placed under United Nations control.[47]

This seemed to be a good example of cause and effect: the president sees a news story and then responds. In the *New York Times*, R. W. Apple wrote: "The frightful television images of the carnage may have broken, or at least dented, the shell of American public indifference. At the least, they have given the President as good an opportunity to act firmly in Bosnia as he is likely to get."[48]

But it may have been more complicated than that. White House communications director Mark Gearan said: "It did not take just the TV coverage of the Sarajevo massacre to push things forward. Things were moving."[49] Secretary of State Warren Christopher likewise said, "Television images moved forward a policy we had clearly started on."[50]

Those claims should be considered in the context of the scrambling by policymakers who do not want to appear to have been pushed out of their vacillation by the news media. The truth is probably to be found on the middle ground. Assistant Secretary of Defense Graham Allison said: "The Sarajevo market massacre crystallized for the Clinton administration that it had to do something; we could not do nothing. Those who wanted to do something seized on it." Allison's remarks underscore the importance of news coverage as a catalyst: "If a shell had fallen in Sarajevo and 68 people had been killed, and there would have been no pictures of it, would the U.S. policy have changed? I do not think it would have."[51]

Plenty of examples bear out Allison's contention. For instance, in April 1993, Serbs shelled the "safe area" of Srebrenica, killing fifty-six persons and wounding ninety. But, as British journalist Nik Gowing has pointed out, "there were no television pictures, and the slaughter led to no dramatic international response."[52]

Besides their direct impact on policymakers, vivid news reports have the indirect effect of getting political leaders' attention by influencing public opinion. Speaking about the Sarajevo attack, U.S. ambassador to the United Nations Madeleine Albright said the "pictures on television have helped to educate the American people about the horrors of people dying. . . . The polls are showing increasing public support" for tougher U.S. action.[53]

Actually, a Gallup poll following the Sarajevo killings found only a 48 to 43 percent margin in favor of air strikes.[54] This middling support was reflected in the lack of Sarajevo-related political pressure emanating from Capitol Hill. According to Clinton administration officials, the most persuasive case for a harder line was made by the French government, which had long been impatient with Serb intransigence. The Sarajevo attack in itself—not news coverage of it—was enough to make the French intensively lobby the Americans to threaten the Serbs.

Judging the significance of the news reports is made more difficult by Clinton's personal reaction. After seeing CNN footage from the Sarajevo market, he reportedly told Secretary of State Christopher, "This is awful." He was, of course, correct, but those television stories should not have been a revelation for the president. The Bosnian war had been "awful" for a long time, and, presumably, Clinton did not need to rely on television newscasts to inform him about events in the Balkans.

His consideration of more forceful action may have been a politician's reaction in anticipation of his constituents' response to the gripping pictures. But an argument can be made that such television-enhanced democracy should be celebrated cautiously. As this case illustrates, consistency is unlikely if policy-making depends on the breadth of the camera's vision and the sharpness of its focus. Television news, with its penchant for the dramatic and its impatience with process, has priorities that are often incompatible with those of the responsible governance of foreign affairs. Even when a president wants to do the right thing, dangers exist in letting television's fickle values define what is right.[55]

In this case, the impulse to order a sharp military response to these Sarajevo killings faded quickly. The presidential directive for air strikes never came. Instead, assistance was provided in evacuating the latest Sarajevo casualties. As *Newsweek* said of this measure, "In the age of TV diplomacy, the medical-evacuation plan at least ensured images of U.S. planes landing in Bosnia."[56]

Sadly, wars such as the one that has ripped apart the former Yugoslavia show no signs of vanishing. The United States and other major powers will inevitably face pressures—enhanced by dramatic news reports—to become involved in these struggles. Such intervention may seem morally essential, even if unjustified by either national strategic interests or prospects for success.

The flurry of attention without substantive policy change in this case illustrates the mirage-like quality of the relationship between news coverage and policymaking. The televised pictures from Sarajevo led only to a relatively insignificant reaction by the Clinton administration. This result was in line with an observation made by Walter Goodman of the *New York Times* the year before: "The coverage [of Bosnia] has amounted to a prolonged plea that something be done and a reprimand to those who were failing to do it. If the power of the television image were as irresistible as it is sometimes assumed to be by the medium's professional observers, the nation would by now have been roaring for intervention. Instead, Americans remain chary about rushing to the rescue. Whatever one's opinion about what should already have been done or must be done . . . the resistance is a sign that the image is not all-powerful, that viewers are not just sponges for the tube's outpourings of emotion."[57]

The emotional power of events crashes into *realpolitik*, as is evident in British Foreign Secretary Douglas Hurd's position on Bosnia: "We have not been and are not willing to begin some form of military intervention which we judge useless or worse, simply because of day by day pressures from the media."[58]

In some cases, those pressures will be resisted. In some others, however, the decision will be made to intervene.

THE SOMALIA MORASS (1992–1993)

As 1992 drew to a close, George Bush was contemplating the end of his presidency. The Gulf War had not been enough to win him reelection but would presumably ensure his place in history as a president adroit in foreign affairs. He had no interest in embarking on a risky, last-minute venture that might tarnish this reputation.

And yet that is precisely what he did. The site was Somalia, a country most Americans had never heard of until they were flooded with news reports depicting heart-wrenching starvation and anarchy. Walter Goodman wrote in December: "Once the pictures appeared of the fly-tormented faces and bloated bellies of dying babies the effect was stunning. The natural reaction of Americans, pity for the dying and rage against the gun-happy druggies who were stealing their food, became too much for Washington to resist. . . . The effort to weigh shadowy future costs against urgent needs is not abetted by the vividly rendered images of pain that, to the ambiguous credit of television, make us all want to do something."[59]

White House press secretary Marlin Fitzwater agreed: "After the election, the media had free time and that was when the pressure started building up. We heard it from every corner, that something must be done. Finally the pressure was too great. The President said, 'I just can't live with this for two months.' TV tipped us over the top at a time when the death rate [from starvation] was over 100 a day."[60]

At the United Nations, this kind of pressure was recognized as part of the decision-making process. Secretary General Boutros Boutros-Ghali noted that public sympathy for dying children could drive governments' policy. Former U.S. Ambassador to the United Nations Donald McHenry said that with graphic news reports "governments are forced to act whether they wish to or not."[61]

Somalia, as opposed to Sudan, which was also ravaged by famine and war, got the Bush administration's attention largely because that was where the television networks had sent their cameras. During 1992, American evening news programs carried six stories about Sudan, 468 about Somalia.[62]

When Bush dispatched a military force to Somalia, Walter Goodman wrote, "every news program hailed the arrival of American troops, which was treated like an old-fashioned Hollywood premiere; a spirit of self-congratulation prevailed."[63]

As this was happening, diplomat George Kennan was perplexed by "the reason for the general acceptance by Congress and the public about what is being done." On December 9, 1992, after watching television coverage of the U.S. troops coming ashore in Mogadishu, he wrote in his diary: "There can be no question that the reason for this acceptance lies primarily with the exposure of the Somalia situation by the American media, above all, television. The reaction would have been unthinkable without this exposure. The reaction was an emotional one, occasioned by the sight of suffering of the starving people in question. That this should be felt as adequate reason for our military action does credit, no doubt, to the idealism of the American people and to their ready sympathy for people suffering in another part of the world."[64] But, continued Kennan, that quick emotional reaction is an inadequate substitute for carefully thought-through policy that has been presented in timely fashion by the president to the Congress and the public.

Kennan was not the only one to comment on this television-based distortion of the policy process. "Television, in particular," noted Walter Goodman, "has a way of touching the heart without reaching the brain."[65] He also wrote: "Even as the pictures prepare viewers for action, they overwhelm analysis. How can ifs and buts compete with the image of a mother and child dying before one's eyes? For the cost of action to come across as forcefully as the cost of inaction requires American casualties."[66]

The lack of thought cited by Kennan and Goodman produced ramifications not for George Bush but for his successor, Bill Clinton, who had inherited the U.S. commitment to Somalia. Bush left office without having defined exactly what the American troops were supposed to do besides alleviate, in ways that remained vague, the suffering that television was displaying. Elizabeth Drew wrote, "Implicit in the Bush administration's mission was that it wouldn't just dump the food and depart, but would try to leave behind something that wouldn't simply return Somalia to chaos, warlordism, and more famine. Left ambiguous was whether one goal was to disarm the warring clans."[67]

Preoccupied with domestic policy and political problems during his first year in the White House, Clinton let the Somalia operation drift along with its goals vaguely specified. In a military operation, that is asking for trouble, which is precisely what he got.

A raid to try to capture clan leader Mohammed Farah Aideed in October 1993 turned into a deadly fiasco. U.S. helicopters were shot down, and a battle erupted in downtown Mogadishu. It was the largest firefight in which U.S. troops had been involved since the Vietnam War. Eighteen Americans were killed, seventy-four wounded, and one was captured. As many as 1,000 Somalis may have been killed.[68]

Television, of course, was there. The next day, Americans watching the news could see Somalis dragging the body of a dead U.S. soldier through Mogadishu's streets and could look into the frightened eyes of the American helicopter pilot being held by Aideed's militia.

The reaction: Thousands of Americans called Capitol Hill demanding that the U.S. get out of Somalia.[69] Members of Congress, most of whom had never been clear on the scope of the Somalia mission, responded quickly to this manifestation of public opinion that had been produced by what R. W. Apple of the *New York Times* called "the journalism of images."[70] Senators and members of the House, wrote Elizabeth Drew, "were in a state of panic—the sort of unproductive and often misguided state they collectively get in from time to time, when events beyond their immediate control are riling up the country."[71]

David Halberstam noted that the images of starving children that had led to the American involvement had now been superseded by "counterimages"—pictures of dead and wounded Americans, the casualties who were the "price of this involvement."[72] Similarly, Marvin Kalb said that the body of the soldier seen by so many Americans was "a symbol of American power being dragged through the Third World, unable to master the new challenges of the post-Cold War era."[73]

Whatever the historical significance of this episode may have been, the Clinton administration was faced with the immediate problem of news-fueled public opinion firming up against the inherited, dysfunctional Somalia policy. It did not matter that the intervention had been a gift from George Bush; it was Clinton's now.

Without any firm commitment within the administration about what to do, news coverage and the public feelings it generated had extra impact. The White House staff and other top administration officials offered the president conflicting advice and then tried to hammer together their foreign policy and political strategy to meet the public's concerns about events in Somalia.

Clinton delivered a speech to the nation from the Oval Office, outlining the case against sudden withdrawal from Somalia and justifying his decision to send additional troops to stabilize the military situation there. He made his argument effectively, if belatedly. Public criticism and interest subsided.

As was to happen the following year with the American reaction to the bloodshed in Bosnia, news reports did not dictate the specifics of policy. Rather, the coverage and the public reaction it produced affected the *process*, pushing Clinton and his administration into more concentrated policy-making.

Testifying before the Senate Foreign Relations Committee in October 1993, when concern about Somalia was high, U.S. ambassador to the United Nations Madeleine Albright said: "Television's ability to bring graphic images of pain and outrage into our living rooms has heightened the pressure both for immediate engagement in areas of international crisis, and immediate disengagement when events do not go according to plan."[74] Her words reflected the sensitivities of the Clinton foreign policy team. But a month later, testifying before the same committee, Secretary of State Warren Christopher added some cautionary words: "Television is a wonderful phenomenon and sometimes even an instrument of freedom. But television images cannot be the North Star of America's foreign policy."[75]

The lesson emerging from these examples is that presidents *can* be pushed by news coverage and the resultant public opinion. But *how far* they will let themselves be pushed remains uncertain.

To a certain extent, this is healthy, responsive, democratic politics—the government reacting to popular opinion. Although this system may be preferable to a government that walls itself off from public sentiment, as happened during the Vietnam War, it may be a symptom of a policy-making process that is intrinsically flimsy.

Ideally, principle and thoughtful long-range planning will counterbalance events and emotions of the moment. For those who shape policy, crafting those principles and plans is made more difficult by the pressures that can be exerted by news coverage.

Images on a television screen may seem too ethereal to knock governance askew, but they are quite capable of capturing the public's interest and guiding the public's attitude. The momentum this power generates will shake any policymaker—bureaucrat or president—who is unprepared to deal with it.

Chapter Four

The President Pushes Back

President George Bush understood how news coverage had exacerbated the crises faced by his predecessors, such as Lyndon Johnson during the Tet offensive and Jimmy Carter during the Iran hostage-situation. When Bush confronted his own most formidable foreign policy challenge—the Persian Gulf crisis of 1990–1991—he was determined not to be buffeted by the news media and placed on the defensive while he decided what he wanted to do. Instead, he took the initiative, using cajolery, controls, and sometimes deception to influence how news organizations covered his response to the invasion of Kuwait and his leadership in the war that followed.

PREPARING FOR WAR

In his book *The Commanders*, journalist Bob Woodward described the significance of a president's judgment about when to take the country into battle: "The decision to go to war is one that defines a nation, both to the world and, perhaps more importantly, to itself. There is no more serious business for a national government, no more accurate measure of national leadership."[1]

George Bush grappled with this decision after Iraq invaded Kuwait on August 2, 1990. In a speech from the Oval Office on August 8, Bush announced that he was sending American troops to Saudi Arabia. He had political, military, and economic reasons for doing so (especially protecting the Saudi oil fields), but he began his speech by citing a higher moral purpose: "In the life of a nation, we're called upon to define who we are and what we believe. Sometimes these choices are not easy. But today as President, I ask for your support in a decision I've made to stand up for what's right and condemn what's wrong—all in the cause of peace."[2]

The mission apparently was to be defensive and limited: deploy enough troops—50,000 was the figure most often mentioned—to signal Iraqi leader Saddam Hussein that he should not think about moving on from Kuwait into Saudi Arabia. This U.S. presence plus diplomacy would, presumably, stabilize the region and push Saddam into a face-saving, nonbloody withdrawal.

A *Washington Post*-ABC News poll (published August 10) found that 74 percent of Americans supported Bush's decision to send troops, while 68 percent opposed invading Iraq to force it to leave Kuwait.[3] But early in the crisis, Bush was already thinking about liberating Kuwait. He knew that public opinion would have to be skillfully massaged if he was to have the domestic political support he needed.

As Jason DeParle reported in the *New York Times*, top Bush administration policymakers discussed earlier military operations in which they thought that relations with the news media had been handled poorly. In addition to considering Vietnam, they looked at brief ventures, such as the 1975 effort to rescue the American ship *Mayaguez*, which had been seized off Cambodia, and the 1989 invasion of Panama. Secretary of Defense Dick Cheney (who had been on President Gerald Ford's White House staff during the *Mayaguez* incident) was put in charge of coming up with a press plan. He said he was guided by two principles: "One was that military needs had to take precedence over journalistic rights, and so the 'lore' of past practice needed to be disregarded."[4]

Cheney found the going easy, at least at the outset. Journalists, like politicians, read the opinion polls; their coverage reflects the public's mood, at least as much as it shapes it. Soon after Bush announced his plan, ABC's Sam Donaldson told the *Wall Street Journal*, "It's difficult to play devil's advocate, especially against such a popular president as George Bush."[5] Donaldson's attitude was reflected in the television networks' coverage. According to the conservative-leaning Center for Media and Public Affairs, 76 percent of all references to Bush during the first two weeks of the crisis were favorable, and many journalists adopted Bush's strong anti-Saddam rhetoric.[6]

The circumstances of the deployment virtually guaranteed news coverage that was favorable to the administration. Not only had the nobility of the venture been accepted by the American public, but this also looked to be the safest kind of heroism: Send the troops to the desert, and certainly the Hitler-clone Saddam would turn and run. The soldiers were not, after all, being sent into combat; no one was shooting at them. While their presence loomed, there was plenty of time for diplomacy, ultimatums, and then perhaps a real war, if Saddam made that necessary.

Until that final step, the build-up could be covered as a painless (although expensive) patriotic exercise. In the years since Vietnam, better and less costly technology had made international coverage feasible for local television stations as well as networks. The Pentagon seized on this change. For example, not only could a Texas television station cover the troops departing from Fort Hood in central Texas; now they could also send a news crew to Saudi Arabia—on a free, Pentagon-provided junket—to cover the homestate soldiers acting soldierly.

Lawrence Grossman, the former president of NBC News, characterized the coverage this way: "The war build-up story was pictured largely in terms of personal vignettes and human interest features. The amount of coverage was overwhelming and people could not seem to get enough of it. News studios . . . sprouted yellow ribbons in support of the troops."[7]

Meanwhile, Bush became increasingly enamored of restoring Kuwaiti sovereignty, which no one had cared much about before, and Kuwaiti democracy, which had not existed at all. The president's concerns were fueled in part by a lavishly funded public relations campaign. The American firm Hill and Knowlton was hired by Citizens for a Free Kuwait, which was supposedly an organization of concerned individuals acting privately, but which had actually secured $11.8 million of its $12 million budget from the Kuwaiti government.[8]

Hill and Knowlton helped orchestrate public sympathy for Kuwait as a first step toward winning an American commitment to go to war if necessary to remove the Iraqis from Kuwait. This campaign involved such measures as organizing a day of prayer for Kuwait in American churches and providing "Free Kuwait" T-shirts.

Among the most successful tactics in this effort was the testimony before a congressional caucus of a fifteen-year-old Kuwaiti who identified herself only as Nayirah. She told of Iraqi soldiers coming into Kuwaiti hospitals, stealing pediatric incubators, and leaving newborns on the floor to die. Bush cited these "incubator atrocities" six times in a month as he rallied public support for his war plan. Citizens for a Free Kuwait also offered members of Congress and the news media graphic evidence of Iraqi atrocities perpetrated in Kuwait: photographs of tortured and bayoneted victims. The photos were grainy and somewhat out of focus, but they were clear enough to inspire hatred of Saddam in anyone who looked at them.

All this information was reported faithfully by much of the news media. But some problems gradually appeared. Nayirah was not just a hospital worker; she was a member of the Kuwaiti royal family and the daughter of Kuwait's ambassador to the United States. Her incubator story was surmise built on rumor; postwar reports by ABC News and Amnesty International concluded that the story was not supported by evidence. In the photographs documenting torture, the "victims" turned out to be mannequins.[9]

As John R. MacArthur has reported in *Second Front*, his book that analyzed the pro-Kuwait propaganda campaign, "there is no doubt that Saddam Hussein's troops did terrible things in Kuwait," but invention tended to displace fact in the public relations effort. These inventions were then passed on to the American public as "news."[10] MacArthur has also noted, "The perceived degree of violence and terror committed had everything to do with America's choice of war." He added that the public's reliance on this propaganda could not have occurred "without the media's overwhelming credulity and willingness to repeat again and again the Hitler analogy. Bush had accused Hussein's troops of 'outrageous acts of barbarism that even Adolf Hitler never committed,' and reporters were unwilling to challenge the obvious speciousness of the comparison."[11]

The administration did not orchestrate the Citizens for a Free Kuwait propaganda campaign but did seize upon it when making the case for going to war against Iraq. The Kuwaitis–as–martyrs imagery was particularly useful in deflecting charges that Bush's war was a "blood for oil" trade-off.[12] The news media remained mostly uncritical throughout all this, succumbing to the administration's coaxing and never forgetting that the opinion of the public—the people who buy the newspapers and watch the televisions—remained pro-Bush.

Sometimes Bush's dominance slipped. On Veterans' Day weekend in November, newspapers featured stories about discord among members of the anti-Saddam coalition and about the problems that would plague a land war in the desert. *USA Today* published a poll, headlined "Bush Support Slim," showing 51 percent of Americans approving of the president's handling of the Gulf crisis, down from 82 percent approval in August.[13]

But even 51 percent was not bad, and Bush's use of the media helped him push his ratings back up. In late November, *Newsweek* featured an article titled "Why We Must Break Saddam's 'Stranglehold,' " written by none other than George Bush. (Media critic John MacArthur has called this "one of the most shameless examples of media war promotion disguised as journalism that occurred during the Gulf crisis.")[14]

On December 16, Bush taped a television interview with David Frost for broadcast on January 2. In the interview, he said (in his unmatched syntax): "When you have such a clear case of . . . good versus evil. We have such a clear moral case. . . . It's that big. It's that important. Nothing like this since World War II. Nothing of this moral importance since World War II."[15]

While the president made his case, antiwar voices were seldom heard. The liberal-oriented watchdog group Fairness and Accuracy in Reporting (FAIR) claimed that "nightly network news programs largely ignored public efforts to oppose the Bush administration's military policies in the Persian Gulf." FAIR reported that, of 2,855 minutes of television coverage from August 8 to January 3, only twenty-nine minutes—roughly 1 percent—dealt with popular opposition to the American military build-up.[16]

In their book about the Bush administration, Michael Duffy and Dan Goodgame of *Time* have written that the president recognized early on that he had the best chance of achieving his goals if he acted secretively and on his own. Bush, they have noted, "knew he was not capable of sustained rhetorical leadership, so he wanted the least possible public involvement in his handling of the Gulf crisis. He was going to prosecute his campaign against Iraq by bold, unilateral action, and if he was successful, public opinion would follow."[17] They have also contended that Bush concealed from both the U.S. public and his allies the extent of the military deployment he had in mind and his goal of liberating Kuwait. "That he managed this global juggling act for as long as he did was nothing short of remarkable."[18]

AT WAR

The air war against Iraq began at an appropriate media-age time—during America's network newscasts on January 16, 1991. Millions listened as correspondents in Baghdad provided live descriptions of the attack (no live pictures were available that night). Meanwhile, the build-up in the Saudi desert continued as the United States and its allies prepared to launch their ground offensive.

The build-up of the American press corps also continued, tightly monitored by the Pentagon. In a postwar report, the Gannett Foundation noted that the news media's coverage of the war evolved "without much planning or reflection and certainly with little historical perspective on the role of the press in wartime. At the same time, the military had made studious preparations for dealing with the press in this war, far beyond what it had ever done before."[19]

Military institutions and leaders had thought a lot about what to do with journalists. A textbook used at the War College suggested, "Seek out the media and try to bring them in to write stories and produce television shows or clips in support" of the effort underway.[20] Along similar lines, General Colin Powell, chairman of the Joint Chiefs, said, "Once you've got all the forces moving and everything's being taken care of by the commanders, turn your attention to television because you can win the battle but lose the war if you don't handle the story right."[21]

In *The Commanders*, Bob Woodward has written of Powell's concern about how to do this: "The reporters and the cameras would be there to record each step, vastly complicating all military tasks. Powell was sure of one thing: a prolonged war on television could become impossible, unsupportable at home."[22] As a result, according to Woodward, Powell determined that "the public and the world were going to see an incredibly limited and antiseptic version of the war."[23]

Powell's outlook reflected his understanding of the linkage between military and political concerns. He said: "A great deal of my time is spent sensing that political environment. . . . There isn't a general in Washington who isn't political, not if he's going to be successful, because that's the nature of our system. It's the way the Department of Defense works. It's the way in which we formulate foreign policy. It's the way in which we get approval for our policy."[24]

The Pentagon's leaders also know that Washington politics is influenced by public opinion. Lieutenant General Thomas Kelly, who was the Pentagon's chief press briefer during the war, has said, "Anybody who doesn't recognize that the support of the American people is a critical element of combat power is pretty dumb."[25]

This political awareness at the Pentagon aided the White House in its efforts to get its message across to the public via the media. According to Brown University professor Stephen Graubard, the administration wanted to deliver a single, clearly defined, self-serving story: "The war would be difficult; only ingenious American military and political planning could cause it to be brief and, no less importantly, virtually casualty-free. So long as the media accepted the idea that only White House intelligence and resolve prevented Saddam Hussein from causing a massacre among the Coalition forces assembled to contain him, they contributed in creating the myth that the President and his close advisers wished them to communicate."[26]

The public was an avid audience for whatever "news" was provided to them. For example, sales of *Newsweek* were up 90 percent over the year before, and the *Los Angeles Times* was printing 200,000 extra copies a day.[27] Opinion research found that "most of the public strongly supported military censorship of war news and that people felt they were getting excellent or at least adequate coverage."[28] People in the news business understood that they had been outmaneuvered. *Washington Post* chairman Katharine Graham recognized that the public believed that it was getting enough news, but, she said, "They don't realize that what they know they know despite the government attempts to delay and disrupt the coverage."[29]

Former NBC News president Lawrence Grossman offered one of the best appraisals of the administration's successful news management:

The government, in effect, commandeered the Gulf War's television coverage and set the tone for almost all the news that appeared each day. The official, sanitized, upbeat version of the war dominated American television screens and neither the public nor the press, which should have known better, was aware that anything was missing at the time. We saw hardly any of the casualties and gore of war. . . . The military's most striking success in controlling the flow of battlefield information, however, came not from its censorship of war news . . . but from its well-planned and inspired decision to flood the world's television screens with fascinating video tapes of smart bomb strikes that never missed and with detailed official briefings.[30]

At the White House, the president was an attentive watcher of the daily televised Pentagon briefings. When Department of Defense officials decided that their principal briefer, Lieutenant General Thomas Kelly, had star potential, they began rehearsing him daily, testing him on the questions reporters would be most likely to ask.[31] Journalists were, for the most part, complaisant in the face of such manipulation. When Joint Chiefs chairman Powell said, "Trust me" at a news briefing, most journalists did.

Later in the war, George Bush remarked, "By God, we've kicked the Vietnam Syndrome once and for all." That statement reflected his administration's obsession with not letting defeatism creep into the public's appraisal of the conduct of the war. As Jason DeParle reported in the *New York Times*, the goal of senior officials, including the president, was "to manage the information flow in a way that supported the operation's political goals and avoided the perceived mistakes of Vietnam."[32]

"Don't upset the public and they'll follow you" seemed to be the premise guiding White House policy. This approach was challenged by some journalists, such as Sydney Schanberg, who wrote, "But a president who is seen to be withholding information is also likely to lose public support over time." Schanberg pointed out that Barry Zorthian, who had been the offical spokesman for the U.S. mission in Saigon from 1964 to 1968, had said that, although about 2,000 correspondents had been accredited to cover that war and had filed hundreds of thousands of stories during those years, only five or six violations of security guidelines had occurred. Most of these, according to Zorthian, had been accidental or had been caused by honest misunderstanding; none to his knowledge had jeopardized military operations or lives.[33]

But the Bush administration was in no mood to take chances. Before the fighting began, it imposed rules that strictly limited correspondents' ability to gather news. Some of the guidelines made sense—such as no reports about specific troop deployments or future operations, although this is the kind of information that news organizations presumably would have had sense enough to withhold anyway. In addition, coverage in many instances would be done only by pools (small groups of journalists who would share the information they gathered with their colleagues) or by reporters accompanied by military public affairs escorts. Once hostilities began, pool reports would be subject to military review "to determine if they contain sensitive information." The guidelines said that material would be reviewed only for true security reasons, "not for its potential to express criticism or cause embarrassment."[34]

In justifying these rules, Assistant Secretary of Defense Pete Williams cited differences between the Gulf War and earlier wars: the reporters might be delivering their stories live and, "at least in the case of CNN, their reports can be seen by the commanders of enemy forces just as easily as they can be seen by American viewers at home in their living rooms."[35] (For more about live coverage of the Gulf War, see Chapter 7.)

Although cloaked in reasonableness, the rules were seen by many journalists as unfairly interfering with their reporting. The use of pools meant that most correspondents would be left behind, dependent on the work of others, and even the perspective of those others on the war would depend on where the pools were allowed to go. The presence of escort officers would almost certainly inhibit interviewing. And the invocation of the multistep security review process could delay publication long enough to wring the newsworthiness out of a story.

In a letter to Assistant Secretary Williams, Burl Osborne, president of the American Society of Newspaper Editors, asked that reporters be given security guidelines rather than having their work subjected to pre-publication review. Osborne also noted that escorts, if needed, should just escort and not be a menacing presence when reporters were trying to conduct interviews. For example, wrote Osborne, a military public affairs officer "declaring chaplains to be off-limits to journalists doesn't do anyone any good."[36]

In practice, the censorship did affect the content of coverage. For instance, Frank Bruni of the *Detroit Free Press* wrote a story about American pilots returning to an aircraft carrier after a bombing raid. Bruni described the pilots as "giddy"; a military censor changed that word to "proud."[37] Moreover, the Pentagon prohibited any coverage of the arrival of caskets of Americans killed in the war at Dover Air Force Base in Delaware, the site of the main military mortuary.[38] The reasoning behind that move was obviously political, rather than being based on security concerns. Not knowing how long or how bloody the war might turn out to be, the Bush administration did not want public support for the war undermined by nightly news video of a stream of caskets coming back from the desert. Journalist Sydney Schanberg called this part of the "concerted attempt to try to edit out all reminders of Vietnam."[39]

As blatant as such attempts were, the public did not object. A Times Mirror poll conducted during the war's first month found that 79 percent of Americans thought military censorship was a good thing, and 57 percent favored even more military control of the news media.[40] Sydney Schanberg offered some reasons for this public sentiment: "We journalists are not a very popular bunch. Some people see us as whiny and self-important, and some even see us as unpatriotic because we take it upon ourselves to challenge and question the government in difficult times like these." But, he added, "We are required to be responsible, not popular."[41]

While the administration had its policy clearly defined, the news business did not come together to speak with one voice. In addition to the protest by the American Society of Newspaper Editors, the editor of *The Nation* magazine and several other journalists filed a lawsuit objecting to the Pentagon's rules. No other national news organizations joined in the litigation, however, or even filed friend-of-the-court briefs.[42]

In the field as well as in court, the press was off balance. *Newsweek* media critic Jonathan Alter noted: "The sad truth is that we 'covered' the war but we didn't report the war. There was very little independent journalism until the last hours of the conflict. Pool coverage is not journalism—it's something else. I'm not quite sure what it is, but I wouldn't call it journalism."[43]

Two former CBS journalists who had covered the Vietnam War understood what the administration was doing. According to Marvin Kalb: "One can just imagine dreadful pictures being relayed back to American living-rooms and if they continue night after night, the impact is going to be inevitable. This is not an American response to a Japanese attack on Pearl

Harbor. This will be a delayed American response to an Iraqi attack on a small Arab sheikdom with which we had no contractual obligation. . . . In that context, the question, 'What are we doing here?' is apt to come from many American lips."[44] Walter Cronkite's comments were even more pointed: "An American citizen is entitled to ask, 'What are they trying to hide?' The answer might be casualties from shelling, collapsing morale, disaffection, insurrection, incompetent officers, poorly trained troops, malfunctioning equipment, widespread illness—who knows? But the fact that we don't know, the fact that the military feels there is *something* it must hide, can only lead to a breakdown in home-front confidence and the very echoes from Vietnam that the Pentagon fears the most."[45]

While the press griped, the Pentagon moved smoothly along. The military, wrote Lawrence Grossman, "gave sympathetic reporters special access, weeding out the critical ones and tending to favor the hometown press. In most cases, the television press not only went along, but also enlisted in the cause. Dan Rather literally saluted the troops in the field during one news broadcast and congratulated Army officers for their outstanding performance while he was interviewing them."[46]

A Gannett Foundation study of newspaper editorials written during the Gulf crisis found that on the whole they were "respectful toward the President and generally supportive. When there was dissent, it was usually over tactics and timing, rather than goals and principles."[47]

When the press was criticized for being too passive, one response was that the coverage reflected the sentiments of the American people: Support the President and go to war if necessary. That rationale, however, leads to an important question: Did the press merely reflect public opinion, or did it help shape (or at least reinforce) that opinion through its uncritical coverage?[48] A definitive answer is elusive, but the impact of coverage on opinion deserves consideration by journalists. Their work *does* have effect, reinforcing or undercutting the conventional wisdom as it takes shape in public opinion.

The White House watched warily to see if its controls were generating public backlash. At one point, Bush aides were considering relaxing some of the restrictions, but after they saw a "Saturday Night Live" sketch lampooning the press (with the show's "reporters" asking ridiculous questions) they decided that the public was on the administration's side and did nothing.[49]

When negative stories were written or even foreseen, the administration responded promptly. One reporter in the war zone later wrote: "Three times near the front I ran into Americans I had quoted earlier in stories, with their permission. They had talked about themselves, not military operations. All three had been hunted down and disciplined."[50] When some news organizations were investigating reports that Soviet satellite photos showed there had been no Iraqi military activity near the Saudi border in September (a month after the invasion of Kuwait), Pentagon spokesman Pete Williams actively discouraged reporters from doing stories about the pictures, saying that they did not accurately reflect the real Iraqi menace.[51]

After the war ended, some journalists questioned the news media's performance. ABC's Ted Koppel said, "I'm not sure the public's interest is served by seeing what seems to have been such a painless war, when 50,000 to 100,000 people may have died on the other side."[52] In *Harper's* magazine, Lewis Lapham analyzed the government's effective press strategy:

The media never subjected the administration's statements to cross-examination, in large part because the administration so deftly promoted the fiction of a "liberal press" bent on spiteful negation of America's most cherished truths. . . . The administration well understood that the media couldn't afford to offend the profoundly conservative sympathies of their prime-time audience, and so it knew that it could rely on the media's complicity in almost any deception dressed up in patriotic costume. . . . If even the well-known "liberal press" could be brought into camp, then clearly the administration's cause was just.[53]

Though some in the press agonized about their performance, President Bush was well pleased. In April 1991, he said: "I think the American people stand behind us. I think they felt they got a lot of information about this war."[54]

The value to the Bush administration of its preemptive strike against independent, inquisitive reporting is difficult to measure because of the war's brevity. The ground war began February 23; Iraq announced a cease-fire February 28. Questions remain about whether the assertive approach to press controls will be a useful precedent for future administrations. What if the war had continued for many months? What if American casualties had been heavy? Would public opinion then have shifted, supporting the demands of an increasingly restive press corp for more information? Would Americans have come to view the administration's censorship as nothing more than a massive cover-up? If coverage had become more aggressive, what would the political ramifications and effects on policy have been?

"What if" speculation can generate an array of theories for future presidents to consider. In this case, at least, George Bush was less a political victim than some of his predecessors considered themselves to be. He had decided to push, rather than let himself be pushed. It worked.

THE BRITISH EXPERIENCE: THE FALKLANDS WAR (1982)

George Bush was not the first political leader to consider the precedent of Vietnam War news coverage when planning foreign policy. Among others, British Prime Minister Margaret Thatcher displayed an appreciation of press power and made every effort not to fall into the "Vietnam trap." She built strong press controls into her political strategy during the 1982 Falklands War.

Situated in the South Atlantic 8,000 miles from Britain, the Falklands had been a subject of a long-running but mostly low-key ownership dispute between Great Britain and Argentina, which calls the islands the Malvinas. Continuous British presence on the islands dates back to 1833. The Falk-lands are home to about 2,000 British subjects, many of whom raise sheep (about 600,000 of them) on 4,700 rugged square miles. On April 2, 1982, Argentine forces seized the islands, overwhelming the small garrison of Royal Marines. Thatcher immediately dispatched British naval forces to the area. The war was underway.

British journalist Robert Harris has written that "the American experi-ence in Vietnam did as much as anything to shape the way in which the British government handled television during the Falklands crisis."[55] A thesis popular within the British military was that news coverage had contributed to the American defeat in Vietnam, and, despite the absence of factual support, this idea did much to shape official British policy about television news coverage of the Falklands fighting.[56] Journalists themselves were conscious of this. According to Harris, "the Vietnam analogy was a spectre constantly stalking the Falklands decision-makers and was invoked privately by the military as an object lesson in how not to deal with the media."[57]

Attitudes within the British military and civilian leadership ranged from pragmatic idealism to pragmatic cynicism. The former view was articulated by Field Marshal Sir Edwin Bramall: "I believe that in a democracy the armed services can only work effectively if their operations are acceptable to the people on whose behalf they are undertaken. So, by definition, the services should seek the support of the media."[58]

That sentiment was echoed by Lieutenant General Sir James Glover, who noted that, during the years of conflict in Northern Ireland, "we learned that part of the Army's role was to educate, in the best sense of the word, journalists about what is going on. We learned that you have to accept the dominant role that the media play in all our affairs."[59] The British navy had no recent press relations experience comparable to the army's work in Northern Ireland. As a result, the navy, as the dominant service branch during the Falklands campaign, proved insufficiently prepared to deal with the news media accompanying the task force.

In practice, this "educating" was shaped to fit the task at hand. Sir Frank Cooper of the Ministry of Defence said: "We aimed throughout not to lie. But there were occasions when we did not tell the whole truth and did not correct things that were being misread."[60]

The hardest line was expressed by Foreign Secretary Francis Pym: "The duty of the government is to help the services win the war. In this sense if information withheld makes it easier to win the war, it should be withheld. There is no such thing as a public right to know information which reduces the possibility of the war being waged successfully."[61] Thatcher's press secretary, Bernard Ingham, remarked that it is "perfectly legitimate in war to seek control of the media." This echoed the maxim attributed to David Lloyd George, who served as prime minister during World War I: "The press must either be squared or squashed."

Information moved slowly from the war zone to the British public. In 1854, during the Crimean War, the Charge of the Light Brigade was described graphically in *The Times* twenty days after it happened. In 1982, some television reports took twenty-three days to get from the Falklands to London. For the entire war, the average delay between filming and availability for broadcast was seventeen days. One television journalist complained that these reports "almost became the Dead Sea scrolls by the time we got them in."[62]

The logistics of the war worked to the advantage of the government censors. With the Falklands 8,000 miles from Britain and 400 miles from the nearest land mass, correspondents could not get to the war unless the Ministry of Defence took them there; in return, they had to live with the government's rules.[63]

The ministry told the navy that journalists on the Falklands task force ships should "feel free to file their stories and material" but were expected to adhere to guidelines for "responsible reporting." Nothing was to be published that "puts at risk lives or success of operation." Commanding officers had the authority to stop journalists' transmissions based on this guideline.[64] The controls on content went beyond security matters. One shipboard press officer told reporters: "You must have been told when you left you couldn't report bad news. You knew when you came you were expected to do a 1940 propaganda job."[65]

Journalists' material was "cleared" (a term the military preferred over "censored" or "vetted") both in the war zone and when it reached Britain. The purported limitation of censoring for security purposes only was frequently ignored. As Robert Harris has reported: "Enraged editors found censorship going far beyond security and straying into questions of 'taste' and 'tone.' The BBC [British Broadcasting Corporation] was told not to use a picture of a body in a bag, not to use the phrase 'horribly burned.' "[66] Some journalists were so annoyed by the military authorities that they tried "to prefix their reports as 'censored'; but the word itself was censored."[67]

These tight controls may have influenced content in the way the government wanted, but the rigidity also created problems. Television companies, starved for footage from reporters with the task force, began to use film from the Argentinians.[68] This practice, plus the news organizations' use of leaks from defense sources in the United States, led the Thatcher government to speed up the flow of information from the task force.[69]

Throughout the war, the Ministry of Defence orchestrated coverage, though it was not always a smooth operation. In their history of the war, journalists Max Hastings and Simon Jenkins wrote, "The ministry's choice of Ian Macdonald as a spokesman, who in his television announcements seemed more like a maiden aunt than a government representative, added a note of eccentricity to what was otherwise merely a farrago of indecision and incompetence."[70]

In the judgment of journalist Phillip Knightley, however, the ministry "was brilliant—censoring, suppressing, and delaying dangerous news, releasing bad news in dribs and drabs so as to nullify its impact, and projecting its own image as the only real source of accurate information about what was happening."[71] Criticism of the ministry, according to Knightley, missed the point. The assumption among much of the public was that the ministry, like the news media, wanted to disseminate information as quickly as possible and failed to do so only because of bureaucratic missteps. But actually the ministry was concerned far more about control than about openness, "and its role in the Falklands campaign will go down in the history of journalism as a classic example of how to manage the media in wartime."[72]

Journalists covering the war were given a Ministry of Defence booklet telling them that they were expected to "help in leading and steadying public opinion in times of national stress or crisis."[73] News organizations sometimes went much farther than "leading and steadying." With their huge circulations, the British tabloids rivaled television as prime sources of information about the war. Many newspapers were so supportive of the government's war policy that they stridently attacked other news organizations that expressed any reservations about the war or dared to introduce "balance" into their coverage.

The tabloids' approach, wrote Simon Jenkins, goaded politicians into supporting a no-compromise, total-victory stance. In many headlines and stories, "warmongering is barely concealed behind the veil of national pride. The *News of the World*'s 'Latest Score: Britain 6, Argentina 0' [referring to warships sunk] pleads with its viewers to treat it all as a game."[74]

From the tabloids came florid rhetoric that was consistently pro-war and pro-Thatcher. The *Daily Mail* wrote: "Forcing Argentina to disgorge the Falklands is a bloody, hazardous, and formidable enterprise. It can be done. It must be done. And Mrs. Thatcher is the only person who can do it. But she will have to show ruthless determination and shut her ears to the siren voices."[75] The *Sun* found what it considered "siren voices" emanating from the Foreign Office: "Since the days of [Neville] Chamberlain, it has been a safe haven for appeasers. . . . The Iron Lady must be surrounded by men of iron!"[76]

Not all the coverage was blindly supportive. Some of it presented balanced reports that included Argentina's point of view. Thatcher promptly attacked these, especially targeting the BBC. Speaking during question time in the House of Commons, she said: "Judging from many of the comments that I have heard from those who watch and listen more than I do, many people are very concerned indeed that the case for our British forces is not being put over fully and effectively. I understand that there are times when it seems that we and the Argentines are being treated almost as equals and almost on a neutral basis. I understand that there are occasions when some commentators will say that the Argentines did something and then 'the British' did something. I can only say that if this is so it gives offence and causes great emotion among many people."[77]

Thatcher's critique drew cheers from the *Sun*, which took her line of thought considerably farther. A *Sun* editorial on May 7 said, in part: "There are traitors in our midst. Margaret Thatcher talked about them in the House of Commons yesterday. She referred to those newspapers and commentators who are not properly conveying Britain's case over the Falklands, and who are treating this country as if she and the Argentines had an equal claim to justice, consideration, and loyalty. The Prime Minister did not speak of treason. The *Sun* does not hesitate to use the word."[78]

On the defensive, BBC chairman George Howard responded: "It needs saying with considerable vigor that the BBC is not and cannot be neutral as between our own country and an aggressor. . . . Strong supporters of the Government side will expect the BBC to be, as it were, 'on our side,' and will accuse us of treason if we are more neutral. Doubters will look for the neutral tone and accuse us of jingoism and warmongering if we adopt any other. We are not in the business of black propaganda or distortion of the truth. All we can do is to proclaim the truth so far as we can."[79] Dick Francis, managing director of BBC Radio, commented more tersely: "Whatever reputation the BBC may have does not come from being tied to the Government's apron-strings."[80]

And still, the vicious dueling continued. After the BBC and ITN (Independent Televison News) carried footage from Argentina of grieving relatives of those who had been killed when the warship *Belgrano* was sunk by the British, Member of Parliament Robert Adley turned up the criticism of television coverage, saying that the BBC was the Argentinian government's "fifth column in Britain."[81] On May 10, the BBC program "Panorama" included interviews with Argentina's representative to the United Nations and with two Conservative Party members of parliament who expressed doubts about Thatcher's policy. The day's show ended with a lengthy interview with Conservative Party chairman Cecil Parkinson, a member of the War Cabinet and a strong supporter of the prime minister's leadership. Despite the program's balance, the next day Conservative M.P. Sally Oppenheim called it "an odious and subversive travesty which dishonored the right of freedom of speech in this country."[82]

Thatcher herself chimed in about "Panorama": "I know how strongly many people feel that the case for our country is not being put with sufficient vigor on certain—I do not say all—BBC programs. The chairman of the BBC has assured us . . . that the BBC is not neutral on this point, and I hope his words will be heeded by the many who have responsibilities for standing up for our task force, our boys, our people, and the cause of democracy."[83]

Thatcher clearly wanted the press to show some deference to her as the country's wartime leader. Just after announcing an important British victory, she was asked by reporters, "What next?" Her reply: "Just rejoice at the news and congratulate our forces." As she walked back into 10 Downing Street, she said again over her shoulder, "Rejoice! "[84]

Beyond such specific incidents, Thatcher and members of her government recognized the need for a certain ambivalence in their attitudes toward the news media. They did not hesitate to restrict coverage to avoid jeopardizing military operations, and they worried about "Vietnam-type" coverage that would undermine public opinion. But they also knew they needed *supportive* news coverage to bolster public backing—domestically and internationally—for their policies.[85] To this end, Thatcher and others relied on gamesmanship, such as giving exclusive interviews to ITN when the BBC's coverage was thought to be overly critical.[86]

Thatcher had reason to pay attention to the BBC. Before the fighting, the BBC's "Nine O'Clock News" had 500,000 fewer viewers than ITN's "News at Ten." During the war, viewers switched: now the BBC attracted 500,000 *more* than ITN.[87] Despite the attacks on the BBC's patriotism, a poll taken after the "Panorama" controversy found that 81 percent of Britons believed that the BBC had behaved responsibly during the Falklands war.[88]

Overall, television newscasts' audiences grew substantially: 2.5 million more viewers in April than in March, an increase of 16 percent.[89] Newspaper readership increased also. It already was high; almost 80 percent of British households saw a national newspaper each day.[90]

As the military news from the Falklands improved, Thatcher mellowed slightly. In an ITN interview in late May, she said about the coverage: "I had one or two rather acid things to say about certain programs. May I say since then it is very much better. It was our decision, you know, to put correspondents on board the ships, and some of them have been very, very helpful indeed and given very, very vivid accounts and helped us all to know what is going on."[91]

Thatcher's sensitivity to news coverage was based in part on her precarious political position. She wrote in her memoirs about Parliament's qualified backing for her Falklands policy: "I obtained the almost unanimous but grudging support of a Commons that was anxious to support the Government's policy, while reserving judgment on the Government's performance. But I realized that even this degree of backing was likely to be eroded as the campaign wore on. . . . And how long could a coalition of opinion survive that was composed of warriors, negotiators, and even virtual pacifists?"[92]

Although the prime minister was on a tightrope, she managed to get across it triumphantly. In the public opinion polls, her personal approval rating had been 24 percent in early 1982. By the end of the war, it had risen to 60 percent.[93] Leading Labor Party politician Denis Healey described this political ascendance: "Just as Reagan used the invasion of Grenada to purge America of the trauma left by Vietnam, so Mrs. Thatcher exploited the victory of our forces in the Falklands to create the feeling, both at home and abroad, that Britain was great again; she portrayed herself as the greatest national leader since [Winston] Churchill, if not since Elizabeth the Virgin Queen."[94]

Thatcher shrewdly used the Falklands victory to fuel her 1983 reelection campaign. Appraising her own leadership style, she said: "People saw the kind of results it produced in the Falklands and I think they began to realize it was the right way to go at home as well. I think people like decisiveness, I think they like strong leadership."[95]

During a trip to the Falklands, Thatcher took full advantage of the television coverage she had disparaged just a few months earlier. Recognizing the political power of footage that showed the prime minister visiting with troops and Falkland residents, her press secretary, Bernard Ingham, made sure that the BBC footage of the event (a BBC crew was the only one on hand) was made available to other broadcasters. When the BBC resisted surrendering its exclusive video, Ingham threatened to bar transmission from the South Atlantic. The footage was shared.[96] Describing this coverage, David Watt wrote in *The Times*, "The hushed reverential tones adopted by the TV announcers, the expensive seconds of television time spent establishing pictorial frames for her patriotic tableaux, the constant references to her troops, all proclaim this is a royal visit."[97]

Such media events further established the "Falklands factor" as a political force. Journalist Peter Jenkins described this in his book about Thatcher: "The psychological need was for a success, a success of some kind, an end to failure and humiliation, to do something well, to win. Nostalgic knee-jerk reaction it may have been, vainglorious posturing in a post-imperial world of Super Powers, but it made people feel better, not worse."[98]

Along the same lines, BBC journalist Michael Cockerell observed that "the Prime Minister felt she was fighting to retrieve the national honor," and therefore she believed that the nation's news organizations should support her.[99] Thatcher was determined not to succumb to the indecision that had ruined Anthony Eden during the Suez crisis of 1956.[100] She would define her objectives and determine the means of achieving them.

Several weeks after the war's end, she spoke to a Conservative Party rally about the success to which she had led her country: "We rejoice that Britain has rekindled that spirit which has fired her for generations past and which today has begun to burn as brightly as before. Britain found herself again in the South Atlantic and will not look back from the victory she has won."[101]

Thatcher's insistence on controlling news coverage of the Falklands War paid dividends during the following year's elections, which she and the Conservatives won handily. Coverage of the brief war had helped to crystallize her political image as a decisive and principled leader. As was to be the case with George Bush nine years later, the brevity of the war and the preemptive imposition of censorship let policymakers work with a relatively free hand.

Looking at the Falklands War and its press coverage, *Washington Post* reporter Leonard Downie, Jr., noted that, even after the fighting had ended, "only a few British journalists questioned whether such pervasive news management, in peace or war, was good for the country." Of those few critics, Downie cited Charles Wintour, writing in the *Sunday Observer*, who observed that "the hidden attitudes of many people in authority toward the media have been exposed. They think the public should be told as little as possible. They don't object to deception on matters both large and small. They dislike reporters. And they prefer that ruling circles should be left to run the state without being bothered by troublesome disclosures and unpleasant truths. In fact, some of them don't really care much for democracy either."[102] Voicing similar concern was another British journalist, Sir Ian Trethowan, who wrote that the politicians' eagerness to restrict coverage "showed an alarming lack of confidence in the emotional sturdiness of the public on whose behalf they claim to govern."[103]

This is an issue that even victory in a short war cannot erase. The news media have an institutional memory of indeterminate capacity. When the next war or other crisis happens, attitudes—and therefore the tone of the coverage—about policymakers may be influenced by what has happened before.

Those who govern should keep this in mind. Pushing the press to gain a free hand in policy-making can have its costs; damaging the long-term relationship between government and the public may be too expensive a price to pay.

Chapter Five

Manipulating the Messenger

Recognizing the news media's impact on public opinion and on the politics of policy-making, government officials—from the president on down—frequently try, subtly or overtly, to shape news coverage. In most instances, this is done while still observing the letter, if not the spirit, of the First Amendment's insistence on freedom of the press. But however nuanced such efforts may be, the intent is clearly to manipulate. However noble the stated purpose, the result is still to obstruct the flow of information to the public.

Sometimes news organizations resist such pressure; sometimes they are only too willing to succumb to it. With phrases such as "a matter of national security" being tossed around, tensions remain high while these decisions are being made.

SECRETS

Secrecy is an integral part of diplomacy, intelligence-gathering, military operations, and other elements of foreign policy. Coexistence of this secrecy and the openness essential in a democratic society is always tenuous.

Journalists may find themselves presented with a difficult choice: Should they reveal a secret to the public or withhold the information to protect the national interest? The journalist's job is to do the former, but that does not mean the latter can be cavalierly ignored, particularly when government officials make a compelling case about security concerns.

Bay of Pigs Invasion (1961)

When John F. Kennedy became president in January 1961, he inherited a plan to have United States–backed force of Cuban exiles invade their homeland and battle Fidel Castro. The effort had been orchestrated by the Central Intelligence Agency (CIA) and was presented to Kennedy as a sure-fire, low-risk operation.

Although getting rid of Castro had great appeal, this scheme was thoroughly flawed, from grand concept to tiny detail. Kennedy, to his lasting discredit, let the invasion go forward. It proved to be a monumental disaster: The invaders were all either killed or captured on their beachhead, and the United States was depicted throughout the world not just as an aggressor, but as an incompetent aggressor. Kennedy later asked one of his aides, "How could I have been so stupid?"[1]

As plans for the invasion advanced, news organizations picked up on the story. *La Hora*, a Guatemalan newspaper, reported the existence of a secret CIA base in that country. In November 1960, an editorial appeared in *The Nation*, citing an American academic who had heard of this base while in Guatemala and had learned that its purpose was to train Cuban exiles.[2]

In early April 1961, the *New Republic* was ready to run an article titled "Our Men in Miami," which, according to Kennedy aide Arthur Schlesinger, Jr., was "a careful, accurate, and devastating account of CIA activities among the [Cuban] refugees." *New Republic* editor Gilbert Harrison sent the article to Schlesinger, asking if there were any reason it should not be published. In his memoir about the Kennedy presidency, Schlesinger wrote: "Obviously its publication in a responsible magazine would cause trouble, but could the government properly ask an editor to suppress the truth? Defeated by the moral issue, I handed the article to the President, who instantly read it and expressed the hope that it could be stopped. Harrison accepted the suggestion and without questions—a patriotic act which left me oddly uncomfortable."[3]

Harrison's deference might be applauded as an example of putting the nation's interest ahead of the journalistic imperative of scooping the competition. It also might be criticized, however, as granting the White House de facto censorship authority and ignoring the magazine's responsibility to tell the public what its government was doing.

When the *New York Times* prepared to run its story about the obvious preparations for an invasion, with training going on in Florida as well as Guatemala, the White House was not asked for its advice about whether to publish or withhold. The managing editor of the *Times*, Turner Catledge, later wrote: "My concern was to supply the same standards of news and accuracy to this story that I would to any story. I was not worried so much about protecting the government as about protecting the *Times*. When people talk about newspapers serving the public interest, I am sometimes forced to admit that I'm never sure what the public interest is, beyond its needs for accurate information."[4]

But, according to Catledge, *Times* publisher Orville Dryfoos *was* concerned about balancing the newspaper's interest with the national interest. Dryfoos wondered: "If we revealed the invasion plans, would we be tampering with national policy? And would we be responsible if hundreds, even thousands, of Cuban exiles died on the beaches of their homeland?" Catledge, meanwhile, "suspected that Castro already knew about the impending invasion, and the real question was not whether we would be responsible for deaths during the invasion, but whether, however unfairly, we might be blamed for them."[5]

The *Times* eventually produced a compromise (some might say compromised) version of the invasion story: The editors removed the predictions about an "imminent" attack, as well as any references to the CIA as the sponsors of the Cuban exile force. Although the story remained on the front page, the dominant four-column headline was reduced to a one-column head.

The word "imminent" was deleted because the timing could not be confirmed. The CIA was not specifically named because Catledge was not certain exactly which American intelligence or military organization was doing the training; the phrase "United States experts" was used instead. The headline size was very important because, according to news editor Lew Jordan, "A multi-column head in this paper means so much."[6] Another writer observed that, to *Times* readers, "a headline of such size would spell something close to war."[7]

The story ran on April 7 under the headline, "Anti-Castro Units Trained To Fight at Florida Bases." It began, "For nearly nine months Cuban exile military forces dedicated to the overthrow of Premier Fidel Castro have been training in the United States as well as in Central America." The invasion was referred to only obliquely, with the words, "when the time comes for a major move against the Castro fortress in Cuba."[8]

The internal debate at the *Times* spawned a continuing controversy: Was the invasion plan story, which had been written by veteran correspondent Tad Szulc, revised because of in-house concerns or because the White House had asked the paper to back off? Many histories of the crisis cite pressure by Kennedy on Dryfoos and say that the *Times* spiked the story or buried it inside. But the story *did* run, and it appeared on page one. In his history of the *Times*, Harrison Salisbury wrote: "The momentous decisions on Szulc were made by the *Times* on its own, acting in what the editors considered to be the broadest national interest. They slightly modified but did not suppress a story, even though it was a story of an *ongoing* military operation. . . . The *Times* believed it was more important to publish than to withhold. Publish it did."[9]

At the White House, the president and his aides reacted angrily to the pre-invasion coverage. Press secretary Pierre Salinger later wrote: "In the weeks before the invasion, hardly a day passed without a story appearing in some newspaper, or broadcast over some radio or television station. It is fair to say that some of the press went after the story as if it were a scandal at city hall, or a kidnapping—not a military operation whose entire success might depend on the elements of surprise and secrecy. . . . [Reporters] were able to publish much information of tactical importance, including exact estimates of the brigade's strength."[10] When the Szulc story ran, Kennedy became livid, saying: "I can't believe what I'm reading! Castro doesn't need agents over here. All he has to do is read our papers. It's all laid out for him."[11]

The invasion began Monday, April 17. By the end of the week, virtually all the United States–backed troops at the Bay of Pigs were either dead or captured. The news coverage—whether softened or overdone—had not affected Castro's preparedness. He had not known in advance the details of the invasion's time and place, but he had known it was inevitable, and he was ready with an overwhelming military response.

Among *New York Times* editors and reporters, the paper's pre-invasion coverage stirred up much speculation, which went on for years. In 1966, Clifton Daniel, then the managing editor, said, "The Bay of Pigs operation might well have been canceled and the country would have been saved enormous embarrassment if the *New York Times* and other newspapers had been more diligent in the performance of their duty—their duty to keep the public informed on matters vitally affecting our national honor and prestige, not to mention our national security."[12]

A different opinion was held by James Reston, the Washington bureau chief of the *Times*. When Szulc was working on his story, Reston talked to CIA director Allen Dulles, "who pooh-poohed the notion that his agency was involved in an invasion of Cuba."[13] Catledge recounted in his memoirs that, the day before the Szulc story was to run, Reston "warned against printing anything that would suggest an invasion was in the works or might otherwise upset the government's plans." Reston, wrote Catledge, had "allowed his news judgment to be influenced by his patriotism."[14] Reston, however, later argued that the decision to run or withhold the story was not as significant as some people made it out to be. "It is ridiculous," he said, "to think that publishing the fact that the invasion was imminent would have avoided this disaster. I am quite sure the invasion would have gone forward."[15]

In his memoirs, published in 1991, Reston defended his cautious approach to the story: "It was one thing . . . to repeat that the anti-Castro legions were mobilizing (Castro had his own agents in their ranks)—but quite a different thing to inform Castro of the timing of the invasion."[16] He also wondered "whether it is the job of a newspaper to make up its front page in such a way as to influence decisions of the president."[17]

A few days after the invasion's collapse, Kennedy told Salinger, "The publishers have to understand that we're never more than a miscalculation away from war and that there are things we're doing that we just can't talk about."[18] Kennedy expanded on this in an April 27 speech he delivered to a meeting of the American Newspaper Publishers Association in New York. Stressing the perilous state of the world, he urged the press not to await a formal declaration of war before imposing "the self-discipline of combat conditions." Implicitly accusing the news media of undermining national security, Kennedy said: "The facts of the matter are that this nation's foes have openly boasted of acquiring through our newspapers information they would otherwise hire agents to acquire through theft, bribery, or espionage; that details of this nation's covert preparations to counter the enemy's covert operations have been available to every newspaper reader, friend and foe alike; that the size, the strength, the location and the nature of our forces and weapons, and our plans and strategy for their use, have all been pinpointed in the press and other news media to a degree sufficient to satisfy any foreign power."[19]

The president went on to ask "the members of the newspaper profession . . . to reexamine their own responsibilities, to consider the degree and the nature of the present danger, and to heed the duty of self-restraint which that danger imposes upon us all. Every newspaper now asks itself, with respect to every story: 'Is it news?' All I suggest is that you add the question: 'Is it in the interest of the national security?' "[20]

The response from journalists to Kennedy's message was quick and largely negative. Editorials criticized the president for raising the specter of official censorship, or at least demanding self-censorship.[21] The Raleigh (NC) *News and Observer* editorialized: "President Kennedy should be thinking more about how the free, informed American people can contribute to the struggle, not how 'greater official secrecy' can be imposed upon them with the connivance of reporters and officials together.[22] Even within the White House, the speech caused concern. Arthur Schlesinger wrote that it "went much too far, and [Kennedy] did not urge the point again."[23]

Despite the tough, cautionary tone of the New York speech, Kennedy showed some wistful ambivalence about press influence. Clifton Daniel said that Kennedy told Orville Dryfoos in September 1962: "I wish you had run everything on Cuba . . . I am just sorry you didn't tell it at the time."[24] Similarly, Turner Catledge said that Kennedy—just two weeks after the New York speech—had told him: "Maybe if you had printed more about the operation you would have saved us from a colossal mistake." Catledge said of this: "His logic seemed to me faulty. On the one hand he condemned us for printing too much and in the next breath he condemned us for printing too little. He wanted it both ways, and he did not change my view that the newspapers, not the government, must decide what news is fit to print."[25]

The dichotomy remained, but, as a practical matter, middle ground could be found. White House press secretary Pierre Salinger argued that "a democratic society, if it is to survive in today's world, must be able to launch covert actions against its enemies."[26] Clifton Daniel of the *New York Times* noted that, "when it comes to matters of national interest, American news-papermen obviously must not be irresponsible in the dissemination of information that might affect the safety and security of our country."[27] Those positions are not too far apart, but the relationship between the administration and the press remained tense.

Cuban Missile Crisis (1962)

A rapprochement of sorts occurred the following year. Again the story was about Cuba, but this time the stakes were far higher.

During the summer of 1962, intelligence reports indicated that the Soviet Union was delivering missiles—the type was not known—to Cuba. State Department and military intelligence concluded that they were merely surface-to-air missiles (SAMs) to bolster Castro's defenses against what he considered a likely American attack. But in August, CIA director John McCone sent a memo to President Kennedy stating his belief that the SAMs were being sent "as a means of making possible the introduction of offensive missiles" that could reach the United States.[28]

By early October, the White House was convinced that the Soviets were indeed establishing an offensive capability on Cuba. U.S. military activity in the Southern states and the Caribbean intensified as a prelude to a possible invasion of Castro's island. On October 16, the president was shown photographs taken from a U-2 reconnaissance airplane that showed construction underway for ballistic missile launch pads in western Cuba.

By October 22, Kennedy and a team of advisers had decided on their course of action: a naval "quarantine" to stop the shipment of offensive weapons to Cuba, plus a clear warning to Nikita Khrushchev and Fidel Castro to stop their military build-up. In a televised speech that night, Kennedy put the matter in stark terms: "It shall be the policy of this nation to regard any nuclear missile launched from Cuba against any nation in the Western Hemisphere as an attack by the Soviet Union on the United States, requiring a full retaliatory response upon the Soviet Union."[29]

Before the president's speech, news organizations had provided sketchy reports about what was happening, based mainly on rumor, surmise, and circumstantial evidence. On October 18, Florida newspapers took note of troop movements in the state.[30] On October 19, White House press secretary Pierre Salinger received queries from journalists about a rumored forthcoming invasion of Cuba by the United States. On the president's instructions, Salinger (who had not yet been briefed on the crisis) told the reporters that they were wrong.[31] On October 20, Salinger was deluged by calls from reporters as the Washington gossip network carried speculation around town.

James Reston of the *New York Times* had done his job well and had a solid story that U.S. forces were being moved into position to blockade Cuba against the delivery of Soviet nuclear missiles. After Reston queried White House officials about his story, the president called him. Kennedy, wrote Reston in his memoirs, "didn't deny what was afoot, but said that if I printed what we knew, he might get an ultimatum from Khrushchev even before he could go on the air to explain the seriousness of the crisis."[32] Reston told the president that he understood his reasons for wanting the story held and that he would pass on the request to his editors.

Kennedy then called *Times* publisher Orville Dryfoos, who had talked with Kennedy the month before about government requests that news be withheld. According to the Clifton Daniel, Dryfoos had told the president then that "what was needed was prior information and prior consultation. He said that when there was a danger of security information getting into print, the thing to do was to call in the publishers and explain matters to them."[33]

In this instance, Kennedy made his case well, and the *Times* did not publish Reston's original version; but instead it printed less than was known. The lead on the story was the vague sentence, "There was an air of crisis in the capital tonight." It noted U.S. military activity and administration denials. Finally, in the sixth paragraph, the veil was lifted a bit: "But the speculation in Washington was that there has been a new development in Cuba that cannot be disclosed at this point."[34] Several days later, Kennedy wrote to Dryfoos, thanking him for helping with the Reston story: "Events since then have reinforced my view that an important service to the national interest was performed by your agreement to withhold information that was available to you."[35] In addition to talking with Dryfoos, Kennedy called Philip Graham, president of the *Washington Post*, and Henry Luce of *Time* magazine. Graham and Luce also pledged cooperation.[36]

Kennedy kept watch on news coverage of the crisis and its aftermath. Soon after praising Khrushchev's "statesmanlike decision" to dismantle the Soviet missiles and ship them home, Kennedy watched a CBS news show on which correspondents David Schoenbrun and Marvin Kalb were talking about the "American victory." Kennedy said to Salinger, "Tell them to stop that." Salinger immediately called CBS and spoke with Schoenbrun during a commercial. "David," he said, "I'm speaking from the Oval Office. The President is right next to me. Please do not let Kalb run on about a Soviet defeat. Do not play this up as a victory for us. There is a danger that Khrushchev will be so humiliated and angered that he will change his mind. Watch what you are saying. Do not mess this up for us." The reporters agreed and toned down their comments.[37]

Beyond such case-by-case White House interventions, systemic measures to influence news coverage had also been put into place. On October 24, two days after Kennedy's address to the nation, the White House sent a memo to news organizations listing twelve categories of information that the government considered "vital to our national security." These included military plans, intelligence estimates, details of troop movements, locations of forces, and so on. The memo went on: "During the current tense international situation, the White House feels that the publication of such information is contrary to the public interest."[38]

This memo was not a legally enforceable edict, just a request to the media not to release military secrets. Presumably, given the seriousness of the missile crisis, news organizations would exercise extraordinary restraint without needing to be asked to do so, but the White House was not sure just what the press's standards might be. Press secretary Salinger recalled that when he released the document, "I clung to the point that our guidelines were not even voluntary censorship, since the press had the final right to make news judgments. But I had the feeling . . . that the press had not been very convinced."[39]

Relations between the news media and the government worsened when the Pentagon's press liaison, Assistant Secretary of Defense Arthur Sylvester, told a *Washington Star* reporter: "In the kind of world we live in, the generation of news by the government becomes one weapon in a strained situation. The results, in my opinion, justify the means."[40] Sylvester also was quoted several months later as citing "the inherent right to lie when faced with nuclear disaster."[41] According to Salinger, Sylvester said he was misquoted, but Sylvester did later tell a Congressional committee that the government had a right to put out false information "intended to mislead the enemy."[42] Sylvester's frank comments did not sit well with the press corps. James Reston wrote, "As long as the officials merely didn't tell the whole truth, very few of us complained; but as soon as Sylvester told the truth, the editors fell on him like a fumble."[43]

(Almost twenty years later, Jody Powell, President Jimmy Carter's press secretary, wrote that the government "has not only the right but a positive obligation to lie" because of the inherent conflict between the government's right to secrecy and the press's right to publish without prior restraint.[44])

The anger about Sylvester's statement resulted in part from journalists' uncertainty about their divided responsibilities during the missile crisis. In the Bay of Pigs story, the issue was government incompetence, which deserved to be covered and could be covered without jeopardizing true national security. By withholding news about the imminence of the invasion or the CIA's role in it, the press had contributed to the fiasco.

Granted, journalists had no way of knowing what a mess the operation would turn out to be, but their reticence had been a mistake for several reasons. As Kennedy pointed out to Catledge and Dryfoos, if they had run the story, he might have decided to put the invasion on hold and during that interval have figured out how ill-conceived the plan was. That might have saved many lives among the anti-Castro fighters. Delaying or canceling the invasion also would have been politically beneficial for the president— something that really should not be the press's concern. Another reason for going with that story *was* simple logic: Castro *was* clearly anticipating an attack; running a story—even about its imminence—would probably not have increased the jeopardy of the invaders. More importantly, the American public should not have been kept in the dark.

If a general rule is to be drawn from this episode, it is this: Absent a compelling reason to withhold information, the story should run.

During the missile crisis, by contrast, that compelling reason probably was present. The points that Kennedy made about Reston's story were sensible; the U.S. strategy was newsworthy, but tipping that information to the Soviets clearly would have hampered Kennedy's efforts. Legitimate national interest cannot be ignored. In this instance, the prospect of the missile crisis leading to a nuclear war was terrifyingly real.

All these concerns produce more questions than answers. If withholding a story is sometimes appropriate, what guidelines should be used to determine when? How is the public to obtain vital information if the press withholds it at the government's behest? What exactly is "national security," and how can journalists avoid being manipulated by government officials who are quick to invoke it?

Given the nature of the events during which such questions arise, the press often has few hard facts on which to base answers and little time to ponder impact. These are not esoteric debate topics, for the news media's actions may have enormous, perhaps devastating, consequences.

Project Jennifer: The *Glomar Explorer* (1975)

Relations between the CIA and journalists have always been uneasy. The CIA is in the business of keeping secrets; journalists may feel compelled to reveal them. That dichotomy would seem to define a clear adversarial relationship.

But these sharp differences sometimes tend to blur. The agency occasionally wants information released through the news media. This "news" may be true or not. In any case, the CIA supplies it not out of any commitment to openness but for its own (perhaps questionable) purposes. For their part, responsible news organizations do not want to endanger the nation's security, so they may temper their instinct for revelation with a dose of realism about the nature and value of intelligence operations.

The relationship becomes even more complicated when individual journalists have divided loyalties. Some may be little more than conveyor belts for CIA leaks, such as a Washington bureau chief for *Newsweek* who regularly accepted as news items material written and delivered by the CIA.[45] CBS News used to let CIA agents review reporters' film and reports that were not used on the air.[46] Presumably such coziness cannot survive in the more frigid press-government relationship that prevails today.

Over the years, most of the collusion has been low-key, between friendly correspondents who would debrief the agency about information that they uncovered during overseas reporting assignments; they would then be rewarded with agency interviews and leaks. This collaboration would be kept secret, sometimes from editors and consistently from the public. Such practices raise significant ethical questions: For whom are these journalists really working—their news organizations or the government? To whom do they owe their principal allegiance—the public or the intelligence agency? These issues have attracted the attention of some members of the news business, most notably Harrison Salisbury, who devoted a substantial part of his book *Without Fear or Favor* (about the *New York Times*) to cataloging and analyzing links between the press and the CIA. Controversy lingers about these matters. In April 1996, CIA director John Deutch told news executives that the agency did not intend to use journalists as agents or use news organizations as cover for agents.

As was the case with President Kennedy and the press during the Cuban crises, maintaining secrecy for some CIA operations has depended on gingerly constructed agreements between government officials and news organization managers. An example of this situation was the CIA's Project Jennifer, an exotic $300 million scheme involving a sunken Soviet submarine, billionaire Howard Hughes, and an underwater salvage vessel—the *Glomar Explorer*—that seemed the stuff of fiction. Only James Bond was missing.

The Soviet submarine was resting on the floor of the mid-Pacific, 16,000 feet below the surface. American intelligence officials knew that it was armed with nuclear missiles and torpedoes; it also carried sophisticated communications devices and coding systems. It was an extremely valuable prize.

The venture began in 1969. Howard Hughes oversaw the construction of the *Glomar Explorer,* ostensibly for undersea mining. In truth, it would be the mother ship for the recovery vessel that would carry the Soviet sub up from the ocean floor.

In the summer of 1974, the secret salvage operation was launched. The *Glomar* found the sub, and the recovery vessel hooked onto it and lifted it toward the surface. But at 5,000 feet, the submarine broke in two; only half the vessel made it to the *Glomar.* That half was worth the effort; it contained two nuclear torpedoes and offered valuable insights into Soviet submarine technology. The CIA planned a second expedition for the following summer to try to recover the rest of the ship.[47]

But the press had picked up the scent. First, Seymour Hersh of the *New York Times* began making calls after receiving a vague tip about a CIA undersea operation. According to Harrison Salisbury, CIA Director William Colby "did not conceal his concern. He said it was a matter of extraordinary national security and asked Hersh not to write anything and, indeed, not even to mention the project to anyone."[48] Both Colby and Secretary of State Henry Kissinger called *Times* executives to ask that the story be withheld.[49]

Several other newspapers were also working on the story. When the *Los Angeles Times* printed a report about the Hughes connection and the effort to raise the sub, CIA officials called the paper's editor, William F. Thomas, even before the first edition hit the streets. Thomas agreed to move the story inside the paper for later editions, but it was picked up by other papers around the country.[50]

Colby then launched an intensive lobbying campaign, calling journalists and asking them to back off and give the agency time to make another run at the remnants of the sub before the Soviets took note and intervened. In a meeting at CIA headquarters, Colby asked Hersh and two *New York Times* editors to agree not to publish anything else about Project Jennifer until the second salvage effort had been completed or aborted, or the story had been published by someone else. The *Times* agreed.[51] A year later, however, editor A.M. Rosenthal had second thoughts about this deference and wrote in a memo, "I think frankly Colby used us."[52]

In his memoirs, Colby wrote, "In practically every instance, my urgings paid off and the press held back."[53] Journalist Jack Anderson, however, would not be swayed, and reported the story on national television. After that, other stories followed and, according to Colby, "the Glomar project stopped because it was exposed." He added, "A real significance of the affair, however, is its indication that most American publishers will cooperate in maintaining a national secret if they understand it really to be one, provided that it does not spread so far as to be uncontrollable."[54]

Colby prevailed in this case, at least temporarily. But after the story appeared, some journalists wondered if his appeals about protecting national security had been merely CIA gamesmanship. Might Project Jennifer have been more successful than the agency let on? Had the reports—carried so eagerly by the press—about only partial recovery of the sub been designed to confuse the Soviets? Or was even the story about limited success untrue, floated to take the heat off the agency once the press reported that the cost of Project Jennifer had been more than $300 million?

In retrospect, journalists wondered if they had been pawns in this game. *Washington Post* ombudsman Charles Seib wrote: "There is no evidence I know of that the executives who agreed to suppress the story made any real effort to find independent evidence to support or refute Colby's claim of national security. It seems to me that they accepted his pitch with disconcerting speed."[55]

For policymakers, this case underscored the flimsiness of the wall of secrecy that had kept most intelligence operations out of the news media. The anger and cynicism generated by the Watergate scandal had reduced journalists' restraint, particularly in dealing with the CIA. The agency came under increasing press scrutiny after the public airing of allegations about its foreign and domestic misconduct.

Project Ivy Bells (1986)

Despite the trend toward more aggressive reporting about intelligence matters, news organizations have remained willing to cooperate with the government when a convincing argument for national security has been made. Coverage of the Ivy Bells project—specifically, about how the venture had been compromised by an American spying for the Soviets—proceeded only after remarkable delays. This pace was dictated not by the investigating journalists' lack of material, but rather by their recognition of the impact that their reports would have on the work of policymakers.

Ivy Bells, which began in the 1970s, was basically a wiretapping operation. The target was an underwater communications cable used by the Soviet military. American intelligence technicians had developed an ingenious eavesdropping device that wrapped around the cable and listened electronically, without penetrating the lines themselves. When the Soviets raised the cable for inspection, the device would break away so the eavesdropping would go undetected. The most difficult parts of the operation were the placement of the device and the retrieval of its tapes, which had to be done by Navy frogmen carried to the target by submarine.

The project went well for several years, providing information about Soviet missile tests and other useful material. Then, in 1981, the Soviets found the American device. Ivy Bells was finished. Four years later, a Soviet defector told the CIA that Ivy Bells had been betrayed from within. This discovery led to the arrest of Ronald Pelton, a former employee of the National Security Agency.

Washington Post reporter Bob Woodward learned of the existence of Ivy Bells before he found out that it had been compromised. *Post* editor Ben Bradlee would not run the initial story: "I found Woodward's story appalling . . . because I could see no useful social purpose whatever in publishing news of our new intelligence capability. It was obviously of enormous value to the country, in avoiding a war, or fighting one if worse came to worst."[56]

After Pelton's arrest in November 1985, however, Bradlee decided that the story should be published to illustrate the damage that could be caused by even a low-level employee of an intelligence agency. But before proceeding, Bradlee wanted to tell U.S. intelligence officials that the story would soon appear.

Bradlee and the *Post's* managing editor, Leonard Downie, Jr., went to see Lieutenant General William Odom, the director of the National Security Agency. That visit began a marathon of negotiations (and occasional threats) lasting more than six months. Every time the government made its national security argument, the *Post* backed off and withheld publication.

The dialogue went this way: The *Post* argued that, since Pelton had betrayed Ivy Bells and the Soviets had found the listening device, no secrets remained and no harm would be caused by telling the story. Odom and other government officials responded that such news stories might tell the Soviets more than they already knew and might damage the improving but still fragile relations between the United States and the Soviet Union.

The *Post* recognized that it was being manipulated. After unearthing a ten-year-old *New York Times* story about the underwater eavesdropping, Odom told Bradlee, "I hoped you wouldn't find that."[57] That irritated Bradlee, who had his reporters keep working on their story.

Time and again, the *Post* consulted with Reagan administration officials and even let some of them see drafts of the story. Time and again, these officials cited "national security," and the *Post* did not publish. When CIA director William Casey misplayed his hand and threatened to prosecute the *Post* if it printed the story, an angered Bradlee vowed to proceed.

But then President Ronald Reagan called Katharine Graham, the *Post* board chairman, asking that the story not be run. Graham took presidential requests seriously. She asked Bradlee if the story really should be published and urged him to be extremely careful.[58] Finally and predictably, in May 1986, the issue resolved itself. The *Post* was scooped when NBC ran the story.

During the six months that the *Post* was working intensively on the Ivy Bells story, Bradlee had about twenty conversations with Casey, plus many others with top intelligence and administration officials. Reflecting on this process, Bradlee wrote that he had learned three lessons: first, that Pelton, not the *Post* or other news organizations, did the damage to national security; second, that the government's interest in preventing publication was simply to avoid embarrassment, since the Soviets already knew all they needed to know about the operation; and third, that "the claim that publication would threaten national security is an insidious one. The public feels entitled to believe that a president, or a CIA director, or a four-star general knows more about national security than a two-stripe editor. It is a formidable task to convince the public that patriotism is not exclusively the province of administration officials."[59]

Despite his belief that he and the *Post* had been manipulated, Bradlee acknowledged the need for self-policing by news organizations. He wrote, "In my time as editor, I have kept many stories out of the paper because I felt—without any government pressure—that the national security would be harmed by their publication."[60]

CIA director Casey remained skeptical about news organizations' behavior. Shortly after the Ivy Bells controversy, Casey said that, while some reporters are careful about covering intelligence matters, "there are some who are in a rush to publish and are not particularly sensitive to national security and intelligence capabilities considerations."[61]

Bradlee's view of self-restraint is based on commonly accepted standards of good citizenship. It is in line with the approach adopted by most responsible news organizations. Editors and television producers know that their constitutional prerogative gives them great leeway. They can even be grossly irresponsible, if they so choose. But that is not the course that most of them follow.

Government policymakers can count on this good faith when the national interest truly mandates caution, but they must recognize that this is not an unlimited guarantee. If journalists' good faith is not reciprocated by the government, then publication—sometimes harmful, sometimes inconsequential—will surely follow.

LEAKS AND DISINFORMATION

"I don't give a damn how it is done, do whatever has to be done to stop these leaks and prevent further unauthorized disclosures; I don't want to be told why it can't be done. This government cannot survive, it cannot function, if anyone can run out and leak whatever documents he wants to. . . . I don't want excuses. I want results. I want it done, whatever the cost."[62]

Those are the words of President Richard Nixon. The anger behind them—if not the tactics that followed—has been shared to one degree or another by virtually all presidents and other government officials who have found supposedly confidential information being trumpeted by the press.

Those who would like to keep secrets while they govern are at a disadvantage in a country where freedom is valued more highly than secrecy. In a deposition in the 1971 "Pentagon Papers" case, Max Frankel of the *New York Times* rejected the notion that secrecy was essential in conducting diplomatic and military affairs, calling the idea "antiquated, quaint, and romantic." He went on to say that "practically everything that our government does, plans, thinks, hears, and contemplates in the realms of foreign policy is stamped and treated as secret—and then unraveled by that same government, by the Congress and by the press in one continuing round of professional and social contacts, and cooperative and competitive exchanges of information."[63]

Journalist Hedrick Smith has also observed that leaking is standard operating procedure: "On Wall Street, passing insider information to others is an indictable offense. In Washington, it is the regular stuff of the power game. Everyone does it, from presidents on down, when they want to change the balance of power on some issue."[64] The quest for power is behind most leaks. Smith has also written: "Those who are in control of policy . . . will try desperately to keep the information loop small, no matter what the issue; those who are on the losing side internally will try to widen the circle. As the audience grows and the circle is widened, control over policy shifts, the conflict spreads, and the very nature of the game changes."[65] Along the same lines, Richard Darman, an aide to President George Bush, has said: "Winners leak out of pride in what they have won. Losers leak to try to change policies."[66]

Journalists are both beneficiaries and arbiters of this process. In addition to digging up information on their own, they are often presented with gifts in the form of newsworthy leaks. But the motives behind leaks vary greatly—a circumstance that often affects the quality of the information provided. Reporters must beware of being manipulated by leakers who want the news media to act as their agents. Leakers sometimes have only the most altruistic reasons for providing their material. For instance, they may be whistle blowers, alerting the public to a malfunctioning Pentagon weapons system. Alternatively, they may have purely selfish motives. For example, they want to sink a policy they oppose or knife a bureaucratic rival.

Sometimes the leak may bear an official imprimatur. Dean Rusk, Secretary of State during the Kennedy and Johnson administrations, held "deep background" briefings to get information out, but his ground rules required that his remarks not be attributed to him and not be identified as coming from the State Department. Rusk's ploy was flawed since the reporters whose bylines appeared on the resulting stories were known to be State Department correspondents. Therefore, guessing their source required little effort.

Another Secretary of State, Henry Kissinger, was particularly adept at using the news media. His ground rules for press briefings included "background" sessions, from which reporters could quote only "a senior American official," and "deep background," which meant no direct quotes and no attribution at all.

Kissinger biographer, Walter Isaacson, has written: "The real danger of the backgrounders was that they often replaced rather than supplemented real reporting, and their popularity arose from two great journalistic sins, coziness and laziness."[67] When Kissinger was engaged in his Middle East shuttle diplomacy, the story was reported principally from his plane. This meant that he was the primary—sometimes the sole—source, and his version of events became certified as "the news."

Usually, the press played by Kissinger's rules. In 1971, however, when he told reporters on deep background that the United States was reconsidering whether to attend a forthcoming Moscow summit, the *Washington Post* attributed the statement to Kissinger himself. The *Post*'s editor, Ben Bradlee, believed that the public needed to know where this information came from in order to decide how credible it was. Bradlee said, "We have engaged in this deception and done this disservice to the reader long enough."[68]

The *Post* soon backed away from this standard. Had the paper not done so, the backgrounders might have ended, at least for *Post* reporters. Diplomacy is too fragile for Secretaries of State to be making frank observations that will be attributed to them. Going on the record means that a pronouncement becomes official and that other nations might respond. Unattributed statements do not normally elicit official responses, and they can be valuable to the public if put in the proper context by journalists.[69]

Secretary of State James Baker, in the Bush administration, was also a skilled user of news coverage as diplomatic tool. He noted that the United States and other nations regularly used news stories to float ideas unofficially—via leaks or background briefings—to see what the reaction would be. "Thus," he said, "is diplomacy conducted."[70]

Taking backgrounding a step farther, what purports to be a leak may actually be part of a carefully contrived strategy to make the release of information seem surreptitious in hopes that journalists will find this aspect appealing and run stories to serve the "leakers'" purposes. The Reagan administration was adroit at releasing questionable information to affect public opinion via the news media. When Congress was considering aid to the Nicaraguan contras, for instance, the White House orchestrated leaks about alleged Soviet construction of airstrips for Nicaragua's Sandinista government. When these reports appeared in print and on the air, at least some members of Congress assumed them to be true and voted accordingly.

Sometimes the Reagan White House got involved in more intricate plotting. In April 1986, the United States launched a bombing raid on Libya, targeting Muammar Qaddafi in retaliation for his involvement in terrorism. In August of that year, several American news organizations—citing "intelligence sources"—reported a new increase in tensions between the United States and Libya, along with the likelihood of further air strikes.

In October, the *Washington Post* reported that the August stories had been inaccurate and had been based on information supplied by the White House as part of a scheme to rattle Qaddafi. The *Post* cited a memorandum written by John Poindexter, Reagan's national security adviser, which outlined a disinformation strategy. "It combines real and illusionary events," wrote Poindexter, "through a disinformation program, with the basic goal of making Qaddafi *think* that there is a high degree of internal opposition to him within Libya, that his key trusted aides are disloyal, that the U.S. is about to move against him militarily." [71] When asked about this, President Reagan denied using contrived media leaks as disinformation, but he added that he wanted Qaddafi to "go to bed every night wondering what we might do."[72]

Journalists do not like being used this way. Their obligation is to publish the truth, and they expect the government to respect that responsibility and not set up journalists to report phony material. Journalists would argue that, in the Libya case, even the undisputed evil of Muammar Qaddafi did not give the government license to be dishonest in dealing with the American news media.

From the policymakers' perspective, however, using news coverage for strategic purposes can be irresistible in the era of communications-oriented modern diplomacy, news organizations have elevated themselves to the status of players, particularly because of the speed and quantity of their coverage. Therefore, argue policymakers, they must be governed by the rules designed for participants as well as observers.

In the Reagan-Qaddafi case, the White House apparently won, at least until the *Post* revealed the administration's plan. But for policymakers to rely on that victory as a precedent may be unwise. If trust between government and the news media is eradicated, good faith cooperation in the national interest will become much more rare. Both sides may suffer as a result.

Sometimes leaking is used by those on the periphery of power as well, as part of a multifaceted effort to force a change in policy. In his post-presidential years, Richard Nixon—once the famous denouncer of leaks—became a master at this, just as he was at orchestrating his own political rehabilitation.

In 1992, Nixon was dissatisfied with the Bush administration's policy toward Boris Yeltsin's Russian government. The former president wanted more assertive support for Yeltsin—a risky position that Bush would have preferred to finesse as he began a presidential campaign featuring a challenge from the Republican right in the person of Pat Buchanan. Nixon nevertheless launched a thorough campaign of indirect pressure on Bush. He appeared on "Nightline" and "Larry King Live," wrote opinion pieces for major newspapers, and lobbied journalists, foreign policy experts, and government officials. He also wrote a memo that criticized Bush and raised the specter of the question, "Who lost Russia?"

In his book *The Nixon Memo*, Marvin Kalb has written that this document "would surely leak and explode on the front page and on the evening news. That was his intention."[73] When Nixon let it get into the hands of journalists and others, it attracted little attention for more than a week. But then, according to Kalb, the leak "flooded the landscape and transformed the debate on Western aid to Russia. The *New York Times* ran two prominently placed pieces on the Nixon memo and accomplished in one edition what the former president had been orchestrating for months."[74]

One official in the State Department said that Nixon "hijacked the press, and the press allowed itself to be hijacked."[75] Most journalists understood what Nixon was doing and how he was using them to advance his agenda. But their job was to deliver news to the public, not to worry about the games politicians' play. A Nixon-versus-Bush policy battle was news, and that was what mattered.

Nixon remained persistent after Bill Clinton took office. He asked for an audience at the White House, got it, and apparently had a greater effect on the Democratic president than he had had on Bush.[76] Overall, Nixon's public relations campaign—a combination of covert leaks and overt lobbying—succeeded in establishing his views about Russia as the conventional wisdom. This case illustrates, according to Kalb, how "the interaction of press, politics, and public policy could be understood as a gigantic loop of information."[77] In this loop, the press provides the channels through which information flows.

As Nixon recognized, shrewd use of the news media was the most expeditious way to affect policy. Not every lobbyist has Nixon's clout—the ability to appear on "Nightline" or on the *New York Times* opinion page at will. But the Nixon memo episode underscores the peril in which policy makers place themselves if they are not alert to the manipulative power that can be exercised by or through the news media.

Chapter Six

Does Anyone Care?

In any context, a major responsibility for journalists is to decide what is newsworthy. Part of that decision is easy. Plenty of stories are covered without a second thought: a presidential campaign, a disaster close to home, the spicy travails of the Prince and Princess of Wales. These are "important," particularly if importance means having a ready audience.

But in many instances, deciding about newsworthiness is more problematic. Stories that are complex, distant, and difficult to cover may be pushed aside, regardless of their intrinsic importance, because they do not meet the economics-driven criteria used by many news organizations: If news consumers are not certain to be instantly intrigued by this story, give them another one that is sure to grab them.

The more ferocious the business competition among news organizations, the more intense the decision making about these matters will be. In an American city with only one major newspaper but three strong television stations, the paper may be willing to run a story that might or might not find interested readers right away. With no direct competition, this risk is acceptable. The television stations, however, may be more likely to shy away from any chance of losing audience to their competition; hence, they may decide to offer only the tested menu of pathos, crime, and soft features. On a national level, the highly competitive weekly news magazines may find it safer to do audience-friendly cover stories about the latest pop music phenomenon rather than about a distant famine.

These decisions affect foreign policy because those who make policy will at least take note of what the public thinks is important. Delaying action about a foreign crisis is much easier in the absence of pressure to act promptly.

Foreign news priorities can be set by journalists themselves. They can decide that particular stories are important and present them to the public, hoping that news consumers will pay attention to them. Alternatively, they can rely on market research to gauge public interest and guide their news judgments. Still another course is to cultivate interest in foreign affairs gradually, making foreign affairs a more significant part of the public agenda. Doing this is not easy, but the investment of time and effort can pay long-term dividends.

HUMANITARIAN CRISES

Much news coverage consists of stories about the sordid side of life: wars, political chicanery, and such. Journalists shine their spotlight on these matters and hope that the information they provide proves useful. But despite their impact on public opinion and perhaps on policymakers, news professionals rarely can take satisfaction in having done something intrinsically good, such as helping people who desperately need assistance.

The opportunity to do so arises, however, with depressing frequency. As with other topics, news coverage of famines and similar disasters can alert the public and prod governments. Sometimes a definite cause-and-effect relationship can be seen between news stories—especially on television—and a surge in relief efforts.

Bosnian's ambassador to the United Nations, Mohamed Sacirbey, noted this influence in 1993: "If you look at how humanitarian relief is delivered in Bosnia you see that those areas where the TV cameras are most present are the ones that are the best fed, the ones that receive the most medicines. While on the other hand, many of our people have starved and died of disease and shelling where there are no TV cameras."[1]

Similarly, Pierre Gassman, head of media for the International Committee of the Red Cross, has said:

The international media, in particular television, must be duly credited for having mobilized the extraordinary solidarity of the international community in the wake of the Somali and Rwanda disasters. Governments and United Nations agencies found themselves under immense pressure produced by the television pictures and radio and newspaper dispatches that emerged from these crises. As a result, they reacted both swiftly and massively. . . . The international media are more and more influential in shaping foreign policy of those countries where TV pictures can create such emotional responses that governments are forced "to do something."[2]

News coverage can stimulate outrage, and outrage can galvanize a sluggish bureaucracy. Relief agencies and other proponents of assistance in a particular case know that when they encounter governmental inaction, the next step is to provide information—the more graphic, the better—to news organizations.

The other side of this issue is the effect of undercoverage or no coverage at all. Television news producer Danny Schechter has written: "There seems a clear link between air time allotted a story and public interest—remove the former and you reduce the latter. When viewers don't see the story, legislators and policy makers don't hear about the issue."[3]

But even considered from that standpoint, this is an inconsistent and unpredictable process. Not every catastrophe will capture the public's interest, regardless of its magnitude; not every government or agency will respond, regardless of the level of public concern. The criteria for eliciting coverage and for interesting news consumers are imprecise. Preconceptions, biases, limited attention spans, the pressures of other matters—all these affect judgments about what is "important news."

Looking at the bloodshed in Africa during the early 1990s, *Newsweek* media critic Jonathan Alter asked: "Why is it that when blacks kill other blacks it doesn't register much on the world outrage meter?" The answer, Alter suggested, is rooted in more than racial attitudes, although these should not be discounted. Geographical proximity, the content of news coverage (dramatic television pictures make a difference), and feelings of futility also are factors in defining principles in and deciding where national interests lie. "If it's immoral to look away from Bosnia," Alter wrote, "then it's immoral to look away from Rwanda."[4]

That makes sense, but public opinion is so fluid that it may resist being confined by standards rooted in ethics or even logic. According to Dr. Rony Brauman, former head of the relief agency Médecins Sans Frontières: "Misery, overpopulation, war, famine, all seem to be mixed together and have become practically interchangeable in the minds of the public, and the media. So that when half a million people were killed in Rwanda, we integrated the massacres into these vague mixed feelings, one more disaster along with all the rest that keep occurring, and will keep occurring, in Africa."[5]

The reaction to horrifying news about Africa and other distant places is often "It's just another war," "It's just some more starvation," "It can't be as bad as they say," or "It doesn't have anything to do with me." If Americans seem particularly susceptible to such moral nonchalance, it may be due partly to their news media's failure to provide consistency and context in their reports from faraway places.

When news stories do appear, they often just skim the garish surface of horrific events. Pierre Gassman of the Red Cross has noted: "If the media fail to make the effort to investigate why the chanceries and the military establishments of key countries let these catastrophes happen, if the wrong assessments, the biased reports, the convenient lies remain hidden from the public view, there is little hope that what happened in Somalia and in Rwanda might not happen again."[6]

As they decide what to investigate and how deeply to probe, news organizations consider their audiences' interests. Giving the public what it wants makes good business sense, but relying on this criterion becomes self-perpetuating. Much of the public may not understand what it is missing. The path of least resistance (and the way to greatest profits) is likely to lead to a parochial world view: Give people O. J. Simpson, and they will not care about or want anything else.

That attitude is patronizing toward the audience, and it may turn out to be wrong.

Famine in Ethiopia (1984)

During the early 1980s, nature and politics combined to create a horrific famine in Ethiopia. Ten million Ethiopians were at risk, and a million of them died. The relief organization World Vision estimated in 1984 that the famine was claiming 2,000 Ethiopian lives every day.[7]

This devastation was no secret, at least not to the news media. African and European journalists covered the story, but American news organizations—particularly the television networks—ignored it, assuming that Americans would not be interested. For this story to find a slot on a network newscast, "it had to slip through a crack in the operating theory that the more distant the place and the darker its people, the slimmer a story's chances of making it on the air."[8]

The BBC aired a story by reporter Michael Buerk in July 1984 that helped stimulate $10 million in donations to relief agencies. Meanwhile, American network producers talked about the story for several months, but they decided that cost, logistics, and presumed audience indifference made the story not worth the effort.

Buerk went back to Ethiopia in October 1984. He returned to London with wrenching footage of what he called "a biblical famine," including pictures of a three-year-old girl, the last of her mother's children, dying on camera.[9] When the story aired in Britain, the public's response was even more generous than it had been in July.

But the American networks still resisted. New York executives of NBC, which had an arrangement with the BBC giving it first rights to BBC reports, initially passed on the story. Paul Greenberg, executive producer of "NBC Nightly News," later commented, "You say, 'Yeah, it's terrible and it's horrible,' and then you get back to your business."[10]

Only when the NBC London bureau took it upon itself to feed the unwanted story to New York did the network's decision makers pay attention. When the story appeared on newsroom monitors, Greenberg, anchorman Tom Brokaw, and others were convinced that it needed to be aired. Greenberg later said: "There are very few times that a newsroom can be brought to complete silence, and this was one of those occasions. . . . Tears came to your eyes and you felt as if you'd just been hit in the stomach."[11] Two other stories were dropped, and the three-and-a-half minute BBC piece ran at the end of the newscast.

Brokaw introduced the story this way: "For some time now, we have been hearing reports of another famine in Africa. This time, in Ethiopia, stories of mass hunger and death. But with all else that's going on these days, so often those reports don't have much impact . . . words from far-off places."[12] If the "words from far-off places" didn't have much impact, the BBC pictures certainly did. NBC and relief agencies were flooded with calls.

The network ran more of Buerk's report the following night, with still more public response. On the third night, Brokaw said, "Last night, after we broadcast the second of two reports on conditions in Ethiopia, the U.S. government announced that it will provide another 20,000 metric tons of grain."[13] The Reagan administration insisted the aid was already in the pipeline, but Brokaw could make a convincing claim that NBC's broadcasts had at least hastened delivery.

Soon after the stories aired, American relief agencies reported that they had not received so many offers of assistance in years. Moreover, government aid to Ethiopia began to rise dramatically: The 1984 allocation from the Agency for International Development (AID) had been $21 million; in 1987, the amount reached $306 million.[14] Of all this, Steve Friedman, executive producer of NBC's "Today" show, said: "This [famine] has been going on for a long time, and nobody cared. Now it's on TV and everybody cares."[15]

Similar observations came from private relief agencies. Brian Bird of World Vision said: "We've been trying to interest the news media in hunger in Africa for two years. But for some reason, until you get a major network to run footage, it's not a news story."[16] Robert McCloskey, a former ambassador who had become senior vice president of Catholic Relief Services, noted: "On most big issues the government leads and public opinion follows. Certain gut issues have the capacity to turn that process around. We are now witnessing a singular example."[17]

Public response to the 1984 famine stories seemed to prove wrong those news executives who thought that few people would care about distressing events in distant places. Given the reaction—the outpouring of donations, the increased flow of government aid—a case might be made that American news organizations, especially the television networks, had been derelict in not doing the story previously. Many lives might have been saved, had the relief effort received its coverage-generated boost during earlier stages of the famine.

In addition, the argument could be made that the public response to these stories might have been sufficient to encourage news organizations to expand their coverage of Africa, humanitarian issues, and foreign reporting generally. That sounds logical, but there is another side to this matter. The public's concern might have been underestimated that time, but that fact in itself did not ensure lasting interest. When another famine hit Ethiopia in 1988, it was covered, but the news stories evoked relatively little response.[18]

Perhaps the prior exposure diminished the shock that news consumers felt the second time around. Perhaps compassion burnout had set in. Whatever the reason for this diminished response, the attitude was noted by the editors and producers who decide what stories the public sees and does not see.

War in Rwanda (1994)

In 1994, a war born of political and tribal enmities ripped Rwanda with a savagery and scope that was incomprehensible to most of the world. Philip Gourevitch described it this way: "Although the killing was low-tech—performed largely by machete—it was carried out at dazzling speed: of an original population of 7,700,000, at least 800,000 were killed in just a hundred days. By comparison, Pol Pot's slaughter of a million Cambodians in four years looks amateurish, and the bloodletting in the former Yugoslavia measures up as little more than a neighborhood riot. The dead of Rwanda accumulated at nearly three times the rate of Jewish dead during the Holocaust."[19]

Rwandans able to escape the fighting poured into neighboring countries. There cholera swept through the refugee camps, killing tens of thousands more. Journalists found the task of covering this horror overwhelming. ABC's Jim Wooten, who reported from refugee camps in Zaire, later wrote: "For seven days human beings were constantly falling all around us. In many cases, we and the lenses of our cameras were the very last things they saw in the very last moments of their lives. It was an excruciating dilemma: at last, a reality so wretched it demanded some degree of personal involvement; and yet a story whose wretchedness was of such epic proportions that any personal involvement was useless. The urge to *do something* was constantly answered by the grim realization that *nothing* would help."[20]

Despite the magnitude of this story, some news organizations were slow to respond. Pierre Gassman of the Red Cross wrote of his frustration: "While at CNN headquarters in Atlanta in early April, 1994 . . . I tried to persuade its assignment editors to cover Rwanda immediately. Yes, of course, they said, they knew about Rwanda, but all their available crews and satellite uplinks were in South Africa. The editors also expressed doubt about the possibility of showing two African topics at the same time as this might confuse their audience."[21]

This response reflected the classic rationale for minimal coverage: The Rwanda war was too remote, both geographically and in terms of its nature and magnitude, to concern Americans. In addition, some might say, the skimpiness of the coverage was because the protagonists were black, which, according to conventional journalistic wisdom, meant most Americans would simply not be interested.

Calculations about how stories from Rwanda might affect ratings or circulation are part of the news business. But a case can be made that the importance of this story deserved considerable weight in the news organizations' decisions about how much coverage to provide. After all, a special U.N. commission found that the "concerted, planned, systematic, and methodical" acts of "mass extermination perpetrated by Hutu elements against the Tutsi group constitute genocide."[22] An even stronger case can be made that, as a matter of journalism's ethical responsibilities, genocide should—indeed, must—be covered, wherever it is and whoever the parties to it may be.

Along these lines, Dr. Rony Brauman of Médecins Sans Frontières wrote: "Although knowing about a crisis does not solve it, the knowledge does at least pave the way for the most basic act of justice. If the guilty cannot be punished, then at least the victims can be recognized."[23]

The American news media—so focused on domestic matters, particularly the scandalous—might consider readjusting their priorities. Jonathan Alter wrote in *Newsweek* about this: "Human brutality must be confronted and denounced everywhere, starting at home but extending all the way around the world. . . . The White House press corps is always looking for something juicy. Indifference to slaughter is a good place to begin. Tiny stories with headlines that read '100,000 Dead in Africa'—now *that's* a scandal."[24]

As demonstrated by the different responses to coverage of the Ethiopian famines of 1984 and 1988, news consumers sometimes apparently suffer from compassion burnout. That fatigue, however, may be induced by the sporadic and frantic coverage of such disasters as starvation and massacres. The story does not build; it suddenly explodes. The reader, listener, or viewer is caught unaware and suddenly thrust into the midst of a crisis, with no contextual foundation for support.

More consistent coverage might give news consumers a firmer intellectual footing, allowing them to consider more thoughtfully the events that are taking place and the possible responses to them. Famine, for example, does not just suddenly happen. The starving Ethiopians shown to the world on television in October 1984 had not been well-fed in September or even in 1983. In Rwanda, there was an unanticipated spark that set off the killing—the President's plane crashed (or was shot down)—but the bloodshed itself should not have come as a surprise. During the previous year, Hutu-versus-Tutsi warfare in neighboring Burundi had left more than 50,000 dead.[25]

But much news coverage is hit-and-run, lacking depth and sometimes even accuracy. "Parachutists"—that is, journalists with little knowledge about a story's background—are dropped into crises that are well underway. British journalist Timothy Weaver has written: "News agencies which move in to cover the story are under great pressure from news editors to get their material out quickly. At best this leads to superficial reporting; at worst it can lead to gross distortions, as lies and propaganda are broadcast with little attempt being made to check the facts."[26]

Even when the reporting is solid, consistency can be a problem. Lou Cioffi, who covered the Ethiopia story for ABC, said: "We're all going to do a great job and get the country aroused and all of that, but what is going to happen three months from now? I don't know. But if we forget about this story, we're going to be wrong."[27] If the news media forget about the story, the public certainly will. And if the public forgets, governments are more likely to follow a politically expedient course and push the issue aside.

Other important players in this process are the relief agencies that count on news coverage to stimulate popular interest and governmental action. According to Timothy Weaver, the agencies that "understand the demands of the media can use the situation to run their charity appeals, knowing that if they provide the right sound bite—a pithy phrase summing up the horror of the event—they will feature in the news."[28]

These agencies and journalists often work in informal cooperation. Weaver wrote: "It is incumbent upon the humanitarian organization to be able to provide credible witnesses for reporters to interview. After all, the role of the reporter should be to act as proxy for his audience, to be their representative at the scene. As such he should be the open book in which the stories of the victims are faithfully reported, not interpreted."[29]

Good journalism may include interpretation as well as straight reporting. It inspires its audience to care about the topic at hand, whatever it may be. Despite the efforts of relief agencies, often the news media are the only effective means of alerting the world to a humanitarian crisis. The sad fact remains, however, that even the best-intentioned news organization cannot report every story. Thus, while coverage of Ethiopia may lead to an outpouring of assistance and the saving of lives, noncoverage of the Sudan may mean the crisis there is overlooked and thousands of lives are lost.

If this result were intentional, it could be criticized as being insensitive and capricious. But as an accident of fate, it is merely sad.

BUILDING A NEWS CONSTITUENCY

Of all the world's major democracies, the United States is the most insular in its outlook toward the rest of the world. Strong isolationist feelings have developed deep roots since the republic's earliest days. The "It's not my problem" attitude may remain dormant for lengthy periods, but it never vanishes. The rest of the world is viewed warily, as a collection of ungrateful allies and unprincipled enemies.

One reason for this tendency toward isolation may be that the United States has been the most unscarred by battle of all the big powers. No foreign soldier has fired a shot on the U.S. mainland since the War of 1812. During World War II, for example, while Great Britain endured the blitz, the Soviet Union lost 20 million dead, and much of the rest of Europe was pulverized in battle, the U.S. mainland remained untouched. In the 1990s, with the demise of the Soviet Union, American disregard for the rest of the world has become more pronounced.

This history has bred a sense of security—a false one, perhaps, but nonetheless influential. Just as this feeling shapes public opinion, so too does it affect American news organizations' judgments about how the world should be covered. If news consumers do not care about most of what goes on beyond the U.S. borders, news providers do not try to force-feed them. Journalist John Maxwell Hamilton has written of this theory that "there is an unwritten rule among journalists that local news is news and foreign news is foreign, and that people want plenty of the former and will tolerate only small doses of the latter."[30]

With some exceptions (such as the *New York Times*), news organizations are content to let that unwritten rule guide decisions about newsworthiness. A self-perpetuating truism has thus evolved: If journalists think their audiences do not want foreign news and therefore do not give it to them, the audiences' appetites for such news will not be whetted; the news media will therefore not change the news menu, and hunger for foreign stories will diminish further . . . and so on.

The result is an underinformed public that has a limited agenda. As Daniel Yankelovich and John Immerwahr have pointed out: "It is important to note that the growth of public awareness on issues is not always automatic; there have been spectacular examples where important issues have failed to capture public attention. The key factor here is almost always the role of the press."[31]

Policymakers can find good and bad results from this weak coverage. The benefit for policymakers is that a disengaged public is unlikely to generate political pressures that require a policy response; those who govern can go about their business unimpeded by the annoyances of democracy. But when policymakers find that they need public support on a particular matter, an uninterested and underinformed public may be hard to rally.

This was one of the topics addressed by the American Assembly during its 1993 session about "Public Engagement in U.S. Foreign Policy After the Cold War." The Assembly's final report stated: "The media also have a critical role in making more explicit the links between events in distant lands and their repercussions for average Americans. Local newspapers and television stations, in particular, need to illuminate the fact that foreign affairs has become a local story."[32]

Recognition of the importance of *local* media is crucial if a broad-based constituency for foreign news is to be developed. From their standpoint, policymakers understand the significance of local press coverage. Professor Bernard Cohen has cited State Department officials. One said, "We all read the press carefully" —a sampling from around the nation—"so we know pretty well what the country is thinking." Another commented that reading articles "in seven or eight of the major metropolitan newspapers" gives one "a sense of what is being said in the country." Still another described reporters as "makers of issues."[33]

Charles Bailey, former editor of the *Minneapolis Tribune*, is among those who believe that logical links exist between foreign news and local reporting. Journalists, he says, "primarily those who work for regional or local newspapers, can transform foreign news into local news. And when they do, they find plenty of interested readers."[34] His view has been echoed by ABC's Peter Jennings: "For while there is no substitute for foreign correspondents, there is also no substitute for the powerful impression the local angle makes in revealing the impact of foreign relations."[35]

Here, in a story from Lincoln, Nebraska, is an example of the local stake in foreign affairs. The issue was cutbacks in loans by major banks to Third World countries. The Nebraska angle: The Lincoln bank "did not make foreign loans and never planned to do so, but it wanted the large banks to keep up their level of loans abroad. Without new capital, the Nebraska bank understood, developing countries would not grow and therefore could not import U.S. products. The bank had traced the escalating number of its local farm loan defaults to the inability of countries to import Nebraska-grown food."[36]

That is an interesting and newsworthy story. It was certain to find an audience in Nebraska because, although it was based on what might seem to be a "foreign" topic—the Third World's economy—it really was a local story. Growing global interdependence makes such stories increasingly common.

For their part, policy makers should recognize the importance of the local angle as a way to win public support for controversial initiatives such as the North American Free Trade Agreement (NAFTA). In the battle over enacting NAFTA, both sides knew that political support depended considerably on local news stories about "why NAFTA will be good for Oklahoma City," "why NAFTA will hurt Des Moines," and other such coverage from around the country.

With the Clinton administration touting the agreement, Ross Perot and labor unions warning about the loss of U.S. jobs, and "experts" pontificating from all sides about all aspects of the treaty, public opinion remained unsettled. The ratification of NAFTA was a complex topic involving economic projections and geopolitical principles that many people either did not understand or did not care about until they saw how they personally might be affected by the measure's success or failure. For this, they depended on news coverage.

Because in many instances the dominant concerns were locally oriented (for example, would the hometown factory lose its business to a Mexican company?), local media were likely to garner the closest attention by the public. Also, because local journalists are seen as being part of their communities (a perception cultivated assiduously by their news organizations), their credibility tends to be greater than that of national media stars.

Another factor in building constituencies for foreign affairs coverage is the presence of large "diaspora" populations in the United States. Many of these immigrants and descendants of immigrants maintain an avid interest in events in their personal or ancestral homelands, and so they can be expected to be good audiences for news stories about those countries.

The clout of the diasporas can be seen in the U.S. foreign policy-making process. Israeli political scientist Yossi Shain has noted that "ethnic influences may help to keep U.S. foreign policy true to Wilsonianism at a time when neo-isolationism is on the rise."[37] One example, according to Shain, was the 1994 U.S. intervention in Haiti: "Many observers assert that Clinton acted more in response to the organized elements of the African-American electorate . . . than to a broader national consensus."[38]

Other examples illustrate the potential markets for international news coverage. Many Jewish Americans pay close attention to reports about Israel and the rest of the Middle East. Hispanic Americans can take advantage of the expanding Spanish-language news media offerings as well as English-language coverage of Latin America.

But different groups are likely to have widely different interests, so "international coverage" may amount to little more than a superficial sampler of stories from mainstream news organizations, with more intensive reporting left to smaller, specialized media. Also, the extent of such interests may be hard to gauge; for example, how many African-Americans want more coverage of Africa?

News organizations may have difficulty addressing these issues, in part because decisions about foreign coverage invariably involve expensive allocation of personnel, equipment, and other resources. Nevertheless, the existence of diverse potential audiences for foreign reporting should be noted by news organizations, just as these audiences' interests are considered by policymakers.

Generally, "foreign news is foreign" only when lazy and unimaginative journalists let it seem so. Whether a news report appeals to economic self-interest or to humanitarian instincts, most significant stories from around the world can find a receptive domestic audience. If that audience's knowledge of world affairs is developed over time, interest in and political responses to foreign policy are likely to become more sophisticated. That trend should prove healthy for news consumers, journalists, and policymakers alike.

Chapter Seven

The World Is Watching: Real-Time News

Time is a priceless asset for the political leader confronting a crisis. A hasty reaction to events is always risky, and it almost always proves, in retrospect, to have been unwise. Time provides a cushion for judgment.

Journalists look differently at time. They constantly strive to shrink the interval between gathering and delivering news. For many stories today, technology reduces that interval to zero. Gathering and delivery are virtually simultaneous. The crisis of the moment arrives immediately, explosively, LIVE! In living rooms around the world, people watch the news not as an after-the-fact report, but as it happens. Those who make policy, therefore, must deal not only with the event itself, but also with the instantaneous public reaction. Time's cushion is gone.

The debate about how policy-making is affected by news coverage becomes more complex when real-time reporting is added to the mix of issues. While governments deal with the compression of response time, journalists also find their role being reshaped by their capability to report news so promptly. Providing context and making responsible editorial decisions becomes far more difficult when reporter and audience get information at the same time.

THEN AND NOW: THE BERLIN WALL

Berlin; Sunday August 13, 1961. At 2:30 A.M., East German troops begin stringing barbed wire and jackhammering post holes at the Brandenburg

Gate, a principal crossing point between the East and West sectors of the divided city. The first stages of the Berlin Wall are being built.

American, British, and French troops in full battle gear arrive. No shots are fired, but the tension of superpower confrontation is palpable.

CBS reporter Daniel Schorr, producer Av Westin, and a film crew are on the scene. They record the drama, then take their film to Templehof Airport. The film will be taken by prop plane from Berlin to London. If this flight is on time, the film can be put on a London-to-New-York Pan Am jet. With the time change, it will arrive in New York in mid-afternoon. There, it will be picked up by a courier and taken to a film-processing lab to be developed. Only after that will CBS producers and editors see it and begin putting it into coherent shape for broadcast. American television viewers will get their first look at the Schorr crew's pictures Tuesday night.[1]

Almost three days from filming to broadcast. In 1961, that was fast turnaround for an overseas story. Of course, newspapers, radio, and television had told their audiences about events in Berlin sooner than that, but the visual images of the East German soldiers at work and the Allied troops poised to respond held the greatest drama. They were "the news" most likely to elicit a demand for forceful American reaction.

Everything moved more slowly in 1961. Fifteen hours elapsed between when the East Germans began their barricades and when President Kennedy—who was at his Hyannis Port, Massachusetts, vacation home—received word from Secretary of State Dean Rusk about what was happening. Kennedy responded carefully. He avoided hot rhetoric, signaling the Soviet Union that he planned to do nothing that might turn Berlin into the first battlefield of World War III.[2] In addition, Kennedy wanted no misunderstood American signal to trigger an East German uprising that would certainly end tragically, as had the 1956 revolt in Hungary.[3]

By the time that American newscast audiences saw the Berlin film, the shock had diminished and Kennedy had embarked on his cautious course. Tensions were to remain high in Berlin for decades to come, but this dangerous flashpoint had passed.

Kennedy continued to move deliberately. He realized that news coverage of events in Germany would lead public opinion in the United States toward support for a firmer military posture, so he did not agree with his staff's advice that he should propose new negotiations about the future of Berlin.[4]

The president knew that domestic political opinion would develop only gradually. For eight days after the border was closed, Kennedy said nothing publicly about events in Berlin, nor did he allow any statement on the subject to be issued in his name. Not a single major publication objected to his silence.5

Imagine the same events with today's television technology available. Any television news organization with a crew in Berlin could transmit live pictures of the wall-building by satellite to the United States and elsewhere. The East Germans' early Sunday morning activity in Berlin would have occurred during television's prime time on Saturday night in America, so the instant audience would have been huge. Those pictures might have stirred emotions, presenting the president with a much more volatile domestic political situation and making a rapid, saber-rattling response appealing.

The public would have gotten the news quickly, but what journalist-historian Theodore H. White has called "the protective filter of time" would have been eliminated. Real-time journalism is simple: "Here is what's happening." Real-time diplomacy, however, is much more complicated and risky.

Berlin; November 9, 1989. The East German government announces on the evening television newscast that its citizens no longer need special permission to leave the country. Within hours, tens of thousands of East Germans are crossing into West Berlin. As historians later described the night, "Jazz bands played under searchlights originally installed to help catch fugitives. East and West Berliners leapt atop the ugly twenty-eight-year-old partition; raising glasses of champagne and beer, they sang, danced, hacked off pieces of the wall, and wept with joy."6

This was televised not three days later but as it happened. "The scene was floodlighted for television cameras. Tom Brokaw of NBC stood by the wall, not reporting as much as celebrating the epic. His broadcast captured the joy on the faces of thousands being released from forty-four years of Communist restrictions. . . . It was a broadcast that showed with utter clarity the welcome end of an era."7

It was captivating, and it held an audience of millions, including President George Bush. When he resisted being swept up in the emotion of the event, television showed that too. Television cameras were brought into the Oval Office, and the president allowed that he was "very pleased" by "the latest news coming out of Germany."8 Chided for this tepid response, Bush said, "I'm not going to dance on the wall."9

Bush's reaction bounced around the world. On ABC, David Brinkley in Washington asked Peter Jennings, reporting live from Berlin, what the Germans thought of Bush's tone. "There's a sense here the United States is a little behind the curve," said Jennings. "The President didn't seem very enthusiastic . . . and the people here wonder why."[10]

Tom Shales of the *Washington Post* wrote: "The anchoring triumvirate [Brokaw, Jennings, and CBS's Dan Rather] was performing its ceremonial, ambassadorial, cheerleadial functions, even as criticism continued at home over George Bush's oddly enervated TV appearance on the day the story broke. . . . It's not unreasonable to expect a president in the age of television to come on television at the right times and say the right things. In that respect, Bush fumbled Berlin as clumsily as he fumbled China earlier this year."[11]

Criticism of Bush also came from political quarters. Senate Majority Leader George Mitchell said that the president should have flown immediately to Berlin to preside over the Wall's destruction. Never mind that the administration's restraint was carefully considered. Bush and Secretary of State James Baker were wary of seeming to gloat, fearing that to do so might undermine post-communist reformers in eastern Europe.

But in the television era, Mitchell's advice seemed perfectly logical. Don't worry about making policy; the first order of business is to make yourself part of the media event.

During the Berlin Wall's twenty-eight-year existence, policymakers' time for responding to crisis was compressed by the capabilities and demands of high-tech media. The time in which a crisis needed to be addressed did not shrink because the inherent circumstances of the incident itself moved more quickly; the pace of events did not accelerate. Nevertheless, the period for shaping a response without facing an expectant public was certainly shortened. John Kennedy's eight-day public silence about the Berlin Wall would be inconceivable today. The drama conveyed by live television coverage would almost certainly make the public feel more part of events than was the case in 1961. Such participation—vicarious though it may be—is enough to generate political heat.

Also worth keeping in mind is the evolution of television news format. Presumably, major television networks now would not just offer live bulletins about a story of the magnitude of the Berlin Wall's construction. Rather, they would offer sustained and expansive coverage, including interviews with relatives of those trapped behind the Wall, speculation from military analysts, and much else to fill the time and enhance the drama.

This quantitative if not qualitative comprehensiveness is a trademark of television news coverage of major events today. News organizations have learned that the public expects immediacy and volume, so they provide them. Those who make policy may not care for such a ubiquitous media presence, but they cannot afford to underestimate the intrinsic power of this kind of coverage.

Moreover, broadcasting's reach greatly expanded between the 1960s and the 1990s. According to BBC estimates, in 1965 there were 530 million portable radios world-wide; by 1990, that number had grown to 2.1 billion. During the same time, the number of televisions had grown from 180 million to more than a billion. In 1965, 80 percent of these broadcast receivers were located in North America and Europe. By 1990, only 55 percent of the much larger number were.[12] In other words, much more of the world is watching the world.

PRIME TIME WAR

The Vietnam War became known as the living-room war because it was the first to be brought into America's homes on television night after night. As Michael Arlen wrote of the phenomenon, on that electronic box in our living rooms, "we were watching, a bit numbly perhaps (we have watched it so often), real men get shot at, real men (our surrogates, in fact) get killed and wounded."[13]

Television reports in the living room had replaced newsreels in the movie theater. This new-style war coverage came to its audience with unprecedented frequency and intimacy, but often without the breadth and context necessary to understanding all that was being seen. Americans looked at Vietnam, Arlen continued, "as a child kneeling in a corridor, his eye to the keyhole, looks at two grownups arguing in a locked room—the aperture of the keyhole small; the figures shadowy, mostly out of sight; the voices indistinct."[14]

Television continues to bring war into living rooms, and the medium's perspective continues to be narrow. The biggest change since the Vietnam era has been not so much in content or quality as in speed. There was no live coverage of the Vietnam War; the technology and logistics of the time meant that at least a day or two would elapse between the gathering and the broadcast of war news. Today, once a few technical needs are met, no such delay is necessary. Bomb Baghdad, and the whole world can be told about it as it happens. Launch some Scud missiles at Saudi Arabia and millions will watch to see if they are intercepted or hit their targets.

Couple this speed of coverage with the vastly expanded reach of the television networks, and the notion of a "global village" truly makes sense. When George Bush ordered the beginning of Operation Desert Storm on

January 16, 1991, he understood that both his constituents and people throughout the world would know what was going on even before he formally announced it. This sequence of events was essential. Bush could not have told the American television audience about the bombing before it began because—thanks to CNN—his announcement would have been heard at the same time in Iraq.

The attack on Baghdad occurred during the networks' evening newscasts. On ABC, for example, correspondent Gary Shepard in Baghdad had reported live by telephone that the city was quiet. Only a few minutes later, he was back on the air, describing the first wave of the air attack. (The time for attack—3 A.M. in Iraq—had been recommended by General H. Norman Schwarzkopf for military, not media-related, reasons.) Later that night, with the need for secrecy past, television as a unifying tool was on display. Sixty-one million American households tuned in to President Bush's speech, the biggest audience for a single event in television history.[15] Millions more around the world also watched.

The reach of CNN, in particular, assured a vast and diverse audience for the Gulf War. If they had chosen to do so, George Bush in the White House and Saddam Hussein in his Baghdad bunker could have watched the same televised images of the war they were waging.

The beginning of this war had been preceded by television-influenced diplomacy, with speed again being a principal characteristic of the coverage and with CNN again being a major player. Even when direct communication between Iraqi and American officials broke down, CNN was available as a de facto diplomatic channel. Spokespersons for each side could talk to CNN and be assured that their counterparts would get the message. On the day before the bombing began, CNN chairman Ted Turner stressed the network's importance in a telephone call to his Baghdad producer, Robert Wiener. "We're a global network," said Turner. "If there's a chance for peace . . . it might come through us. Hell, both sides aren't talking to each other, but they're talking to CNN. We have a major responsibility."[16]

CNN was being watched by more than politicians. When CNN anchor Bernard Shaw reported from Baghdad that an Iraqi official had expressed a willingness to discuss all issues, the American stock market soared. Viewers interpreted the story as containing more encouraging news than it actually did.[17]

The content of news stories was also affected by the high-speed communication between Iraqi officials and American journalists. For example, CNN broadcast a story from Atlanta referring to Iraq's National Assembly as "Saddam Hussein's rubber-stamp parliament." The powers that be in Iraq watched that report and did not care for it. One of their information officers called CNN's Baghdad producer to object; the producer then called Atlanta to relay the complaint.[18] No thinking it over, writing official letters of protest, and waiting for the message to work its way halfway around the globe. The information loop can now be completed almost instantaneously.

Messages were also being sent in the other direction, from Washington to Baghdad. After the war, Lieutenant General Thomas Kelly, who conducted Pentagon news briefings, told NBC's Garrick Utley: "Every single time I mentioned the use of chemical weapons in a press briefing, I would look into the camera and say, 'You must understand, any commander who uses chemical weapons is going to be held accountable for his actions.' I knew they watched CNN in Iraq, and I wanted those guys to hear that."[19]

In all these cases, the technology of the medium shaped the content and impact of the message. A few years before, using the news media as a diplomatic messenger might have meant leaking information to the *New York Times* and then gauging reaction as policymakers mulled over the story that ran the next day. Now, hours have become minutes, and diplomats find themselves electronically face to face.

Once the Gulf War began, CNN brought its viewers extensive live coverage from what CNN reporter John Holliman said was "like the center of hell."[20] The young CNN (which had been referred to by its competitors as the "chicken noodle network") dominated the early coverage in part because its planners had provided the network's Baghdad staff with the technical tools needed to circumvent Iraqi-controlled equipment. CNN also received preferential treatment because the Iraqi government wanted to have a way to get its own messages to the rest of the world quickly.

For the first two weeks of the war, CNN broadcast its audio live. The Iraqis had allowed CNN to use a "four-wire" satellite telephone that did not depend on local switching connections. This enabled CNN's Baghdad team to stay on the air for sixteen hours when the bombing began, while their competitors were cut off after just a few minutes.

At the end of January, with the permission of Saddam Hussein's government, CNN began using its own flyaway (portable by truck) satellite uplink, allowing it to broadcast live pictures from Baghdad. Local American affiliates of the big three networks frequently switched over to CNN when their own networks lagged. As the supplier of news to more than 100 countries, CNN was the world's primary source of televised war coverage.

Although reports about American military activity were constrained by tight censorship, reporters still found plenty to discuss. Sometimes, however, the quest for daily drama displaced thoughtful judgment about newsworthiness, and the emphasis on speed pushed aside the checking of facts. Lawrence Grossman, who was president of NBC News from 1984 to 1988, said television viewers experienced "the illusion of news" because "the on-the-scene cameras and live satellite pictures at times served to mask reality rather than shed light on what was happening." He added, "Rumors, gossip, speculation, hearsay and unchecked claims were televised live, without verification, without sources, without editing, while we watched newsmen scrambling for gas masks and reacting to missile alerts."[21]

The political impact of such flaws in coverage makes them more important. In the days before the war, even Secretary of Defense Dick Cheney admitted that he was getting much of his information about happenings in the Gulf region from CNN. Reportorial lapses in such circumstances thus are not merely fuel for future academic debates about journalistic responsibility; they can have an immediate impact if policymakers rely on them.

Such reliance may be unwise. For example, soon after the air war against Iraq began, CNN reported that the Iraqi Air Force and the Republican Guard (reputedly the Iraqis' best troops) had been "decimated" and their missile launchers knocked out. That was incorrect. General Schwarzkopf later said that he had "turned the TV off in the headquarters very early on because the reporting was so inaccurate I did not want my people to get confused."[22]

Live coverage of Iraq's Scud missile attacks against Israel and Saudi Arabia sometimes provided examples of speed-induced problems. Former NBC president Lawrence Grossman wrote: "In their impatience to get on the air live rather than wait to find out what was going on, television reporters wondered aloud on-screen about what they were seeing and what was happening. No longer did they perform as reporters trying to filter out true information from false. Instead, they were merely sideline observers, as ill-informed as the rest of us. Was it the sound of 'thunder,' or a 'lethal rocket attack' outside? Was it the odor of 'nerve gas' or 'conventional explosives' that was seeping into the TV studio in Tel Aviv? (It turned out to be bus exhaust.)"[23]

The inconsistent mix of timely, accurate journalism and hurried, misleading reports is something that policymakers must factor into their calculations. A story such as the Gulf War will attract a massive audience—the same audience that a president needs to be supportive of his administration's policy. This means that government officials must try to direct and correct coverage as the need arises, promoting their version of events with the same emphasis on speed that drives electronic journalism. As was detailed in Chapter 4, a president sometimes can do much to influence coverage. What a president cannot afford to do, however, is underestimate the potency of live reporting of a war or similar foreign policy event. Policymakers will find themselves at a political disadvantage if their efforts lag too far behind the pace set by news coverage.

COUPS AND OTHER CONTROVERSIES

The Gulf War was not the first occasion for television to be a broker in high-speed, high-stakes diplomacy. In 1977, CBS anchor Walter Cronkite conducted separate interviews, via satellite, with Egypt's president, Anwar Sadat, and the Israeli prime minister, Menachem Begin. Sadat told Cronkite that he would be amenable to an American-arranged invitation to travel to Israel for peace talks. Several hours later, Begin told Cronkite that he would send the invitation the next day via the American ambassador in Israel. CBS edited the interviews together (telling viewers that it had done so) and put the dramatic product on the air. This breakthrough in Israeli-Egyptian relations was hailed as "Cronkite diplomacy."[24]

When Sadat went to Jerusalem later that year to meet with Begin, ABC's Barbara Walters was able to cajole the two into a joint interview. (Sadat was reluctant but agreed when Begin said, "Let's do it for the sake of our good friend Barbara." That's star power.)[25]

The Cronkite and Walters interviews were not broadcast live, as they probably would be today, with the anchor's commanding presence looming over the conversation. But even with the brief delays that the technology of the 1970s required, this was still a remarkable media intrusion into the foreign policy process.

In this short-circuiting of traditional diplomatic mechanisms, the complex niceties of negotiation give way to dueling sound-bites. This can produce fast and dramatic breakthroughs, but the risks are great, too. A rhetorical misstep in such a face-to-face situation, with the world looking on, might do inordinate damage. When a television anchor assumes the role of diplomatic mediator and when policymakers agree to perform in this forum, the danger exists that the thirst for controversy (to garner higher ratings) will overcome the discipline required to avoid counterproductive provocations. Perhaps the likes of Larry King and Ted Koppel (or Phil Donahue and Oprah Winfrey?) are wise enough to appreciate the ramifications of televised negotiating, but it is no wonder that professional diplomats shudder at such goings-on.

Television diplomacy of this kind is imbued with gimmickry. Even when all parties have the best of intentions, this is, after all, *television*, as ephemeral as it is gripping. Its use displaces process, which may be more mundane but has its own built-in safeguards.

While most negotiating may benefit from a deliberate pace, during some crises, speed is essential. Television can alert the world to trouble and can be the vehicle for a rhetorical response that might prevent a crisis from turning into a catastrophe.

Soviet Coup (1991)

Events in the Soviet Union during August 1991 illustrated television's role as high-speed diplomatic messenger. In a coup d'état, President Mikhail Gorbachev was placed under house arrest at his vacation home in the Crimea, and a junta tried to take control of the Soviet government. Although the coup leaders apparently had substantial support within the military, they met immediate popular resistance. Their most potent opponent was Russian Federation President Boris Yeltsin, who, though no fan of Gorbachev, climbed atop one of the tanks that had moved against his political headquarters and denounced the coup as unconstitutional.

Television immediately played an important role in the unfolding drama. In the United States, national security adviser Brent Scowcroft watched CNN reports about the first TASS (the Soviet news agency) announcements on August 19 concerning Gorbachev's "ill health" and his replacement by vice president (and coup principal) Gennadi Yanayev. Scowcroft relayed that news to President Bush.[26] As events developed, General Colin Powell, chairman of the Joint Chiefs of Staff, "kept one eye on CNN and another on intelligence reports that were still flowing in."[27] And in the White House Situation Room, staff members "used both CNN and U.S. intelligence reports to monitor the movement of troops, tanks, and war planes."[28] This careful watching of television reports illustrates how thoroughly television news has been integrated into the array of intelligence sources on which policymakers rely.

Even more important, television news—especially CNN—was used in this case as an important diplomatic tool. One Bush administration official (who declined to be named) told the *Washington Post* that "his first consideration on hearing about the coup was not how to cable instructions on U.S. reaction to American diplomats, but how to get a statement on CNN that would shape the response of all the allies. 'Diplomatic communications just can't keep up with CNN,' he said. . . . 'We had also sent a signal to Yeltsin and the people on the street that we are going to work toward elimination [of the coup], that we are with you. Yeltsin finds out that Bush is on his side—he finds out publicly before we could even get a message to him. You get a statement out as fast as you can.' "[29]

The heavy television coverage of the coup—much of it featuring live reports—made a prompt public response from Bush essential. He did not have the luxury of time and silence that John Kennedy had enjoyed thirty years before during the Berlin Wall crisis. Just a few hours after he and the world had learned of the coup, the president held a briefing for reporters at his home in Kennebunkport, Maine. It was carried live to the world via CNN. Still uncertain of the coup's chances of success or its leaders' long-term plans, he sent a cautious signal, calling the coup "extra-constitutional," rather than "illegal" or some other harsher term. Bush also said: "We're not going to overexcite the American people or the world. And so, we will conduct our diplomacy in a prudent fashion, not driven by excess, not driven by extreme."[30] And, he might have added, not driven by television coverage.

But television's intrusiveness cannot be wished away. Moments after Bush's news conference, broadcast commentators were criticizing the President for the lack of assertiveness in his response, a charge that particularly rankled because it seemed to echo accusations that he had been soft in his reaction to the Tiananmen Square massacre two years before. Referring to the news coverage, Scowcroft told Bush, "We may have a problem developing here."[31] Bush then changed his plans for the day and returned to Washington, where he could look presidential in full view of the television cameras.

Yeltsin was desperately trying to build opposition to the coup at home and abroad. He knew that television would carry his message and up-to-date information to foreign leaders, but he faced the problem at home that coup supporters had seized the Soviet media. Again, CNN (and other Western networks) came into play. When, for example, Yeltsin made his fiery appearance atop a tank, he expected world leaders to see him doing so. George Bush, via CNN, did and began adjusting the U.S. position to bolster the anti-coup forces.[32]

Furthermore, Yeltsin knew that, although Soviet television might not report his doings, the coverage from CNN and other networks would be beamed back to the Soviet people.[33] By 1991, CNN had established a presence in the Soviet Union. Government agencies, news organizations, hotels, and others could already receive it. About 100,000 members of the Soviet intelligentsia could thus follow the coup events live on the American network.[34] This group made up a critical mass in the contest for public support during the critical early hours of the coup. Former foreign minister

Eduard Shevardnadze wrote of this: "Praised be information technology! Praised be CNN. Anyone who owned a parabolic antenna able to receive this network's transmissions had a complete picture of what was happening."[35]

The situation worked as Yeltsin hoped it would. By the first evening of the coup, 25,000 anti-junta Soviets had joined Yeltsin in the streets. That number grew rapidly. On Tuesday, August 20, when he first talked to Bush on the telephone, Yeltsin estimated that the crowd of supporters surrounding his headquarters had reached 100,000. In a dramatic boost for Yeltsin's cause, Bush announced at a White House news conference that he had spoken with Yeltsin and had voiced U.S. support for the restoration of Gorbachev. Bush, wrote Secretary of State James Baker, "had used the fastest source available for getting a message to Moscow—CNN."[36]

By contrast, when the coup leaders tried to use television themselves, the attempt proved counterproductive. Yanayev, with some of his colleagues, held a news conference at which he looked shaky, uncertain, and even drunk (which was later confirmed).[37] This news conference was carried live by both CNN and Soviet television.[38] As Soviet viewers watched, the coup's credibility declined, and the plausibility of the Yeltsin-led resistance rose.

Even after the coup had ended and Gorbachev had returned to Moscow, television coverage remained essential to policymakers intent on keeping abreast of the fluid situation. On August 23, Gorbachev and Yeltsin appeared together before a televised session of the Russian parliament. In what had been billed as a display of solidarity, Yeltsin clearly was the dominant figure, ordering Gorbachev to respond to reform proposals. As Bush and Scowcroft watched this, Bush said of Gorbachev, "I'm afraid he may have had it."[39]

Another part of the coup's aftermath illustrated the pervasiveness of television's influence. Soviet Foreign Minister Alexander Bessmertnykh was accused by Gorbachev of being too passive in his resistance to the coup, so he resigned. Soon after, during an interview with ABC's Ted Koppel (which was not carried live, but was broadcast a few hours later), Bessmertnykh telephoned his American counterpart, Secretary of State James Baker, to tell him that he was leaving his post. Baker, who was unaware of the ABC crew's presence, commiserated with Bessmertnykh as the now ex-foreign minister proclaimed his innocence of any complicity with the junta. Bessmertnykh skillfully took advantage of his televised forum to make the case for his honor.[40]

Various lessons emerge from the coverage of the Soviet coup. Most important, such a venture no longer can be carried out without the entire world knowing about it and probably being able to watch it happen. The only way to prevent this situation is to implement a fierce and well-organized suppression of news coverage, which is difficult to do and in itself virtually ensures adverse public reaction around the world. Moreover, to avoid coverage-generated pressures, those who undertake a coup or other such act must move so rapidly that they can present the world with a *fait accompli*.

Television coverage also can be a deterrent to ruthlessness. For example, in hindsight, the perpetrators of the Soviet coup may wish that they had ordered Yeltsin shot as he stood on the tank. After all, his firm opposition was a key factor in the coup's unraveling. But the immediate impact of such an assassination would have been felt far beyond Moscow's streets. George Bush and other world leaders would have been watching as it happened, and they would have had to deal with inflamed opinion among their own constituents. This circumstance would have made any kind of friendly gesture toward the junta politically unpalatable, if not impossible.

In pretelevision days, such an execution would still have caused problems for those ordering the act, but, absent pictures, the perpetrators might have been able to weather the storm. The intrinsic power of the television image has changed the rules of the game. The camera can thus be an inhibiting force.

This is particularly true when live coverage evokes immediate and strong public reaction. Another lesson from the Moscow coup is that the allowable response time to a crisis shrinks in direct proportion to the promptness and quantity of news coverage, especially by television. Those who govern cannot escape this pressure. The contrast between John Kennedy's reflective reaction to the Berlin Wall and George Bush's hurried response to the Moscow coup was not a matter of choice. Instead, the contrast reflects a technology-driven change in the nature of the presidency.

Tiananmen Square (1989)

Television's inhibitive influence has its limits. It evaporates quickly when those wielding power simply do not care what the world thinks about their actions. This was the case in June 1989, when the Chinese government used military force to crush a student demonstration in Beijing's Tiananmen Square.

The demonstrators were well aware of their international television audience and had designed part of their strategy to influence American public opinion. They waved signs written in English, quoting the likes of

Patrick Henry. Their much-photographed "goddess of liberty" was modeled on the Statue of Liberty.

These Chinese protests represented the first time that a major breaking story was covered without interruption for a worldwide television audience. With the presence of CNN, the wire services now had live competition, so they no longer could unilaterally determine the pace at which information would be gathered, edited, and reported.[41] CNN also intruded into the wire services' traditional role as the primary source for other news organizations.

The cumulative power of this coverage was particularly noteworthy. Walter Goodman wrote about this in the *New York Times*: "Beginning Saturday night and resuming Sunday morning, the networks had been running still photographs and televised scenes from China as they came in. They conveyed action, confusion, crisis. What exactly was going on was not always clear, but that in a way added to their immediacy. Taken together they told a strong story—soldiers, so many soldiers, moving in on the protesters; students pounding with sticks on an armored troop carrier; burned-out buses and stranded bicycles; the improvised barricades crushed by the military machines; recorded voices of witnesses describing beatings of students by the soldiers."[42]

The real-time policy-making loop was much in evidence in this case. When the Chinese government ordered a halt to live television transmissions, President Bush issued his formal protest—via CNN—about the events he had been witnessing . . . on CNN.[43] Both CNN and CBS broadcast their own shutdown being ordered by "official representatives of the Chinese Government, embarrassed and clearly aware that they were losing face on live television."[44]

The Chinese government found a way to put some of the American networks' live coverage to its own use. When NBC's Tom Brokaw interviewed government spokesman Yuan Mu, both NBC and China's state-run television carried it live. Yuan insistently denied that government troops had massacred students. As he said this, NBC rolled videotape of the Tiananmen violence. On the Chinese broadcast, however, only the picture of Yuan appeared.[45] Presumably, Chinese officials thought their credibility with their own people would be enhanced if Yuan was seen being grilled by an American. They, of course, had no intention of showing the incriminating pictures from the square.

Responses to the Tiananmen brutality were further indications of the transformation in policy-making since the early 1960s. When a huge audience is watching troops move against demonstrators, policymakers must respond immediately and decisively or be prepared to pay a political price for their perceived sluggishness. Besides, Bush administration officials knew the CNN coverage was being seen worldwide, so they needed to react quickly to maintain America's policy leadership position.

Despite presumably understanding all this, Bush was restrained in his response. He thought that "posturing" about human rights would do no good and would cost too much in terms of long-term relations between China and the United States.[46] But for much of the public, intense television coverage of dramatic events overwhelms such cautious arguments. Whatever logic Bush's position contained looked puny in comparison with the harsh televised realities of the moment.

No longer is responding to events such as those in China just a matter of interaction between two nations, at whatever pace they decide to set, with however much openness they decide to allow. To a considerable extent, the entire world becomes a participant, watching what is happening and passing judgment on the principals' actions and reactions.

Television-enhanced ripple effects travel far and can have profound impact. The protests in China were watched with particular attention in East Germany. That they could even be seen in what had long been a bastion of rock-ribbed communist rule was in itself evidence of technology-fostered change. East German Chancellor Erich Honecker wanted to keep his countrymen and women from viewing the democratic surge in China, so East German television initially did not carry the Tiananmen pictures. But West German television did, and East Germans watched that. Honecker had to respond, and, typically, he did so by supporting the Chinese government's vicious intolerance. He apparently did not understand that his words paled in comparison to the images from China, as well as those that had been coming from recently reborn Poland and Czechoslovakia.

The time was long past when East Germans would merely accept their leader's pronouncements. Television producer Tara Sonenshine has written of this change: "Television was, for the people of East Germany, a window through which they could witness the revolutionary changes taking place around them. It allowed them to take part in the broad movement to unseat communism around the world. It filled them with the courage to confront a police state known for its brutal repression of dissent. It gave them information and knowledge—with which they could challenge the old ways of looking at the world."[47]

But even information traveling through the airwaves cannot always reach all of those who need to see it. Although the Chinese students provided the impetus for revolutionary change in Eastern Europe, they could not see what they had helped bring about. According to Sonenshine: "The Chinese leadership, unlike Erich Honecker, understands fully the impact of television. The dramatic images of the crumbling of the Berlin Wall were barely seen in the homes of ordinary Chinese citizens."[48]

That fact is sadly ironic. But the day is not too distant when even an autocratic government will be overmatched by technology and will not be able to keep broadcast images from reaching China's hundreds of millions of homes.

REAL-TIME ETHICS

Live coverage brings news to the public quickly and often dramatically. These two characteristics are generally positive; people are kept informed and interested.

But these attributes may be accompanied by ethical problems. Just as policymakers may lose their cushion of time under the pressure of the rapid reporting of events, so too do journalists sometimes surrender the time they need to ensure precision and responsible news judgment in their reports. As competitive pressures and public expectations grow, speed may displace accuracy as news organizations' top priority.

Journalism does not merely provide a mirror image of events. It includes context and supporting material so that the news consumer can understand, not simply be awash in, the news. Reflecting on coverage of the Gulf War, Lawrence Grossman, a former president of NBC News, wrote, "The networks' chief role should be to provide thoughtful, expert reporting after the fact, rather than mere live narrative over an endless stream of satellite pictures."[49]

Control of content is essential to journalistic integrity. Live broadcasting is irresistible to those who work or play at politics, in part because of its immediacy, but also because, when broadcast journalists "go live," they partially surrender their gatekeeper role. Politicians see news organizations as tools waiting to be used. Their attitude is nothing new; real-time coverage just adds a dimension to this phenomenon.

For example, when the United States sent troops into Panama in 1989, the Soviet foreign ministry, rather than sending a formal protest through diplomatic channels, called CNN to arrange for a Soviet official to broadcast a statement condemning the invasion.[50] In this instance, using the diplomatic pouch would have been slower but adequate. It would, however, have been far less helpful in terms of propaganda benefits for the Soviets. The target audience of their protest was the world as well as the American Department of State.

Even when extraneous efforts to influence content are not at issue, decisions about what to cover require ethics decisions in which governments may have a substantial vested interest. During the Gulf War, news organizations' live coverage capabilities posed immediate problems when Iraq launched its Scud missiles against Israel. Consider this scenario: A missile has just struck downtown Tel Aviv. A reporter does a live stand-up a few blocks from where the missile hit. In the background are recognizable landmarks and smoke from the explosion. If this is on CNN or another network that the Iraqis receive, the reporter—however inadvertently—is serving as a spotter for the Iraqi missile targeters. They can get a good idea from the television picture where their missile hit and make adjustments accordingly before they launch the next one.

The Israelis did not take long to figure this out. The Israeli government quickly worked out the following rules with CNN and other networks:

- An Israeli censor would be in the network's workspace, reviewing and censoring live shots as they were set up and actually aired.
- If the live location was outside, the reporter could be shown only in a tight head shot, with no identifying background location visible. If the live shot was done within the workspace, any framing of the shot would be acceptable.
- The number of missiles landing could not be reported unless the number was provided by Israeli authorities. No reference could be made about whether any missiles actually exploded on impact.
- No specific locations could be shown: no rising smoke, no wide shots of attack scenes, no shots that would allow even a general neighborhood to be identified.
- No maps or other graphics of the attack sites could be used.

The last three of these rules applied to taped as well as live stories.

Was this censorship? Certainly. But no responsible journalist could object to the Israelis' logic. From their standpoint, this was not about news or openness; the issue was the self-preservation of a nation under attack.

Whether the censorship is self-imposed or ordered by others, some controls will inevitably accompany live reporting. In the Gulf War, no American military commander could even contemplate allowing a live broadcast—which might be viewed in Baghdad as well as in Boston—announcing, "An American tank column has just moved north toward the Kuwaiti border."

As was discussed in Chapter 4, controls on coverage sometimes go beyond military security and are based on protecting political self-interest. In those cases, news organizations should resist being pushed around. But overall, journalists' common sense must keep pace with their profession's technology.

The live coverage of combat will raise issues beyond those of grand strategies. Suppose that, in the Gulf War, during a live report from an American base in Saudi Arabia, a Scud slammed into a barracks, killing many Americans. If this event were covered live, consider the horrible impact on the families of the dead and wounded if they saw their relatives being carried from the rubble. News about casualties is always terrible, even when delivered as gently as possible by the formal military notification process. That process, however, is more humane than suddenly seeing "live death" on television. Once again, this is a matter requiring journalistic self-restraint, meaning compassionate self-censorship. The rush to be "live" should not overwhelm decency.

As another matter of journalists' professional judgment, the ability to present a story live should not be the sole factor in determining the extent of coverage such a story receives. As media critic Tom Rosenstiel has written, "Breaking news is not always hard news; being 'live' does not mean being serious."[51] Even if the public has a *right* to know whatever news can be delivered quickly, it may not have a true *need* to know. When a news organization possesses whiz-bang technology, it tends to want to show it off. This may not, however, be the best way to define newsworthiness for a public that may reasonably assume that an event carried live is of special significance.

These ethical questions complicate not only the decisions of journalists, but also the work of those who make policy about the issues that journalists cover. Granted, those who craft and implement foreign policy may make arbitrary decisions themselves, relying on politics, not rating points or the availability of satellite time. British journalist Nik Gowing has offered this example: "While the world focussed on Sarajevo and Bosnia in March, 1994, it is estimated one thousand people died in one violent two-day period in Burundi. At the same time, a U.S. diplomat was describing Sudan as 'Somalia without CNN,' with a humanitarian situation worse than that in Somalia."[52] The policymakers may need to resist the allure of the televised trouble spot, using their own—not television's—criteria to decide what is important and what to do.

British Foreign Secretary Douglas Hurd, speaking in 1993 about Bosnia in this context, said, "We have not been and are not willing to begin some form of military intervention which we judge useless or worse, simply because of day by day pressures from the media."[53] Again, this kind of problem for policymakers is not solely a function of real-time coverage, but the audience-grabbing drama inherent in live reporting makes the pressure to which Hurd referred far harder to resist.

FOREIGN POLICY AS THEATER—THE SOMALIA LANDING (1992)

On December 8, 1992, U.S. forces came ashore on the beach at Mogadishu, Somalia. They were greeted not by hostile fire, but by blazing television lights.

This seemed at first to be an example of gross irresponsibility on the part of the news media, but the Department of Defense had actually encouraged the media presence. The beach was not sealed off, as could easily have been done. Instead, military officials were giving interviews to ABC's Ted Koppel, CBS's Dan Rather, and NBC's Tom Brokaw—all broadcasting live from Mogadishu—while the landing was in progress.[54] Ed Turner, CNN's vice president for news, said: "No one should have been surprised that there was a crowd of journalists on the beach, because they were told what time and where, and encouraged to be there in briefings at the Pentagon and State Department. The briefers made it pretty clear they'd like to have the story reported. They wanted the coverage to show the troops in action."[55]

Television pictures of Somalia's agony had helped to spur U.S. intervention. Now the intervention itself had become a media event, more so than anything in the previous year's Gulf War. The Bush administration simply decided to showcase its foreign policy on live television.

George F. Kennan, who has influenced and analyzed foreign affairs for much of the twentieth century, wrote this in his diary on December 9, 1992: "When I woke up this morning, I found the television screen showing live pictures of the Marines going ashore in Somalia. . . . If American policy from here on out, particularly policy involving the uses of our armed forces abroad, is to be controlled by popular emotional impulses, and particularly ones provoked by the commercial television industry, then there is no place not only for myself, but for what have traditionally been regarded as the responsible deliberative organs of our government."[56]

In warning against a foreign policy based on "an emotional reaction, not a thoughtful or deliberate one," Kennan spoke to the unsettling complexities imposed on diplomacy by satellite-speed journalism. As his words point out the intrinsic conflict between television journalism and government, they also underscore the need to reconcile their respective powers.

Chapter Eight

After the Devil Has Been Saved

The dissolution of the Soviet Union and the end of the Cold War dramatically transformed American foreign policy. For a half century, America's view of the world had been defined by the superpowers' rivalry. Virtually every American foreign policy decision had taken into consideration the impact on or reaction of the Soviets.

The news media could not stand wholly outside the arena. Coverage of foreign affairs was similarly influenced by the tense realities of the nuclear-shadowed U.S.–Soviet relationship. When, for instance, President Kennedy asked for press restraint during the 1962 Cuban missile crisis, his request had to be taken seriously. The prospect of imminent nuclear war was very real and frightening. No journalist could, in good conscience, wholly divorce his or her reporting from considerations of the national interest during this superpower face-off.

Even coverage that was critical of American policy acknowledged Cold War realities. For example, tough reporting about the Vietnam War rarely challenged the fundamental assumption that Southeast Asia was a testing ground for the superpowers.

James Hoge, Jr., editor of *Foreign Affairs*, wrote of this practice: "Events and trends were calibrated by how much they added to or subtracted from America's security versus its ideological superpower rival. . . . Pretensions to the contrary, the press traditionally has covered international affairs from the perspective of America's perceived interests. This has meant explaining U.S. foreign policy and U.S. engagements, laced with criticism only when policy execution appeared to ill serve the nation's defined interests."[1]

Then, during Mikhail Gorbachev's regime, the Soviet Union's world view changed. Prior to its own implosion, the U.S.S.R. relaxed its hold on its satellites and moved toward a more benign relationship with the United States.

With incredible suddenness, the pressure was off. As he left office in January 1993, Secretary of State Lawrence Eagleburger said, "We are in the middle of a global revolution, a period of change and instability equaled in modern times only by the aftermath of the French and Russian revolutions."[2]

America's national interests would have to be redefined, and, with the threat of global nuclear war greatly reduced, at least for the moment, policymakers, their critics, and those who covered them enjoyed new flexibility. Gone was the fear that any small crisis might escalate into a planet-threatening nuclear confrontation. The cost of error was drastically reduced, as was the deference accorded to those who made the crucial decisions.

In December 1992, *New York Times* foreign editor Bernard Gwertzman sent a memo to his staff about how these sweeping changes in the world were affecting their job as journalists. Referring to the superpower rivalry, he wrote: "There was a credible, overarching relevance to covering every aspect of this competition. Without this threat of nuclear destruction, there is an obvious need to question some of our assumptions about coverage."[3]

The framework on which coverage decisions rested had been rendered obsolete. "In the old days," Gwertzman wrote, "when certain countries were pawns in the Cold War, their political orientation alone was reason enough for covering them. Now with their political orientation not quite as important, we don't want to forget them, but we have an opportunity to examine the different aspects of a society more fully."[4]

Consider Poland, for example. After World War II and throughout the Cold War, almost all news stories about Poland had been grounded in the East-West struggle: Poland as Soviet satellite; Poland struggling to escape Soviet domination; Poland as homeland of the Pope who did so much to undermine communism. When the Cold War ended, Poland's relationship with the remnants of the Soviet Union lost much of its relevance. The country's newsworthiness now was to be found in its emerging democratic capitalism and its role as a trade partner for its former adversaries in the West. No longer in the Soviet shadow, its national character and national culture began to be seen as truly independent. Just as the Poles could conduct their nation's business without worrying about Soviet interference, so too could journalists now do stories about Poland without even mentioning the Kremlin.

While journalists altered the lenses through which they viewed the world, American policymakers were making more difficult changes. Presidents, secretaries of state, and other foreign policy leaders were deprived of their most reliable rationale for defense spending, foreign aid, and much else. The use of overt or covert military force, which could almost always be justified somehow by a purported communist threat, now became a less usable tool.

If Dwight Eisenhower wanted to overthrow the government of Iran or Ronald Reagan wanted to harass the Nicaraguan Sandinistas, each had in the Soviet specter a convenient excuse for his actions. When the Soviet Union crumbled, however, the foreign policy establishment and the news media stumbled forward together, one trying to justify its initiatives, the other trying to establish a context for its reporting. Bill Clinton found that this readjustment could be politically painful, as Professor Michael Mandelbaum of Johns Hopkins University has described: "If the decision to intervene was not easier during the Cold War, it was simpler: U.S. presidents did not necessarily know when to use force, but they always knew why—to combat the Soviet Union, its allies, and its clients, and thus defend American interests. The argument for intervention was not always universally persuasive, but it was always plausible. In Bosnia, Somalia, and Haiti in 1993 it was not even plausible."[5]

TRAVELING WITHOUT A COMPASS

In this new world, journalists had to inch their way along without a compass. Jack Matlock, who served as the American ambassador in Moscow during the Soviet Union's demise, said in a 1993 interview: "The Cold War did provide benchmarks, navigation points, which are not there now. So when you look at a situation like Bosnia and other struggles, it's much harder to say, 'OK, who are the good guys and who are the bad guys?' The challenge is even greater now because the press, if it is reporting these stories responsibly, has got to dig deep enough to understand the nuances."[6]

Some of the early verdicts about news organizations' efforts to meet these new demands have not been favorable. Stephen Hess of the Brookings Institution has said: "The networks are now basically out of the foreign news business. The networks are not covering the world, they're covering conflagration points."[7] James Hoge has written: "Except for the dramas of starving people and extreme violence brought into living rooms sporadically by television, the public is seizing the opportunity to turn inward."8

At the *New York Times*, Bernard Gwertzman asked important questions: "We have chosen to invest major resources in covering the former Yugoslavia, but is this the correct move? Should we care what happens to Serbs, Croats, and Bosnians?"9 Questions similar to Gwertzman's were, presumably, being asked at the White House, the State Department, and the Pentagon as well.

In shaping policy and planning news coverage, "caring" about distant peoples involves the merging of conscience and self-interest. Sometimes, however, this merger is made difficult by disparities between the two elements. Conscience may dictate sending U.S. troops to Somalia to impose order and deliver food, but no national interest requires intervention. So is it the right move?

For a president who contemplates putting American troops at risk in Somalia, the stakes are high. For a news organization determining where to deploy its reporters, the question is more an accounting problem than a moral one. Nevertheless, each party's decision influences the other's. If a television network sends crews to Somalia, its reports about starvation and chaos may influence public opinion and the president. If the president acts first, the news organization may choose simply to follow the troops.

This let-someone-else-decide approach may be expedient, but it fails to come to grips with the basic questions about priorities: What should drive policy, and what is "newsworthy"? In debates about the Clinton administration's foreign policy, the lack of a philosophical foundation has often been criticized. At issue are basic judgments not only about *where* to act, but also *how* to act.

When fears arose in 1994 about North Korea's potential nuclear capability and evidence was presented of North Korean violations of the nuclear Nonproliferation Treaty, Clinton apparently wanted to impose sanctions, but he was unable to find international support or even consensus within his own administration for such measures. Were sanctions necessary? What should they be? If imposed, would they lead to war, and would they be worth it? Those questions were not answered. Eventually, former President Jimmy Carter was able to broker a deal with the North Koreans, but the whole episode reinforced impressions that Clinton's foreign policy lacked substance.10

This was not the only instance of Clinton's foreign policy being plagued by uncertainty. In both Somalia and Bosnia, American intentions remained unclear. When Clinton tried to send U.S. Navy Seabees to Haiti to help build that country's infrastructure, an angry crowd on the Haitian docks blocked the navy ship from landing for two days; Clinton then ordered it to sail home, its mission abandoned.[11]

Clinton deserves some, but not all, of the blame for these problems. He has been criticized by the press and politicians, but few constructive suggestions have been offered. His difficulties were compounded by the lack of guiding principles comparable to the anti-communist gospel that had dominated American foreign policy during the Cold War.

While Clinton struggled, the impact of news coverage on policy-making was also less consequential. Although journalists did not hesitate to evaluate particular incidents, such as the failed mission to Haiti, broader judgments have been made difficult by the journalists' own lack of a reliable measuring stick. Other than keeping the lid on the crisis of the moment, what is the goal of foreign policy? What constitutes success and failure?

CREATING A NEW COMPASS

In the interplay between those who make and those who report foreign policy, the question always exists about who is influencing whom. As the world takes its post-Cold War shape, the answer to that question is likely to be determined by who acts more promptly and assertively.

Some drifting is to be anticipated. But eventually—and before too long—a new world view will evolve, whether defined by policymakers, the news media, or both.

Beyond Bipolarism

Even before the fall of the Soviet Union, assumptions about a bipolar world were outdated. East versus West was only one level of competition; North versus South friction had become more significant as well. The Third World was commanding increased attention, collectively and as an array of independent entities. They were no longer merely prizes for competing superpowers; with strategic and economic priorities changing, they were increasingly becoming players in their own right.

For policymakers and the news media alike, decisions need to be made about how to deal with the evolving and often volatile global constituency. Some countries command notice, such as Pakistan, a potential nuclear power. Some cry out for help and coverage, such as the Sudan, plagued by war and famine. Mexico, generating emigrants and struggling as a U.S. trade partner, may finally get the attention it deserves from its northern neighbor. The enormous power of China is maturing, and Japan's economic prowess becomes ever more sophisticated. Vietnam is evolving from enemy to investment magnet. South Africa is politically transformed. A number of Muslim states blend religious faith with political forcefulness. The list is long and keeps expanding.

Government and news media are alike in their tendency to ignore many nations until crises explode. Then a diplomat's cable or a freelancer's story alerts the government or the public, and suddenly East Timor has become important. Government officials and news consumers need to be brought up to speed about yet another place that many of them probably had not even heard of before.

A logical foreign policy in this new world must be built on a firm foundation of general principles with a superstructure that is flexible and can be remodeled as the need arises. No policy can address in advance all possible contingencies; not every political development or natural disaster can be anticipated.

News organizations must operate with even greater flexibility. While the State Department may have desk officers who can keep some kind of watch on even the most obscure places, no news organization can match that. To a considerable degree, the "parachutist" approach to crises—sending in a barely prepared correspondent who must instantly deliver coverage—is certain to continue.

But those news organizations that want to cover the world comprehensively may recognize the need to broaden their perspective. Bureaus in London, Moscow, and Tokyo will increasingly find themselves far removed from the action. As reliance on far-flung stringers grows more necessary, quality control will become more important too. In addition, according to Associated Press president Louis Boccardi, foreign bureaus will have a "changed mandate, from guardians of their own areas to participants in broader regional coverage. We now see our bureau in Islamabad, Pakistan, for instance, as more than our protector on Pakistan news or as the northern pole of the India-Pakistan story. It is the eastern anchor of the crescent of Muslim states that stretches off to the Maghreb, a natural partner of bureaus all across that area in developing regionwide stories."[12]

Similar needs exist among those who make policy and plan news coverage. No White House or State Department official wants to be blindsided by news reports about political unrest or starvation in some distant place. If that happens, and if the public gets interested, then policy will have to respond to the coverage. Similarly, no journalist enjoys "parachuting" into an unanticipated major story after the government has already acted.

"Keep your eye on Washington and Moscow" was a convenient approach to planning the policy and news agendas of the Cold War world. That world is gone.

Geo-economics

Just as the geographic scope of policy-making and news coverage is expanding, so too is the range of subject matter involved. During the Cold War, superpower military strategy was at least the backdrop—if not the driving force—behind most aspects of American foreign policy. Considering the nuclear stakes, that approach made sense.

Now, however, military matters are not as dominant. The proliferation of nuclear weapons remains an issue, as does America's ability to fight a war in the Persian Gulf or organize a rescue mission in Somalia. But, absent the threat of nuclear war between the United States and the Soviet Union, policy and news priorities are changing.

In broad terms, the shift is from military to economic affairs. Competition between nations has almost always been rooted in economics, even if that competition became manifest in armed struggle. Now the economic aspect is more dominant, because nations' relative holdings of tanks and bombers and warheads are comparatively less important.

American policy toward the former Soviet Union, for example, recognizes that prospects for those republics depend largely on their ability to reform their economic systems, moving away from the failed precepts of communism and into some form of a free market. News coverage has roughly paralleled this emphasis.

Other facets of foreign economic policy and the coverage of it are even more complicated. Reporting about the tensions in economic relations between the United States and Japan, for example, influences public opinion, which then generates political pressures, which in turn exacerbate the original tensions. George Bush's 1992 visit to Japan, with eighteen American corporate chief executives in tow, was an example of letting political posturing for an American audience take precedence over a diplomacy driven by logic. Bush tried to look tough, but he was demanding concessions for products that simply were not competitive in the Japanese market. He ended up looking more plaintive than assertive.[13]

During the 1993 debate about the North American Free Trade Agreement (NAFTA), the interplay between news and policy was again on display. The news media were seen by supporters and opponents of the treaty as crucial in shaping public opinion and influencing Congress's vote on ratification.

As the complexities of U.S.-Mexican relations moved to the top of the public agenda, journalists had the always difficult task of reporting the pronouncements of the pro- and anti-NAFTA politicians while providing nonpartisan analysis of the issues involved.

Beyond the mainstream media, "new news" was important in the NAFTA battle. A debate between Vice President Al Gore and NAFTA opponent Ross Perot on the "Larry King Live" television program was a triumph for Gore and NAFTA. Talk radio potentate Rush Limbaugh—reaching 20 million listeners each week—performed an on-air dissection of Perot's anti-NAFTA book. Neither King nor Limbaugh is a journalist, but their programs are relied upon as information sources by vast audiences.

Perot's and Limbaugh's strengths with their constituencies were based primarily on the domestic aspects of NAFTA, which, not surprisingly, generated broader public interest than did traditional international policy concerns such as improving relations with Latin America and aiding political reform in Mexico. Of this, James Hoge has written: "More candid attention needs to be given to deep domestic worries about job loss, immigration flow, and preservation of English as the nation's language. The latter might seem like an odd element in a discussion of trade negotiations, yet NAFTA promoters say it is one of the most frequently asked questions out on the hustings."[14]

The NAFTA struggle was a forerunner of even more complex economic issues to come:

- America's relationship with the European Union will be a major policy topic in the coming years, and the news media's depiction of an evolving Europe is certain to affect the politics of that relationship. Prospects for a Trans-Atlantic Free Trade Agreement (TAFTA) will depend largely on media-driven public perceptions of potential gains and losses from redesigned ties to Europe.

- If NAFTA proves successful, the next step may be to expand it to include the entire Western Hemisphere.

- As the door to China's massive market gradually opens, the quest for economic advantage will be undertaken against a backdrop of political concerns about China's military intentions and its attitude toward human rights.

Economic issues such as these will redefine the world's power relationships. According to Ronald Steel: "The days of deference by allies to American military power are over. In a world without a single menacing enemy, alliances are deprived of meaning. And in trade wars, unlike military confrontations, there are no allies, only rivals."[15]

New Tensions, New Battlegrounds

The world may be different, but it is not more peaceful than it was during the Cold War. The superpowers, when they thought it useful, would sponsor relatively small "proxy wars" in places such as Angola, but they would try to prevent major upheavals that might threaten their own interests. For example, they probably would not have let Yugoslavia disintegrate, at least not so explosively.

The purposes driving American foreign policy have changed. "Containment" of communist expansionism was the dominant premise underpinning U.S. policy during the half-century following World War II. That premise may now be obsolete, but its replacement has yet to be defined.

"Doing good" seemed to motivate the Clinton administration's early diplomacy, and this principle (if not its execution) found a certain level of approval from journalists who yearn to be altruistic, even though their profession does not often lend itself to high-mindedness. But beneficence cannot always be squared with national interest. Peter Rodman of Johns Hopkins University has warned that "our moral impulse will outreach our strategic sense."[16]

Journalists, like policymakers, are trying to find intellectual footing on this strange and shifting ground. National Public Radio reporter Sylvia Poggioli has noted that, during this time of transition, "reporters had to confront new problems that most of them had never explored before, such as ethnic self-assertion, tribalism, religious conflicts, and the rights and limits to self-determination."[17] Policymakers, as well, have seen less emphasis on the "big picture" and have had to monitor many more small pictures.

Picking sides used to be a matter of ascertaining a country's or a faction's loyalty—to Washington or to Moscow. Once that allegiance was determined, policy decisions fell more easily into place, and news coverage acquired a readily understandable framework. The labels "pro-Western" and "pro-communist" were overbroad, but that did not keep them from being widely used.

Now those labels are quaint antiques. A much larger repertoire of names and places is needed to keep track of the world's troubles. Sunni Muslims versus Shi'ite Muslims; Croats versus Serbs; Inkatha versus African National Congress; Tutsis versus Hutus; Ulster Unionists versus Democratic Unionists; the list stretches on. Geography also has become more challenging: Where is Dagestan? KwaZulu-Natal? Chiapas? Qatar? This is more than a trivia quiz; all these groups and locales have recently been in the news.

New alignments are taking shape, but they are not likely to follow the patterns of the past. Homogeneity is less a factor than it once was. *The Economist* has put the shift in historical perspective: "The 19th century's great powers (Britain, France, Germany, Russia, and Austria-Hungary) were all European, all Christian of one sort or another, and all sharers in the pleasures of Mozart, Goethe, and Turgenev; in short, they knew each other pretty well. The 21st century's probable contenders for power (Russia; China; Europe and America either separately or together; and some new Muslim entity) have far less in common. They are therefore more likely to misunderstand one another, and to miscalculate the others' reactions to what they do."[18]

The realignments that this shift represents will mean comparable difficulties for those who make and those who cover foreign policy. The jugglers will have more balls to keep in the air and more distractions to challenge their coordination.

A frightening precursor of the problems of the twenty-first century can be seen during the closing years of the current century: the bloody chaos that has plagued the former Yugoslavia.

THE DISINTEGRATION OF YUGOSLAVIA (1990–)

This, said veteran foreign correspondent Peter Arnett, is "the war of the future."[19]

Perhaps, but the fighting that began in earnest in 1991 in what had been Yugoslavia was just as ugly as wars of the past. The country had been patched together after World War I as a haven for South Slavic peoples who wanted to escape domination by Austrians and Ottomans. During World War II, schisms within Yugoslavia were bloodily apparent, as Croat fascists killed thousands of anti-Nazi Serbs, and partisans fought the Germans and their surrogates. Enmities were controlled during the postwar communist rule of Josip Broz, known as Tito. His was an anti-Moscow and nonaligned communism. With great political adroitness and resolute firmness, he held his country together. He played off East against West to Yugoslavia's advantage during the Cold War.

After Tito's death in 1980, however, the country began to slide toward dissolution. In 1987, Serbian leader Slobodan Milosevic began a power-grab disguised as nationalism. In 1991, Croatia and Slovenia seceded from Serb-dominated Yugoslavia, followed in 1992 by Bosnia-Herzegovina. But the political boundaries did not match the ethnic map. Combat and forced relocations of civilians followed. As what had been Yugoslavia tore itself apart, tens of thousands of people died while the world watched.

When Bill Clinton moved into the White House in January 1993, the fighting—especially in Bosnia-Herzegovina—was well underway. Clinton's top foreign affairs officials were split about what to do; there was no controlling policy.

This was the classic post-Cold War dilemma: Without having to worry about how the Soviet Union might use the situation to its advantage (and to American detriment), there was no vital U.S. interest at stake that might justify intervention. On the other hand, civilians were enduring horrible suffering, so, as the lone superpower, the United States may have had a moral responsibility to stop the fighting, even if that meant using force.

News coverage of the conflict had been relatively skimpy and appeared to have had minimal effect on public opinion. Most Americans paid little attention to whatever it was that was going on in these places with unpronounceable names that they could not find on a map.

Clinton's foreign policy team recognized at least some of the dangers involved. The war had the potential to overflow the Balkans and pull in Greece, Turkey, and other neighboring countries. Moreover, helping or ignoring the beleaguered Bosnian Muslims would affect relations with other Islamic states.[20] Needing to do something, Clinton authorized increased U.S. participation in humanitarian aid efforts and in attempts to negotiate an end to the fighting.

Chapter 3 has addressed the impact of news coverage on Clinton's Balkans policy in 1994, after graphic reports about civilian casualties in Sarajevo appeared. More to the point here is examining the interaction of policy and coverage as a possible paradigm for coverage of future conflicts. One of the few certainties about the state of the world is that the war in the former Yugoslavia will not be the last of its kind.

Regardless of potential political impact, a primary task for the news media is to let the public know what is going on. After that, political pressure may or may not evolve, but at least people will have information to use in making relatively informed judgments about government policy decisions. Carol Williams of the *Los Angeles Times* noted in 1992 that "stories that might have prepared people and educated them about this conflict early on didn't get the space. If the world had gotten the picture that what happened in Croatia was a one-sided war of aggression, action might have been taken to prevent the spread to Bosnia."[21]

Providing that picture is made more difficult when the subjects of coverage, such as Serb, Croat, and Bosnian Muslim political leaders, are intent upon shaping news coverage and using it to their advantage. From Zagreb, Croatia, in December 1994, Roger Cohen reported in the *New York Times* that "attempts to manage and manipulate the press are now accorded as much importance by Muslims and Serbs as maneuvers on the battlefield."[22] This manipulation of journalists distorts the information that news consumers receive and rely on, and it complicates policymakers' jobs.

As has been illustrated throughout the Balkan conflict, journalists must constantly be alert to traps laid by politicians. As Marco Altherr of the International Red Cross noted: "It's the first time I've seen strong and effective propaganda from [all] sides. When you're talking to either side, they're absolutely convinced they'll be slaughtered by the other side."[23] Lord David Owen, the British diplomat who tried to bring the war to an end, has written: "Never before in over thirty years of public life have I had to operate in such a climate of dishonour, propaganda and dissembling. Many of the people with whom I had to deal in the former Yugoslavia were literally strangers to the truth."[24]

Although most news reports blamed the Serbs for the February 1994 mortar shelling of a Sarajevo market that killed many civilians, Owen was more cautious in his opinion: "Having now been exposed for eighteen months to the three parties' claims and counter-claims, I was capable of believing that any of them could have been responsible."[25] This was not the only occasion on which parties to the war were suspected of launching disguised attacks—even if that meant killing their own people—in order to elicit international sympathy or to spur an outside power to take military action against their enemies.[26] (None of these charges have been proved.)

Alternatively, the perpetrators of such outrages have sometimes tried to manipulate the press and public opinion by preventing any coverage at all. Roger Cohen has reported: "Acutely aware that a strong press report can affect U.N. sanctions or NATO's role, the Serbs have taken to sealing off areas under their control. . . . The Muslim-led Bosnian government has also become more restrictive, limiting access to advances in central Bosnia, perhaps out of concern that its image as victim could be affected."[27]

Against such a backdrop of bloody duplicity, journalists can easily become pawns. Seeing the unsettled state of world opinion and of governments' policies toward the Balkan states, the protagonists in the war could be expected to try to use news coverage to shape opinion and policy in ways favorable to themselves. Television pictures of the victims of atrocities might thus be provided or even created in this effort.

When those pictures appear and leaders offer the public no cues about policy, the graphic images have an even greater impact. ABC's Peter Jennings has noted that "political leadership trumps good television every time. As influential as television can be, it is most influential in the absence of decisive political leadership."[28]

The effect of coverage can be amplified by semantic choices. For example, one night in 1995, Jennings started his newscast with the words: "We begin tonight with cruelty and outrage." On another night's newscast, Jennings said, "Once again Bosnian civilians are forced to leave their homes in terror while the Western European nations and the United States do nothing about it." Meanwhile, Dan Rather introduced one edition of the "CBS Evening News" with, "Bosnia tonight is the scene of brutality without end."[29] At about the same time, the lead story in *Newsweek*—about "safe areas" in Bosnia falling—was headlined "For Shame," accompanied by a full-page color photograph of a crying Muslim refugee and her child.[30]

Some news stories included detailed descriptions of the horrors. Roy Gutman, a leader in reporting the victimization of Bosnian civilians, wrote in *Newsday* in August 1992: "The Serb conquerors of northern Bosnia have established two concentration camps in which more than a thousand civilians have been executed or starved and thousands more are being held until they die, according to two recently released prisoners interviewed by *Newsday*. The testimony of the two survivors appeared to be the first eyewitness accounts of what international human rights agencies fear may be systematic slaughter conducted on a huge scale."[31]

The choice of words in such stories is important. "Executed," "systematic slaughter," and—most significantly—"concentration camps" will grab readers' attention, reminding them of Nazi evils and of promises that "never again" would the world allow such horrors to happen.

British journalist Ed Vulliamy of the *Guardian* described one of the camps in similar terms: "The men are at various stages of human decay and affliction; the bones of their elbows and wrists protrude like pieces of jagged stone from the pencil-thin stalks to which their arms have been reduced. . . . There is nothing quite like the sight of the prisoner desperate to talk and to convey some terrible truth that is so near yet so far, but who dares not. Their stares burn, they speak only with their terrified silence, and eyes inflamed with the articulation of stark, undiluted, desolate fear-without-hope."[32]

All these pictures and words are bound to have an effect. The power of such stories is accentuated by their going beyond statistics, showing the wounded woman lying in the Sarajevo street or the sobbing child walking along a country road in a column of refugees. When governments are contemplating intervention, this coverage is helpful to those who want public support for taking action but it is detrimental to those who want to move slowly or do nothing.

British Foreign Minister Douglas Hurd and other officials have referred to the journalists who produce such coverage as "the something-must-be-done brigade." Easy to espouse and effective in eliciting public sympathy, the attitude that "something must be done" frustrates policymakers who know they cannot do merely "something"; they can act only when they have a very specific thing to do. Is the "something" to be a full-scale intervention, an air strike, an economic embargo, or a new push for negotiations? These "somethings" (and there are many more) require very different plans of action and may have very different outcomes.

On the other hand, politicians sometimes succumb to inertia, and so press-generated pressure may be essential if any movement is to take place. In 1992, for example, officials of the NATO governments had said that reports about Serb-run "death camps" were exaggerated. Then the public had a chance to see for themselves the video from the camps. Such news footage tends to be more believable than pronouncements from government officials.

One of the major complaints from policymakers about the pressures created by news coverage is the tendency of the press to oversimplify and to draw crisp boundaries delineating "good guys" and "bad guys." In a war such as that in the former Yugoslavia, such categorization is dangerously simplistic. There are no good guys; everyone is wearing a black hat.

The dichotomy between "good Bosnian Muslims" and "bad Bosnian Serbs" was avidly fostered by the increasingly publicity-savvy Bosnian Muslim leadership and was accepted as conventional wisdom by many in the news media. In the U.S. Congress and within the Clinton administration, this became the path of least resistance, so it was followed. Many in the news media also went this way. By the time that the Bosnian Muslims' own tactics came into question, changing course was too difficult. As a result, little was done by the press or policymakers that might have challenged or modified the simplistic image of the Bosnian Muslims as besieged victims.[33]

But, on occasion, news coverage has underscored the real complexities of the conflict in the former Yugoslavia. In April 1993, Croat militiamen moved into the Bosnian Muslim village of Ahmici and murdered dozens of civilians, including women and children. British troops that were part of the U.N. force in the area discovered what had happened. News crews were there, and their pictures showed the world the bodies, as well as the British unit commander's angry confrontation with Croat soldiers.[34]

This episode presented an unexpected complication for a public that had come to see the Serbs as the villains. Now some new bad guys—the Croats—were added to the mix. This distraction diluted the mounting public pressure for air strikes aginst the Serbs, which NATO policymakers had been resisting.[35]

The world's appraisal of the war in the former Yugoslavia has been shaped by a combination of incomplete news coverage and inchoate foreign policy. Depictions of good and evil have been blurred, as have definitions of national interest. Even after a half-decade of fighting, few convincing answers have emerged about why the war happened and what other nations should do about it.

There will be other wars like this one. The warped nationalism—perhaps tribalism is a better word—that led to the disintegration of Yugoslavia may prove to be a common characteristic of the post-Cold War world. The convulsions occurring in the states of the former Soviet Union provide further evidence of this new instability, as do the tides of bloodshed surging through parts of Africa.

Until governments adjust their foreign policies to the realities of the new geopolitics, news coverage is likely to have an enhanced influence on public opinion. Without the familiar context of the Cold War, the public is less certain how to interpret what is going on in the world. When political leaders fail to provide clearly defined policies as a foundation for considering the events reported by the news media, a vacuum results. News coverage fills at least part of it.

Chapter Nine

Spheres of Influence

The florid journalism that William Randolph Hearst employed to help create the Spanish-American War seems archaic now. But how much distance is there, really, from Hearst's pronouncements about the plight of Cuba to the thinly disguised editorials by today's network anchormen about horrors in the former Yugoslavia? Bill Clinton may not have been subjected to a barrage of inflammatory reporting such as William McKinley had to endure, but clearly he was nudged along the path toward intervention by news coverage that elicited Americans' sympathy for civilians caught up in the Balkan war. That coverage and that reaction made a more assertive U.S. policy politically appealing.

Between the close of the nineteenth century, when Hearst called for war against Spain, to the final years of the twentieth, journalists' practices have changed almost as thoroughly as the world they cover. But the fact remains: The news media do influence foreign policy.

Not determine, but influence; the semantic distinction is important. By revealing—or sometimes not revealing—what is going on in distant places, journalists help to shape public opinion, which in turn helps to shape policymakers' behavior. No neat formula defines this process. News coverage is just one of many factors that affect policy decisions. Although a news report may capture the immediacy of the moment's crisis, it may also reflect little of the complexity of the issue at hand.

The making of foreign policy is a marathon, not a sprint, and news coverage is just one of many factors affecting its outcome.

THE PUBLIC'S VIEW OF FOREIGN AFFAIRS

Any American political leader proposing a foreign policy intiative must be prepared to answer a difficult question: Why is it any of our business? That is the public's way of demanding a definition of "national interest." Officials who cannot offer an articulate, convincing reply will find their policy plans in instant political trouble.

This is another aspect of post-Cold War uncertainty. Absent the need to anticipate and respond to Soviet actions, most anxieties about the nation's future are now rooted in domestic concerns, which overshadow worries about the rest of the world. The results of the 1992 presidential election underscored this. George Bush learned that his foreign affairs prowess was insufficient to get him reelected, while Bill Clinton found that minimizing foreign policy issues was no hindrance to winning the White House.

As Ronald Steel has written: "Our domestic troubles are not in a realm separate from our foreign policy. They are an integral part, even a product, of it. A nation that seeks not only to protect the world but also to inspire other countries with its values and achievements must be able to offer at least as much to its own people as to those it seeks to guard."[1]

This philosophy constrains policymakers. Adventurous internationalism, even if based on the best of intentions, finds little support. In 1994, President Clinton's national security adviser, Tony Lake, said the enemies of the United States include "extreme nationalists and tribalists, terrorists, organized criminals, coup plotters, rogue states and all those who would return newly free societies to the intolerant ways of the past." Looking at that list, Ronald Steel wrote in 1995, "After thus lining up the United States for a crusade against most of the world, the Clinton administration, unsurprisingly, has had to retreat in one area after another, upon discovering that it was standing alone."[2]

People unsure of their own economic future and unhappy about problems such as pervasive crime and a foundering educational system do not want to be bothered by distant crises. Although an occasional humanitarian emergency may evoke a willingness to act, the dominant feeling seems to be that leadership, like charity, should begin at home.

A national opinion poll (1,492–person sample), conducted in October 1994 by the Gallup Organization for the Chicago Council on Foreign Relations, measured American attitudes about foreign policy issues.[3] The survey found the following:

- The percentage of the public interested in news about other countries declined from 36 percent in 1990 to 33 percent in 1994, while those interested in news about U.S. relations with other countries lessened from 53 percent to 50 percent. By contrast, respondents interested in news about their own communities rose from 55 to 65 percent.

- In the respondents' lists of the "biggest problems facing the country today," no foreign policy matter made the top ten.

- 65 percent of the respondents favored an active U.S. role in world affairs, up from 62 percent in 1990. But the respondents' perception of this role was based mostly on U.S. self-interest; stopping the flow of illegal drugs into the country and protecting American workers' jobs topped the list. More altruistic goals— such as protecting weaker nations against aggressors and promoting human rights—declined to the lowest level in two decades.

- Of possible "critical threats" to the United States, the top three cited were unfriendly nations becoming nuclear powers, large numbers of immigrants and refugees coming to the United States, and international terrorism.

- The belief that the United States has a vital interest in Japan and China rose, while opinion that the United States has a vital interest in Europe declined.

- Support for tariffs declined from 54 percent in 1990 to 48 percent in 1994.

- Backing for the use of U.S. troops was 54 percent if Russia invaded Western Europe, 52 percent if Iraq invaded Saudi Arabia, and 42 percent if Arab forces invaded Israel.

The survey's conclusion notes that "the end of the Cold War has not shaken America's fundamental commitment to maintaining an active role in world affairs," but apparently "active" is narrowly defined. The analysis of the survey's findings cites a "pragmatic internationalism," which is not "a rejection of international involvement, but focuses attention on goals that bear directly on the well-being of Americans." For policymakers and journalists alike, these findings make clear that foreign policy remains a hard sell, in terms of both enlisting public support and cultivating an interested news audience.

THE NEWS MEDIA'S ROLE

In a 1995 *New York Times* column, Max Frankel wrote that the unsettled state of the world "should be good news for the media, because so long as the world remains a mysterious and dangerous place, there will be exciting stories to report." The mysteries and dangers have changed since Cold War days, but they have not vanished. For example, noted Frankel, "surely the threat of tens of thousands of nuclear weapons is greater now that they lie scattered in unfamiliar hands than when their masters could be addressed by phone or hot line."[4]

The proliferation of weapons is an important news story, as are threats to the environment, changes in the role of the blue-collar worker in the evolving world economy, and many other topics that, if not truly new, at least have new angles to be covered. Reporting these stories, however, can fall prey to a journalistic Catch-22: If the public is not interested in these matters, they will not be covered; but unless they are covered, the public is unlikely to become interested in them.

Along those lines, NBC's Tom Brokaw has argued that the news media have not caused the new isolationism in America but rather are victims of it.[5] His premise is valid up to a point. News organizations are both perpetrators and victims, but most important for the future is that they not exacerbate the problem.

The corollary to this Catch-22 is that noncoverage perpetuates itself. If Americans' world view—which is largely defined by the news media—narrows, it will be difficult to expand it. An explosive crisis can force an urgent broadening of perspective, but reliance on such an approach is flawed. Iraq's invasion of Kuwait in 1990, for instance, should not have found an American public unable to locate the protagonist nations on a map. The regional political turmoil from which that crisis evolved had been alternately boiling and simmering for years. American news consumers should not have been so surprised by what happened.

This is not merely a matter of developing and satisfying the public's intellectual curiosity. In ventures such as the Gulf War, public support or disapproval should be based on information from diverse sources, including both journalistic and governmental ones. It should not be controlled by politicians who might manipulate constituents lacking the information on which to base logical judgments about what should be done. The democratic process is undermined by inadequate knowledge.

The news media are not wholly to blame for this situation; there are limits to how much they can force-feed their audience. The public has to take some responsibility and indicate that it wants information. As former *New York Times* publisher Arthur Hays Sulzberger observed, "Along with responsible newspapers, we must have responsible readers."[6]

But still, journalists have considerable influence in helping the public decide what news is important. In their role as information-providers, the news media are not entirely neutral. Every day, news executives make important choices: what to cover and what to ignore; what resources to expend in coverage; how to play stories—page one, top of newscast, or in less visible places; whether to do follow-up reports. These and similar decisions are often driven by economics as well as by judgments about what the public wants and needs to know.

Media analyst Stephen Hess has observed that news organizations do not need to spend great amounts on foreign coverage. They get a steady flow of international stories from the wire services to which they subscribe. "The reason for the lack of international news in newspapers," has written, "is indifference, not greed," adding: "Undoubtedly, many readers do not care about the world beyond U.S. shores. But editors take the selection responsibility for publishing other matters they think are in their readers' best interests. Why not print more international news?"[7]

These new judgments also should be based on journalists' recognition of their responsibilities as prods to their audience's conscience. If the news media do not tell the public about the barbarism of the war in the former Yugoslavia or about the scope of starvation in the Sudan, it is unlikely anyone else will (or, at least, anyone else with comparable reach and influence). The question arises: If a battle is fought or a child starves, but it is not covered by the news media, has it really happened? Of course it has, but not in the public's consciousness.

These matters become still more complicated because news coverage is vulnerable to manipulation. Sometimes when the public becomes interested in a humanitarian issue, governments will respond with mere gestures, not with substantive policy. For example, after stories about a famine, a government may order a one-day airdrop of supplies. This action will be dutifully recorded by the television cameras to show the public that the government is appropriately compassionate and responsive. Then, when the press's short attention span expires, nothing further gets done.

Superficial coverage is likely to be met with superficial policy: a one-day emergency airdrop instead of a plan for long-term assistance or agricultural reform. When the news media stoke a constant sense of crisis, first about one event, then another, politicians respond in kind, fighting fires rather than preventing them. That is unlikely to be the wisest way to address underlying problems.

American news organizations' overseas reporting rests in the hands of roughly 400 correspondents. Thus, too many people depend on the eyes of too few.[8] Television, constrained by the newscast format and by the breadth of vision of its cameras, presents a particularly narrow, simplified world to its viewers. The controlling principle seems to be to deliver news quickly, even if incompletely.

Perceiving their audience as not expecting sophisticated international coverage, television news organizations have backed away from aggressive, innovative reporting about the world. Lamenting this trend, Max Frankel has written, "What's been lost at the television networks is perspective on the world, the passion to learn, to explore, to employ the educational force of the camera."[9]

Because of this, Americans remain underinformed about their nation's place in the world and give little thought to what they want America's foreign policy—generally and specifically—to be. Appraising this intellectual vacuum, former U.S. ambassador to Moscow Jack Matlock has noted: "This is one of the problems of the post-Cold War era—if we are to get some coherence into international law and into our own attitudes, we're going to have to work on developing a new consensus. Those who concentrate on the big issues are worth listening to, and I think this is a very important role for the media."[10]

Ambassador Matlock's point deserves serious thought by journalists. He is not asking that the press adhere to an official line but rather that the news media take seriously their role as providers of a forum for policy debate and, eventually, policy creation. The Cold War era's "rules of the game" are largely obsolete; the news media can play an important part in formulating new ones.

NEW FACTORS

The post-Cold War expansion of freedom has enhanced the power of journalism, most notably in places where the news media had previously been censored. A good example of this change is the coverage by Russian news organizations of the war in Chechnya.

The last Soviet war was in Afghanistan, and the coverage that reached the Soviet public was thoroughly sanitized by the state-controlled news media. In post-Soviet Russia, with at least some news organizations relatively free to report what they want, the government is learning how unpleasant it can be to have official pronouncements undermined by press coverage. For instance, in January 1995, Russian officials in Moscow told reporters that the bombing of Grozny, the Chechen capital, had stopped, but NTV, a new private television network, showed video of continuing air raids.[11]

Chechnya has been called "Russia's Vietnam," partly because Boris Yeltsin has felt the sting of news coverage in much the way Lyndon Johnson did. This facet of democratization surprised Russian political leaders, because neither they nor their country had ever had any first-hand experience of press freedom.

Government and military leaders who thought they could ride out even the worst military setbacks with political impunity have learned what problems arise when newscasts carry pictures of dead and wounded Russian soldiers and of wailing civilian victims of the war. Demonstrations by the mothers of dead Russian soldiers have created unprecedented political problems for the Russian leadership. Unless the new press freedoms are rolled back (which could happen), the Russian political system will have to adapt to the news-driven contentiousness that is part of any true democracy.

In addition to newly liberated national news media, global television will put increasing pressure on governments that would prefer to control what their people know. As cable systems and satellite dishes become more common throughout the world, international networks, such as CNN International and BBC World Service Television, will compete with national and local news providers for audiences.

The outcome of such competition may depend on the freedom and quality of domestic television. Where local news sources are good, the public tends to prefer them to international news providers. In Western Europe, for example, the domestic networks are more popular than outsiders.[12] Of course, those countries enjoy press freedom, so their citizens do not have to rely on outside sources for the truth.

In nations that rigidly control information, however, sources such as CNN and BBC are likely to be relied upon more heavily, assuming that the public has the means to receive them. The struggle for access to international television broadcasts is similar to the radio battles of the Cold War, when transmissions of Radio Free Europe and Radio Liberty penetrated the communist bloc despite efforts to jam their signals.

Cable television provides an expanding venue where policy-oriented groups can raise their visibility and proselytize. Jim Lederman, in his study of media coverage of the Palestinian intifada, has observed that use of cable television by advocacy groups "may create new international information loops outside the control of the journalists and political elites. The use of cable services, when combined with the increasing spread of computer billboards and direct satellite broadcasting, may create a new, visual form of the traditional political leaflet. . . . For the first time, political advocacy groups may be able to communicate directly to audiences worldwide in real time—and circumvent established media outlets."[13]

An example of this kind of advocacy jounalism is Al Manar ("the beacon"), a Lebanese television station run by the Shia Muslim Hezbollah militia. Hezbollah troops take video cameras with them on patrol and provide viewers with footage of attacks on Israeli convoys and other combat scenes, plus political stories that reinforce official Hezbollah doctrine. Al Manar is one of fifty private stations established by various militia groups during Lebanon's turbulent 1980s. According to *The Economist*, in early 1995, Al Manar was the fourth-most-watched television station in Lebanon. (Although programming is controlled by a Shia cleric, the station even carries American films, but only after cutting out virtually all scenes that include women.)[14]

The principal advantage of having such a station is its power to circumvent both traditional news media and the policymakers those media cover. Al Manar, for example, is used to offset information originating from Israeli sources. Hezbollah can reach a substantial audience with its broadcasts, deciding what to show and what to withhold, which political figures to feature and which to ignore.

Such stations are the electronic descendants of special interest newspapers, printed openly or clandestinely to serve journalistic and political purposes. This print genre is centuries old; television is simply catching up. In a television-dependent society, the proliferation of advocacy programming will ensure that voices from outside the mainstream will be harder to ignore. This will put new pressure on news organizations and governments as they seek to address the interests of their various constituencies.

Yet another information venue is also on the rise. For broad as well as narrow constituencies, computer networks will provide a flow of information from diverse sources to diverse recipients. As this young medium expands into more households around the world, the news consumer will supersede the news organization in determining how much detail about which stories he or she will receive.

What people will do with all the information that becomes available is far from certain. Those who avail themselves of this resource may become more skeptical about material they receive in traditional formats from governments and the established news media. They may challenge politicians' speeches and newspapers' stories, always asking for more.

Interactive telecommunications may make "public opinion" far more tangible and may revitalize direct democracy, as opposed to representative government. If this happens, news organizations' role as intermediary between the public and policymakers may become less significant.

All this remains highly speculative; the new technologies are still taking shape and winning popular acceptance. But, based on the brief history of these media so far, they may become a significant new factor in the policy-making equation. Depending on the eye of the beholder, this may be seen as useful democratic self-assertiveness or disconcerting intrusiveness.

POLICY TASKS

The uncertain prospects of the Central Intelligence Agency underscore the larger uncertainties about how the government and the public perceive America's place in the world. During the mid-1990s, the CIA has drawn steady fire from congressional critics and others who contend that the agency is unproductive, unreliable, and too expensive. With the Soviet Union gone and intelligence stakes lowered, say critics, needed information can be obtained from diplomats and "open sources," such as the international news media.[15] The counterargument is that plenty of "core threats" remain, from the former Soviet republics, China, and an array of Third World countries. The "next Saddam Hussein" is almost certainly lurking somewhere and ought to be spied upon.

Similar theories affect news organizations' outlook. A perceived absence of menace makes withdrawing into the cocoon of journalistic isolationism seem reasonable. But as appealing as such retrenchment might be to both government and the news media, it is almost certain to prove shortsighted. Wishful thinking has little effect on reality.

During Bill Clinton's first three years in the White House, his critics said he had no real foreign policy, while his defenders said he was moving carefully through uncharted waters. His deputy national security adviser, Samuel "Sandy" Berger, has cited three lessons emerging from Clinton's experience:

• In Europe, even absent the Soviet Union, American leadership and muscle were required when dealing with situations such as the war in the former Yugoslavia. The premise of the NATO partnership—the United States and its European allies working together—remained valid.

• Foreign policy achievements do not come quickly; they require patience and a certain amount of trial-and-error maneuvering, as was the case in the Middle East peace talks and the intervention in Haiti.

• The end of superpower-dominated bipolarity not only makes the practice of diplomacy more difficult but also makes it harder to define the philosophy on which foreign policy is built.

According to Berger, "It is a chimera to search after a one-sentence doctrine that answers every question we are faced with in this world."[16]

In this new context, convenient terms such as "containment" are less useful to government officials and journalists who have the common responsibility of explaining foreign policy.

News organizations should recognize the long-haul nature of foreign affairs and plan their coverage accordingly. Anne Nelson, former director of the Committee to Protect Journalists, addressed this topic at a 1994 Columbia University forum, noting the absence of an international context for considering world events: "What we're increasingly missing, as a culture, is connective tissue to bind us to the rest of the world."

She also cited the limited effectiveness of intervention: "It can only accomplish simple things. It can reopen oil pipelines. It can remove or restore a head of state—on a good day. But it can't do complicated things, like creating a functioning democracy where none ever existed, or dismantling a billion-dollar drug industry that is the only crutch for a crippled third world economy." Journalists should understand this, she added, because their coverage may push the public toward demanding intervention in a particular case. The question that should be answered in such news stories is, "What is present in this situation that intervention can actually fix?"[17]

In many cases, intervention may be little more than trying to impose a short-term solution on a long-term problem. Sending troops into the trouble spot of the moment is likely to prove far more problematic—meaning complex, bloody, and lengthy—than the Hollywood-style good-guys-versus-bad-guys struggle in which the outcome is preordained. On the movie screen, two hours is plenty of time for the forces of good to triumph. In the real world, two *years* might not be enough time even to decide who the forces of good are.

A sophisticated and realistic world view must include a philosophy of intervention. Absent this recognition that intervention may sometimes become necessary, foreign policy may become paralyzed. Thomas Friedman of the *New York Times* illustrated this potential problem in his definition of a "Gulf War syndrome": "The U.S. will engage in military operations abroad only if they take place in a desert with nowhere for the enemy to hide, if the fighting can be guaranteed to last no more than five days, if casualties can be counted on one hand, if both oil and nuclear weapons are at stake, if the enemy is a madman who will not accept any compromise, and if the whole operation will be paid for by Germany and Japan." Friedman then pointed out that the occurrence of all these factors happens about as frequently as a visit from Halley's Comet and that relying on this standard "as a criterion for engagement abroad is a covert prescription for isolationism."[18]

Of the elements constituting Friedman's "syndrome," the reluctance to incur military casualties is noble, but it can prove to be an unrealistic constraint when events demand the use of force in the cause of order. In addition to the moral issues involved in sending military personnel into war, political leaders now must worry about television pictures that transform "combat" from a distant abstraction to a living-room reality. Similarly, footage of civilian casualties can undermine political will. When the air war against Iraq began in January 1991, the allied governments worried that pictures of dead Iraqi civilians might undermine public support for the war before the ground assault to liberate Kuwait could begin.

This linkage between military concerns and news coverage strengthens the significance of General Colin Powell's thesis that, if war becomes necessary, it should begin only when such overwhelming force is amassed that the fighting will be as brief as possible. That is both good military strategy and good media strategy. In the era of intense media scrutiny, ordering troops into combat without preparation adequate for quick and definitive victory is likely to leave those who execute policy in a politically untenable position.

Whether military action or diplomatic maneuvering is involved, the media can be disregarded only at policymakers' peril. While he was chairman of the House Foreign Affairs Committee, Congressman Lee Hamilton held a hearing to address the impact of news coverage—especially television reports—on foreign policy. In his opening statement, Hamilton asked three important questions: "What can be done, if anything, to counter the impact of television on our policy? What should policy makers do, if anything, to prevent television from setting their agenda? What, if anything, should the media do to avoid inadvertantly skewing American foreign policy one way or the other?"[19]

In his testimony at the hearing, Ted Koppel, anchor of ABC's "Nightline," said that news coverage has a significant impact only if those responsible for making policy have not defined that policy clearly and have not marshaled public support for it. "If an administration has thought its own foreign policy through," said Koppel, "and is prepared and able to argue the merits and defend the consequences of that policy, television and all its technologies can be dealt with. If, on the other hand, the foreign policy is ill-conceived and poorly explained, it does not much matter whether the news arrives by satellite or clipper ship. Eventually the policy will fail."[20]

Historian Michael Beschloss, also testifying at the hearing, noted that television, because it "focuses on the tangible and dramatic, tends to reward crisis management over crisis prevention. . . . In peacetime, if a president and Congress do not work very hard to frame international issues for the public all the time, television can do a lot to frame them instead, and in ways that may very much limit the flexibility of our political leadership."[21]

In simple terms, a sliding scale can be employed to evaluate the extent of news media influence on foreign policy: The less the government does to present a carefully reasoned position and to convince the public of its wisdom, the more the public will rely on news sources for information about what issues are important and which policies are valid. Conversely, strong foreign policy leadership will not leave an opinion vacuum that the news media will fill.

That formula should not surprise anyone; it is simply common sense. But there is much equivocation about these matters because the parties involved are possessive about their respective responsibilities and at the same time hesitant about infringing on the prerogatives of others. No State Department official wants to admit to having been pushed into a decision by television coverage. Likewise, journalists are reluctant to admit that they help shape policy rather than just report about it.

These pretensions aside, a de facto partnership (although not always an amicable one) does exist. The public, which rarely cares about the niceties of institutional boundaries, absorbs information originating from both government and news organizations and decides whether to believe some or all or none of it. From that process emerges "public opinion," the amorphous but potent political force to which policymakers and the news media pay varying degrees of attention.

The imprecision of all this may frustrate those who like to see policy-making as an orderly, predictable process, but democracy does not lend itself to such orderliness. Give-and-take prevails, even when the process seems to verge on intellectual anarchy, until policy finally is firmed up enough for the public to understand it and the news media to devise a plan for covering it.

Examples of this contrast can be seen in the Bush administration's Desert Storm policy, which took shape during six months of preparation for war, compared with the Clinton administration's vagueness in its first two years of peace-making efforts in the former Yugoslavia. Bush and his advisers refined his policy to the point at which it could be "marketed" successfully to the American and international publics. The Clinton White House apparently lacked the discipline to do that.

For those who make and those who cover foreign policy, these issues deserve more than casual interest. Politicians cannot escape press scrutiny, at least not for long, and their policies may be exalted or trashed by journalists. Likewise, the press cannot divorce its journalistic concerns from the national interest. Just as the public must be informed, so too must the security of the country be respected. Irresponsible reporting about a Cuban missile crisis or an ongoing intelligence operation may not be just bad journalism, it may be dangerously bad citizenship.

As contributors to the public's issues agenda, journalists must throw their news-gathering net far enough to reach events that otherwise would go undiscovered. They also should present those events in ways that will make the public care about them. Humanitarian issues, in particular, are too important to be left wholly in the hands of politicians.

The dynamics of the relationship between the news media and the policymakers are made more interesting by constant change. Evolving technology has altered journalists' capabilities and duties. Live global coverage is wondrous, but it becomes frightening if speed in reporting outdistances responsible editorial judgment. Similarly, political evolution has changed the scope and complexity of coverage. Cold War news patterns became obsolete once the Soviet Union collapsed. The world may now be safer, but it does not lend itself to an easily prescribed regimen of coverage.

Such changes in the news business influence the policy business. How journalists change the way they do their jobs will necessitate changes in the way policymakers do theirs. This relationship is symbiotic. No one is truly in control, and that is probably how it should be.

Walter Lippmann wrote of the connection between news and policy: "The press is no substitute for institutions. It is like the beam of a searchlight that moves restlessly about, bringing one episode and then another out of darkness into vision. Men cannot do the work of the world by this light alone. They cannot govern society by episodes, incidents, and eruptions. It is only when they work by a steady light of their own, that the press, when it is turned upon them, reveals a situation intelligible enough for a popular decision."[22]

This passage affirms the distinction between reporting and governing. For many journalists, "the news" is intrinsically episodic. But for those who are responsible for foreign affairs, such fragmentation is not good policy. Consistency and coherence—as elusive as they may be—are the hallmarks of productive diplomacy.

The relationship between journalists and policymakers is not the equivalent of a closed club. The public should not be shut out, because, as Lippmann noted, the work of the news media and government ought to lead to the public's being able to make knowledgeable "popular decisions" about policy.

This process demands much of all who are involved in it. The very different responsibilities of those who cover the news and those who make policy should be acknowledged and respected. Professionals in one field will continue to influence the work of their counterparts in the other. Having different missions does not preclude constructive coexistence.

Notes

PREFACE

1. Walter Lippmann, *U.S. Foreign Policy* (Boston: Little, Brown, 1943), 10.
2. W. B. Allen, *George Washington: A Collection* (Indianapolis: Liberty Classics, 1988), 620.
3. George F. Kennan, *American Diplomacy* (New York: New American Library, 1952), 5.
4. Ibid., 6.
5. James Reston, *The Artillery of the Press* (New York: Council on Foreign Relations/Harper & Row, 1967), viii. (Italics in original.)

CHAPTER 1

1. Quoted in Charles H. Brown, *The Correspondents' War* (New York: Scribners, 1967), 4.
2. Quoted in Marcus M. Wilkerson, *Public Opinion and the Spanish-American War* (New York: Russell and Russell, 1932), 47.
3. Quoted in Ibid., 65.
4. Joseph E. Wisan, *The Cuban Crisis as Reflected in the New York Press* (New York: Columbia University Press, 1934), 457.
5. Wilkerson, *Public Opinion and the Spanish-American War*, 62.
6. W. A. Swanberg, *Citizen Hearst* (New York: Scribners, 1961), 135.
7. John Dobson, *Reticent Expansionism* (Pittsburgh: Duquesne University Press, 1988), 24.
8. Ibid., 26.

9. Quoted in Brown, *The Correspondents' War*, 104.

10. Quoted in Kennan, *American Diplomacy*, 14.

11. Ibid.

12. Brown, *The Correspondents' War*, 8.

13. Quoted in Ibid., 108.

14. Quoted in Phillip Knightley, *The First Casualty* (New York: Harcourt Brace Jovanovich, 1975), 55.

15. Quoted in Swanberg, *Citizen Hearst*, 108.

16. Brown, *The Correspondents' War*, 101.

17. Michael Emery and Edwin Emery, *The Press and America*, 7th ed. (Englewood Cliffs, NJ: Prentice Hall, 1992), 200.

18. Quoted in Henry F. Pringle, *Theodore Roosevelt* (New York: Harcourt, Brace, and World, 1956), 122.

19. Brown, *The Correspondents' War*, 112.

20. Quoted in Ibid., 78.

21. Wilkerson, *Public Opinion and the Spanish-American War*, 54.

22. Dobson, *Reticent Expansionism*, 24.

23. Swanberg, *Citizen Hearst*, 160.

24. Quoted in Ibid., 162.

25. Ibid., 166.

26. Ibid., 165.

27. Quoted in Ibid., 168.

28. Wilkerson, *Public Opinion and the Spanish-American War*, 103.

29. Ibid., 113.

30. Quoted in Swanberg, *Citizen Hearst*, 170.

31. Ibid., 155, 162.

32. Edmund Morris, *The Rise of Theodore Roosevelt* (New York: Coward, McCann, and Geoghegan, 1979), 601.

33. Swanberg, *Citizen Hearst*, 170.

34. Wilkerson, *Public Opinion and the Spanish-American War*, 115.

35. Quoted in Brown, *The Correspondents' War*, 145.

36. Quoted in Mitchell Stephens, *A History of News* (New York: Viking, 1988), 262.

37. Quoted in Wilkerson, *Public Opinion and the Spanish-American War*, 126.

38. Quoted in Ibid., 125.

39. John L. Offner, *An Unwanted War* (Chapel Hill: University of North Carolina Press, 1992), 123.

40. Swanberg, *Citizen Hearst*, 163.

41. Quoted in G. J. A. O'Toole, *The Spanish War* (New York: W. W. Norton, 1984), 125.

42. Kennan, *American Diplomacy*, 15.

43. Quoted in Swanberg, *Citizen Hearst*, 171.

44. Brown, *The Correspondents' War*, 141.
45. Offner, *An Unwanted War*, 124.
46. Swanberg, *Citizen Hearst*, 171.
47. John Tebbel, *The Life and Good Times of William Randolph Hearst* (New York: E. P. Dutton, 1952), 190.
48. Quoted in Pringle, *Theodore Roosevelt*, 124.
49. Quoted in Mario R. DiNunzio, ed., *Theodore Roosevelt: An American Mind* (New York: St. Martin's, 1994), 177.
50. Ibid., 193.
51. Brown, *The Correspondents' War*, 145.
52. Quoted in Pringle, *Theodore Roosevelt*, 125.
53. Quoted in Swanberg, *Citizen Hearst*, 164.
54. Quoted in Ibid., 191.
55. Quoted in Ibid., 201.
56. Brown, *The Correspondents' War*, vi.
57. Kennan, *American Diplomacy*, 12.
58. Ibid., 16, 24.
59. Quoted in O'Toole, *The Spanish War*, 142.

CHAPTER 2

1. Don Oberdorfer, *Tet* (New York: Avon, 1972), 33.
2. Ibid., 200.
3. Kathleen J. Turner, *Lyndon Johnson's Dual War* (Chicago: University of Chicago Press, 1985), 217.
4. Quoted in Twentieth Century Fund Task Force on the Military and the Media, *Battle Lines* (New York: Priority Press, 1985), 67.
5. Clark Clifford, *Counsel to the President* (New York: Random House, 1991), 479.
6. Twentieth Century Fund, *Battle Lines*, 69.
7. Daniel C. Hallin, *The "Uncensored War"* (Berkeley: University of California Press, 1989), 171.
8. Quoted in Peter Arnett, *Live from the Battlefield* (New York: Simon and Schuster, 1994), 255.
9. Herbert Y. Schandler, *The Unmaking of a President* (Princeton: Princeton University Press, 1977), 81.
10. Twentieth Century Fund, *Battle Lines*, 62.
11. Ibid., 64.
12. Hallin, *The "Uncensored War,"* 173.
13. William C. Westmoreland, *A Soldier Reports* (Garden City, NY: Doubleday, 1976), 328.
14. Walter Lippmann, "Defeat," *Newsweek*, March 11, 1968, 25.
15. Quoted in Oberdorfer, *Tet*, 264.

16. Quoted in Ibid., 269.

17. Quoted in Ibid., 288.

18. Quoted in Turner, *Lyndon Johnson's Dual War*, 231.

19. Hallin, *The "Uncensored War,"* 169.

20. Quoted in Oberdorfer, *Tet*, 291.

21. Quoted in Townsend Hoopes, *The Limits of Intervention* (New York: David MacKay, 1969), 149.

22. Ibid.

23. Turner, *Lyndon Johnson's Dual War*, 219.

24. Oberdorfer, *Tet*, 259.

25. Ibid., 264.

26. "The War: Debate in a Vacuum," *Time*, March 15, 1968, 13.

27. Peter Braestrup, *Big Story* (Novato, CA: Presidio, 1994), 467.

28. Quoted in Schandler, *The Unmaking of a President*, 202.

29. Lyndon Baines Johnson, *The Vantage Point* (New York: Holt, Rinehart, and Winston, 1971), 384.

30. David Halberstam, *The Best and the Brightest* (New York: Random House, 1972), 648.

31. Clifford, *Counsel to the President*, 474.

32. Quoted in Schandler, *The Unmaking of a President*, 81.

33. Quoted in Ibid., 82.

34. Braestrup, *Big Story*, 471.

35. Ibid., 468.

36. Johnson, *The Vantage Point*, 383.

37. Schandler, *The Unmaking of a President*, 84.

38. Quoted in Clarence R. Wyatt, *Paper Soldiers* (New York: W. W. Norton, 1993), 186.

39. Hoopes, *The Limits of Intervention*, 147.

40. Ibid., 157.

41. Austin Ranney, *Channels of Power* (New York: Basic Books, 1983), 5.

42. Quoted in Robert J. Donovan and Ray Scherer, *Unsilent Revolution* (New York: Cambridge University Press, 1992), 102.

43. Quoted in Turner, *Lyndon Johnson's Dual War*, 232.

44. Quoted in Merle Miller, *Lyndon* (New York: G. P. Putnam's, 1980), 502.

45. Johnson, *The Vantage Point*, 415.

46. Stanley Karnow, *Vietnam: A History* (New York: Viking, 1983), 562.

47. Johnson, *The Vantage Point*, 416, 418.

48. Ibid., 437.

49. Quoted in Ranney, *Channels of Power*, 134.

50. Quoted in Clifford, *Counsel to the President*, 474.

51. Quoted in Schandler, *The Unmaking of a President*, 198.

52. Oberdorfer, *Tet*, 346.

53. Braestrup, *Big Story*, 508.

54. Ibid., 509, 517.

55. Ibid., 517.

56. Ibid., 505.

57. Clifford, *Counsel to the President*, 474.

58. Ann McDaniel and Evan Thomas, "The Rewards of Leadership," *Newsweek*, March 11, 1991, 30.

59. David Gergen, "The President's Finest Hour," *U.S. News & World Report*, March 4, 1991, 64.

60. Ann Reilly Dowd, "How Bush Decided," *Fortune*, February 11, 1991, 45.

CHAPTER 3

1. Quoted in Robert D. McFadden, Joseph B. Treaster, and Maurice Carroll, *No Hiding Place* (New York: Times Books, 1981), 234.

2. Donovan and Scherer, *Unsilent Revolution*, 145.

3. Quoted in Washington Post, *The Pursuit of the Presidency 1980* (New York: Berkley, 1980), 43.

4. Donovan and Scherer, *Unsilent Revolution*, 141.

5. Washington Post, *The Pursuit of the Presidency 1980*, 43.

6. Barry Rubin, *Paved with Good Intentions* (New York: Oxford University Press, 1980), 363.

7. Quoted in Frederic B. Hill, "Media Diplomacy," *Washington Journalism Review*, May 1981, 24.

8. Hamilton Jordan, *Crisis: The Last Year of the Carter Presidency* (New York: Putnam, 1982), 55.

9. Steven R. Weisman, "U.S. Aides, Shunned in Iran, Complain of TV Diplomacy," *New York Times*, December 11, 1979, A 4.

10. Dan Nimmo and James E. Combs, *Nightly Horrors* (Knoxville: University of Tennessee Press, 1985), 142.

11. James Deakin, *Straight Stuff* (New York: Morrow, 1984), 88.

12. "NBC Reporter Resigns Over Hostage Interview," *New York Times*, December 14, 1979, 6.

13. Les Brown, "NBC News Defends Interview with Hostage as 'Public Service,' " *New York Times*, December 12, 1979, 4.

14. Ibid.

15. Quoted in Hill, "Media Diplomacy," 24.

16. Quoted in Donovan and Scherer, *Unsilent Revolution*, 146.

17. Quoted in Don Oberdorfer, "Now That It's Over," *Washington Journalism Review*, May 1981, 38.

18. Donovan and Scherer, *Unsilent Revolution*, 142.

19. Hill, "Media Diplomacy," 27.

20. Michael J. Arlen, "The Air: Tourists in Teheran; or, Cameras in Command," *The New Yorker*, January 21, 1980, 98.

21. Donovan and Scherer, *Unsilent Revolution*, 147.

22. Weisman, "U.S. Aides, Shunned in Iran," A 4.

23. Quoted in Stansfield Turner, *Terrorism and Democracy* (Boston: Houghton Mifflin, 1991), 84.

24. Jack Anderson, "Assessing Carter's Caution in Crisis," *Washington Post*, January 7, 1980, B 12.

25. Donovan and Scherer, *Unsilent Revolution*, 150.

26. Quoted in McFadden, Treaster, and Carroll, *No Hiding Place*, 232.

27. Rubin, *Paved with Good Intentions*, 363.

28. Bill Green, "Iran and the Press: First Questions," *Washington Post*, January 23, 1981, A 16.

29. Jimmy Carter, *Keeping Faith* (New York: Bantam, 1982), 568.

30. Theodore H. White, *America in Search of Itself* (New York: Harper & Row, 1982), 417.

31. Quoted in John Bulloch and Harvey Morris, *No Friends But the Mountains* (New York: Oxford University Press, 1992), 30.

32. Daniel Schorr, "Ten Days that Shook the White House," *Columbia Journalism Review*, July/August 1991, 22.

33. Deborah Amos, "Foreign Policy by Popular Outrage," *Nieman Reports* Vol. 48, no. 2 (Summer 1994), 74.

34. Schorr, "Ten Days," 22.

35. Ibid., 23.

36. James A. Baker III, *The Politics of Diplomacy* (New York: Putnam's, 1995), 434.

37. Schorr, "Ten Days," 23.

38. Ibid.

39. Nik Gowing, "Real-Time Television Coverage of Armed Conflicts and Diplomatic Crises," Working Paper 94–1, Joan Shorenstein Barone Center, John F. Kennedy School of Government, Harvard University, June 1994, 38.

40. Amos, "Foreign Policy by Popular Outrage," 74.

41. Quoted in Walter Goodman, "The Images that Haunt Washington," *New York Times*, May 5, 1991, B 2.

42. Quoted in Schorr, "Ten Days," 23.

43. Goodman, "The Images that Haunt," B 2.

44. Schorr, "Ten Days," 23.

45. Amos, "Foreign Policy by Popular Outrage," 75.

46. Goodman, "The Images that Haunt," B 2.

47. Elizabeth Drew, *On the Edge* (New York: Simon and Schuster, 1994), 411.

48. R. W. Apple, Jr., "Shelling Gives Clinton Chance To Change," *New York Times*, February 8, 1994, A 1.

49. Quoted in Gowing, "Real-Time Television Coverage," 70.

50. Quoted in Ibid., 72.

51. Quoted in Ibid., 73.

52. Ibid., 74.

53. Quoted in Ibid., 28.

54. Ibid.

55. Philip Seib, "Coverage Shapes Bosnia Policy," *Dallas Morning News*, February 14, 1994, A 23.

56. Tom Post, "Blood Bath," *Newsweek*, February 14, 1994, 20.

57. Walter Goodman, "Inspiring Compassion, If Not Action," *New York Times*, May 6, 1993, B 4.

58. Quoted in Gowing, "Real-Time Television Coverage," 85.

59. Walter Goodman, "Re Somalia: How Much Did TV Shape Policy?" *New York Times*, December 8, 1992, C 16.

60. Quoted in Gowing, "Real-Time Television Coverage," 68.

61. Walter Goodman, "Silent Partner Emerging in Policy Councils: TV," *New York Times*, March 6, 1993, B 47.

62. Ibid.

63. Ibid.

64. George F. Kennan, "Somalia, Through a Glass Darkly," *New York Times*, September 30, 1993, A 23.

65. Goodman, "Silent Partner," B 47.

66. Goodman, "Re Somalia," C 16.

67. Drew, *On the Edge*, 319.

68. Ibid., 318.

69. Jacqueline Sharkey, "When Pictures Drive Foreign Policy," *American Journalism Review*, December 1993, 14.

70. Quoted in Ibid., 16.

71. Drew, *On the Edge*, 327.

72. Quoted in Sharkey, "When Pictures Drive Foreign Policy," 17.

73. Quoted in Ibid., 19.

74. Quoted in Gowing, "Real-Time Television Coverage," 20.

75. Quoted in Ibid.

CHAPTER 4

1. Bob Woodward, *The Commanders* (New York: Pocket Books, 1992), xviii.

2. Quoted in Stephen R. Graubard, *Mr. Bush's War* (New York: Hill and Wang, 1992), 10.

3. Jean Edward Smith, *George Bush's War* (New York: Henry Holt, 1992), 103.

4. Quoted in Jason DeParle, "Long Series of Military Decisions Led to Gulf War News Censorship," *New York Times*, May 5, 1991, 1.

5. Quoted in Gene Ruffini, "Press Failed To Challenge Rush to War," *Washington Journalism Review*, March 1991, 21.

6. Arthur E. Rowse, "Covering the Gulf War: The Guns of August," *Columbia Journalism Review*, March/April 1991, 27.

7. Lawrence Grossman, "A Television Plan for the Next War," *Nieman Reports*, Summer 1991, 28.

8. John Martin, "The Plan To Sell the War," on ABC News program "20/20," January 17, 1992.

9. John R. MacArthur, *Second Front* (New York: Hill and Wang, 1992), 47.

10. Ibid., 69.

11. Ibid., 70.

12. Jarol B. Manheim, *Strategic Public Diplomacy and American Foreign Policy* (New York: Oxford University Press, 1994), 54.

13. Woodward, *The Commanders*, 311.

14. MacArthur, *Second Front*, 96.

15. Quoted in Woodward, *The Commanders*, 331.

16. Ruffini, "Press Failed To Challenge," 21.

17. Michael Duffy and Dan Goodgame, *Marching in Place* (New York: Simon & Schuster, 1992), 148.

18. Ibid., 153.

19. Everette E. Dennis et al., *The Media at War* (New York: Gannett Foundation Media Center, 1991), 1.

20. Quoted in DeParle, "Long Series of Military Decisions," 1.

21. Quoted in Woodward, *The Commanders*, 130.

22. Ibid., 300.

23. Ibid., 364.

24. Quoted in Ibid., 130.

25. Quoted in W. Lance Bennett and David L. Paletz, eds., *Taken By Storm* (Chicago: University of Chicago Press, 1994), 17.

26. Graubard, *Mr. Bush's War*, 135.

27. Dennis et al., *The Media at War*, 68.

28. Ibid., 2.

29. Quoted in MacArthur, *Second Front*, 208.

30. Grossman, "A Television Plan," 29.

31. DeParle, "Long Series of Military Decisions," 1.

32. Ibid.

33. Sydney H. Schanberg, "Censoring for Political Security," *Washington Journalism Review*, March 1991, 23.

34. Hedrick Smith, ed., *The Media and the Gulf War* (Washington: Seven Locks, 1992), 8.

35. Quoted in Ibid., 33.

36. Quoted in Ibid., 15.

37. Mort Rosenblum, *Who Stole the News?* (New York: John Wiley, 1993), 123.

38. Schanberg, "Censoring for Political Security," 23.

39. Ibid.

40. David Lamb, "Pentagon Hardball," *Washington Journalism Review*, April 1991, 33.

41. Schanberg, "Censoring for Political Security," 23.

42. Dennis et al., *The Media at War*, 1.

43. Ibid., 70.

44. Quoted in Ed Siegel, "TV Coverage Would Add New Immediacy to War," *Chicago Tribune*, December 13, 1990, 45.

45. Walter Cronkite, "What Is There To Hide?" *Newsweek*, February 25, 1991, 43.

46. Grossman, "A Television Plan," 29.

47. Dennis et al., *The Media at War*, 63.

48. Ibid., 52.

49. DeParle, "Long Series of Military Decisions," 1.

50. Quoted in Rosenblum, *Who Stole the News?*, 122.

51. MacArthur, *Second Front*, 175.

52. Quoted in DeParle, "Long Series of Military Decisions," 1.

53. Lewis H. Lapham, "Trained Seals and Sitting Ducks," *Harper's Magazine*, May 1991, 10.

54. Quoted in DeParle, "Long Series of Military Decisions," 1.

55. Robert Harris, *Gotcha!: The Media, The Government and the Falklands Crisis* (London: Faber and Faber, 1983), 62.

56. Derrik Mercer, Geoff Mungham, and Kevin Williams, *The Fog of War* (London: Heinemann, 1987), 126.

57. Harris, *Gotcha!*, 62.

58. Quoted in Mercer, Mungham, and Williams, *The Fog of War*, 62.

59. Quoted in Ibid., 66.

60. Quoted in Leonard Downie, Jr., "How Britain Managed the News," *Washington Post*, August 20, 1982, B 2.

61. Quoted in Mercer, Mungham, and Williams, *The Fog of War*, 23.

62. Quoted in Harris, *Gotcha!*, 56.

63. Phillip Knightley, "The Falklands: How Brittania Ruled the News," *Columbia Journalism Review*, September/October 1982, 51.

64. Mercer, Mungham, and Williams, *The Fog of War*, 156.

65. Quoted in Michael Cockerell, *Live from Number 10* (London: Faber and Faber, 1988), 270.

66. Harris, *Gotcha!*, 60.

67. Glasgow University Media Group, *War and Peace News* (Milton Keynes, United Kingdom: Open University Press, 1985), 9.

68. Cockerell, *Live from Number 10*, 274.

69. Mercer, Mungham, and Williams, *The Fog of War*, 97.

70. Max Hastings and Simon Jenkins, *The Battle for the Falklands* (New York: W. W. Norton, 1983), 332.

71. Knightley, "The Falklands," 52.

72. Ibid., 51.

73. Ibid., 51.

74. Simon Jenkins, "When Soldiers Play Journalist and Journalists Play at Soldiers," *The Times* (London), May 10, 1982, 8.

75. Quoted in Harris, *Gotcha!*, 38.

76. Quoted in Ibid., 40.

77. Quoted in Ibid., 75.

78. Quoted in Ibid., 50.

79. Quoted in Cockerell, *Live from Number 10*, 271.

80. Quoted in Ibid.

81. Quoted in Ibid., 272.

82. Quoted in Ibid.

83. Quoted in Mercer, Mungham, and Williams, *The Fog of War*, 132.

84. Quoted in Cockerell, *Live from Number 10*, 270.

85. Mercer, Mungham, and Williams, *The Fog of War*, 59.

86. Ibid., 134.

87. "Oh, What a Lovely War," *The Economist*, June 26, 1982, 63.

88. Paul Eddy, Magnus Linklater, and the *Sunday Times* Insight Team, *The Falklands War* (London: Sphere Books, 1982), 214.

89. "Oh, What a Lovely War," 63.

90. Harris, *Gotcha!*, 40.

91. Quoted in Cockerell, *Live from Number 10*, 273.

92. Margaret Thatcher, *The Downing Street Years* (New York: HarperCollins, 1993), 184.

93. Cockerell, *Live from Number 10*, 275.

94. Denis Healey, *The Time of My Life* (New York: W. W. Norton, 1990), 495.

95. Quoted in Cockerell, *Live from Number 10*, 275.

96. Ibid., 277.

97. Quoted in Ibid.

98. Peter Jenkins, *Mrs. Thatcher's Revolution* (Cambridge, MA: Harvard University Press, 1988), 163.

99. Cockerell, *Live from Number 10*, 269.

100. Kenneth Harris, *Thatcher* (Boston: Little, Brown, 1988), 136.

101. Margaret Thatcher, *The Revival of Britain* (London: Aurum Press, 1989), 164.

102. Quoted in Downie, "How Britain Managed the News," B 2.

103. Quoted in Cockerell, *Live from Number 10*, 275.

CHAPTER 5

1. Quoted in Theodore C. Sorensen, *Kennedy* (New York: Bantam, 1966), 346.

2. Peter Wyden, *Bay of Pigs* (New York: Simon & Schuster, 1979), 46.

3. Arthur M. Schlesinger, Jr., *A Thousand Days* (Boston: Houghton Mifflin, 1965), 261.

4. Turner Catledge, *My Life and The Times* (New York: Harper & Row, 1971), 261.

5. Ibid.

6. Quoted in William McGaffin and Erwin Knoll, *Anything but the Truth* (New York: Putnam, 1968), 204.

7. Quoted in Wyden, *Bay of Pigs*, 154.

8. Tad Szulc, "Anti-Castro Units Trained To Fight at Florida Bases," *New York Times*, April 7, 1961, 1.

9. Harrison E. Salisbury, *Without Fear or Favor* (New York: Times Books, 1980), 163.

10. Pierre Salinger, *With Kennedy* (Garden City, NY: Doubleday, 1966), 146.

11. Quoted in Ibid.

12. Quoted in McGaffin and Knoll, *Anything but the Truth*, 206.

13. Quoted in Catledge, *My Life and The Times*, 260.

14. Ibid., 262.

15. Quoted in Ibid., 265.

16. James Reston, *Deadline* (New York: Random House, 1991), 325.

17. Ibid., 326.

18. Salinger, *With Kennedy*, 155.

19. *Public Papers of the Presidents of the United States: John F. Kennedy, 1961* (Washington: Government Printing Office, 1962), 336.

20. Ibid., 337.

21. Salinger, *With Kennedy*, 157.

22. Quoted in Ibid.

23. Schlesinger, *A Thousand Days*, 296.

24. Quoted in McGaffin and Knoll, *Anything but the Truth*, 205.

25. Catledge, *My Life and The Times*, 264.

26. Salinger, *With Kennedy*, 150.

27. Quoted in McGaffin and Knoll, *Anything but the Truth*, 208.

28. Quoted in Richard Reeves, *President Kennedy* (New York: Simon & Schuster, 1993), 339.

29. Theodore C. Sorensen, ed., *"Let the Word Go Forth"* (New York: Dell, 1991), 275.

30. Reeves, *President Kennedy*, 384.

31. Salinger, *With Kennedy*, 251.

32. Reston, *Deadline*, 294.

33. McGaffin and Knoll, *Anything but the Truth*, 207.

34. "Capital's Crisis Air Hints at Development on Cuba; Kennedy TV Talk Is Likely," *New York Times*, October 22, 1962, 1.

35. Quoted in Salisbury, *Without Fear or Favor*, 161.

36. Reeves, *President Kennedy*, 391.

37. Ibid., 424.

38. Quoted in Deakin, *Straight Stuff*, 180.

39. Salinger, *With Kennedy*, 292.

40. Quoted in Ibid., 285.

41. Quoted in Bernard C. Cohen, *The Press and Foreign Policy* (Princeton: Princeton University Press, 1963), 198.

42. Quoted in Salinger, *With Kennedy*, 287.

43. Quoted in Cohen, *The Press and Foreign Policy*, 199.

44. Jody Powell, *The Other Side of the Story* (New York: Morrow, 1984), 223.

45. Ben Bradlee, *A Good Life* (New York: Simon & Schuster, 1995), 453.

46. Charles B. Seib, "CIA's Media Connection," *Washington Post*, June 4, 1977, A 11.

47. John Ranelagh, *The Agency* (New York: Simon & Schuster, 1986), 602.

48. Salisbury, *Without Fear or Favor*, 540.

49. Ibid., 541.

50. Ibid., 544.

51. Ibid., 546.

52. Ibid., 555.

53. William Colby, *Honorable Men* (New York: Simon & Schuster, 1978), 416.

54. Ibid., 418.

55. Charles B. Seib, "Lessons from a Submerged CIA Story," *Washington Post*, October 29, 1977, A 13.

56. Bradlee, *A Good Life*, 470.

57. Quoted in Bob Woodward, *Veil* (New York: Simon & Schuster, 1987), 451.

58. Ibid., 462.

59. Bradlee, *A Good Life*, 474.

60. Ibid.

61. Katherine Winton Evans, "National Security and the Press: An Interview with CIA Chief William Casey," *Washington Journalism Review* July 1986, 15.

62. Quoted in Ranney, *Channels of Power*, 120.

63. Quoted in Elie Abel, *Leaking* (New York: Priority Press, 1987), 34.

64. Hedrick Smith, *The Power Game* (New York: Random House, 1988), 81.

65. Ibid., 84.

66. Quoted in Ibid., 440.

67. Walter Isaacson, "The 'Senior Official,' " *Washington Journalism Review*, November 1992, 30.

68. Quoted in Ibid.

69. Ibid.

70. Baker, *The Politics of Diplomacy*, 154.

71. Quoted in Abel, *Leaking*, 137.

72. Quoted in Ibid.
73. Marvin Kalb, *The Nixon Memo* (Chicago: University of Chicago Press, 1994), 67.
74. Ibid., 84.
75. Quoted in Ibid., 114.
76. Ibid., 159.
77. Ibid., 191.

CHAPTER 6

1. Quoted in Gowing, "Real-Time Television Coverage," 11.
2. Quoted in Edward R. Girardet, ed., *Somalia, Rwanda, and Beyond: The Role of the International Media in Wars and Humanitarian Crises* (Dublin: Crosslines Global Report and the Italian Academy for Advanced Studies at Columbia University, 1995), 150.
3. Danny Schechter, "South Africa: Where Did the Story Go?" *Africa Report*, March/April 1988, 28.
4. Jonathan Alter, "When the World Shrugs," *Newsweek*, April 25, 1994, 34.
5. Quoted in Girardet, *Somalia, Rwanda, and Beyond*, 136.
6. Quoted in Ibid., 158.
7. Donovan and Scherer, *Unsilent Revolution*, 156.
8. Peter Boyer, "Famine in Ethiopia," *Washington Journalism Review*, January 1985, 19.
9. Ibid., 21.
10. Quoted in Ibid.
11. Quoted in Ibid.
12. Quoted in Ibid., 20.
13. Quoted in Ibid., 21.
14. Donovan and Scherer, *Unsilent Revolution*, 158.
15. Quoted in Boyer, "Famine in Ethiopia," 19.
16. Quoted in Ibid., 21.
17. Quoted in Donovan and Scherer, *Unsilent Revolution*, 158.
18. Ibid.
19. Philip Gourevitch, "After the Genocide," *The New Yorker*, December 18, 1995, 78.
20. Jim Wooten, "Parachuting into Madness," *Columbia Journalism Review*, November/December 1994, 46.
21. Quoted in Girardet, *Somalia, Rwanda, and Beyond*, 157.
22. Quoted in Gourevitch, "After the Genocide," 78.
23. Quoted in Girardet, *Somalia, Rwanda, and Beyond*, 37.
24. Alter, "When the World Shrugs," 34.
25. Gourevitch, "After the Genocide," 79.
26. Girardet, *Somalia, Rwanda, and Beyond*, 205.

27. Quoted in Boyer, "Famine in Ethiopia," 21.

28. Quoted in Girardet, *Somalia, Rwanda, and Beyond*, 205.

29. Quoted in Ibid., 210.

30. John Maxwell Hamilton, *Main Street America and the Third World* (Washington: Seven Locks, 1986), 1.

31. Daniel Yankelovich and John Immerwahr, "The Rules of Public Engagement," in Daniel Yankelovich and I. M. Destler, eds., *Beyond the Beltway* (New York: W. W. Norton, 1994), 51.

32. American Assembly, "Final Report of the Eighty-Third American Assembly," in Daniel Yankelovich and I. M. Destler, eds., *Beyond the Beltway* (New York: W. W. Norton, 1994), 286.

33. Quoted in Bernard C. Cohen, *The Public's Impact on Foreign Policy* (Boston: Little, Brown, 1973), 108.

34. Charles W. Bailey, "Foreign Policy and the Provincial Press," in Simon Serfaty, ed., *The Media and Foreign Policy* (New York: St. Martin's, 1991), 182.

35. Quoted in Hamilton, *Main Street America*, x.

36. John Maxwell Hamilton, *Entangling Alliances* (Washington: Seven Locks, 1990), 22.

37. Yossi Shain, "Multicultural Foreign Policy," *Foreign Policy* Vol. 100, (Fall 1995), 70.

38. Ibid., 72.

CHAPTER 7

1. Av Westin, *Newswatch* (New York: Simon & Schuster, 1982), 22.

2. Reeves, *President Kennedy*, 211.

3. Michael R. Beschloss, *The Crisis Years* (New York: HarperCollins, 1991), 273.

4. Ibid., 275.

5. Ibid., 278.

6. Michael R. Beschloss and Strobe Talbott, *At the Highest Levels* (Boston: Little, Brown, 1993), 132.

7. Donovan and Scherer, *Unsilent Revolution*, 311.

8. Duffy and Goodgame, *Marching in Place*, 189.

9. Quoted in Beschloss and Talbott, *At the Highest Levels*, 135.

10. Quoted in Tom Shales, "Three Cheers in Berlin," *Washington Post*, November 13, 1989, B 1.

11. Ibid.

12. Zbigniew Brzezinski, *Out of Control* (New York: Macmillan, 1993), 50.

13. Michael Arlen, *Living-Room War* (New York: Penguin, 1982), 82.

14. Ibid., 83.

15. Richard Zoglin, "Live from the Middle East," *Time*, January 28, 1991, 70.

NOTES

167

16. Quoted in Robert Wiener, *Live from Baghdad* (New York: Doubleday, 1992), 253.

17. Ibid., 252.

18. Ibid., 194.

19. Quoted in Donovan and Scherer, *Unsilent Revolution*, 314.

20. Quoted in Ibid., 312.

21. Grossman, "A Television Plan," 27.

22. Quoted in Ibid., 28.

23. Ibid., 27.

24. Westin, *Newswatch*, 138.

25. Quoted in Ibid.

26. Beschloss and Talbott, *At the Highest Levels*, 422.

27. Ibid., 431.

28. Ibid., 435.

29. Quoted in David Hoffman, "Global Communications Network Was Pivotal in Defeat of Junta," *Washington Post*, August 23, 1991, A 27.

30. Quoted in Beschloss and Talbott, *At the Highest Levels*, 430.

31. Quoted in Ibid.

32. Duffy and Goodgame, *Marching in Place*, 194.

33. Donovan and Scherer, *Unsilent Revolution*, 317.

34. Lewis A. Friedland, *Covering the World* (New York: Twentieth Century Fund, 1992), 43.

35. Eduard Shevardnadze, "The Tragedy of Gorbachev," *Newsweek*, September 9, 1991, 30.

36. Baker, *The Politics of Diplomacy*, 520.

37. Beschloss and Talbott, *At the Highest Levels*, 430.

38. Friedland, *Covering the World*, 44.

39. Quoted in Beschloss and Talbott, *At the Highest Levels*, 438.

40. Ibid., 439.

41. Friedland, *Covering the World*, 4.

42. Walter Goodman, "Many Big Stories To Tell, but the Biggest of All Is China," *New York Times*, June 5, 1989, B 2.

43. Friedland, *Covering the World*, 6.

44. Reuven Frank, "On Tiananmen Square, Echoes of Chicago in '68," *New York Times*, June 4, 1989, A 23.

45. Tom Shales, "China: The Networks' Closing Chapter," *Washington Post*, June 21, 1989, G 1.

46. Duffy and Goodgame, *Marching in Place*, 184.

47. Tara Sonenshine, "The Revolution Has Been Televised," *Washington Post*, October 2, 1990, A 19.

48. Ibid.

49. Grossman, "A Television Plan," 30.

50. Tom Rosenstiel, "The Myth of CNN," *The New Republic*, August 22 and 29, 1994, 28.

51. Ibid., 33.

52. Gowing, "Real-Time Television Coverage," 17.

53. Quoted in Ibid., 85.

54. Howard Kurtz, "TV Viewers Join Military Critics of Media Spectacle on Beach," *Washington Post*, December 10, 1992, A 33.

55. Quoted in Ibid.

56. Kennan, "Somalia, Through a Glass Darkly," A 23.

CHAPTER 8

1. James F. Hoge, Jr., "The End of Predictability," *Media Studies Journal* vol. 7, no. 4 (Fall 1993), 2.

2. Quoted in Jon Vanden Heuvel, "For the Media, a Brave (and Scary) New World," *Media Studies Journal* vol. 7 no. 4 (Fall 1993), 11.

3. Bernard Gwertzman, "Memo to the *Times* Foreign Staff," *Media Studies Journal* vol. 7, no. 4 (Fall 1993), 34.

4. Ibid., 38.

5. Michael Mandelbaum, "Foreign Policy as Social Work," *Foreign Affairs* vol. 7, no. 1 (January/February 1996), 20.

6. Jack Matlock, "The Diplomat's View of the Press and Foreign Policy," *Media Studies Journal* vol. 7, no. 4 (Fall 1993), 53.

7. Quoted in Vanden Heuvel, "For the Media," 14.

8. Hoge, "The End of Predictability," 3.

9. Gwertzman, "Memo," 36.

10. Drew, *On the Edge*, 429.

11. Ibid., 334.

12. Louis D. Boccardi, "Redeploying a Global Journalistic Army," *Media Studies Journal* vol. 7, no. 4 (Fall 1993), 46.

13. Duffy and Goodgame, *Marching in Place*, 244.

14. Hoge, "The End of Predictability," 8.

15. Ronald Steel, "The Domestic Core of Foreign Policy," *Atlantic Monthly*, June 1995, 88.

16. Quoted in Vanden Heuvel, "For the Media," 19.

17. Quoted in Leon Hadar, "Covering the New World Disorder," *Columbia Journalism Review*, July/August 1994, 28.

18. "Situation, Mission, Execution," *The Economist*, December 24, 1994, 17.

19. Quoted in Sherry Ricchiardi, "Covering Carnage in the Balkans," *Washington Journalism Review*, November 1992, 20.

20. Drew, *On the Edge*, 144.

21. Quoted in Ricchiardi, "Covering Carnage," 21.

22. Roger Cohen, "In Bosnia, the War that Can't Be Seen," *New York Times*, December 25, 1994, Sec. 4, 4.

23. Quoted in Ricchiardi, "Covering Carnage," 21.

24. David Owen, *Balkan Odyssey* (New York: Harcourt Brace, 1995), 1.

25. Ibid., 257.

26. Ibid., 244.

27. Cohen, "In Bosnia," 4, 4.

28. Quoted in Michael Dobbs, "Foreign Policy by CNN," *Washington Post National Weekly Edition*, July 31, 1995, 24.

29. Quoted in Walter Goodman, "Images of Horror and Despair from the Balkans," *New York Times*, July 25, 1995, B 2.

30. Tom Post, "For Shame," *Newsweek*, July 31, 1995, 21.

31. Quoted in Laura Silber and Allan Little, *The Death of Yugoslavia* (London: Penguin/BBC, 1995), 275.

32. Quoted in Ibid., 276.

33. Gowing, "Real-Time Television Coverage," 63.

34. Silber and Little, *The Death of Yugoslavia*, 239.

35. Gowing, "Real-Time Television Coverage," 58.

CHAPTER 9

1. Steel, "The Domestic Core," 86.

2. Ibid., 87.

3. John E. Rielly, ed., *American Public Opinion and U.S. Foreign Policy* (Chicago: Chicago Council on Foreign Relations, 1995), 9–37.

4. Max Frankel, "Beyond the Shroud," *New York Times Magazine*, March 19, 1995, 30.

5. Ibid.

6. Quoted in Ibid.

7. Stephen Hess, "Our Foreign Failing," *Presstime*, February 1996, 26.

8. Max Frankel, "The Shroud," *New York Times Magazine*, November 27, 1994, 43.

9. Ibid., 42.

10. Matlock, "The Diplomat's View," 53.

11. Russell Watson, "Russia's TV War," *Newsweek*, February 6, 1995, 32.

12. Richard Parker, "The Future of Global Television News," Research Paper R-13, Joan Shorenstein Center, John F. Kennedy School of Government, Harvard University, September 1994, 22.

13. Jim Lederman, *Battle Lines* (New York: Henry Holt, 1992), 328.

14. "Holy Message from the Front," *The Economist*, February 25, 1995, 42.

15. Stephen Engelberg, "Spy Agency Under Siege," *New York Times*, December 29, 1994, A 10.

16. Quoted in Michael Dobbs, "The Year-End Report from Foggy Bottom," *Washington Post National Weekly Edition*, January 1, 1996, 18.

17. Anne Nelson, "World News: Truth and Consequences," *Columbia Journalism Review*, January/February 1995, 4.

18. Thomas L. Friedman, "Global Mandate," *New York Times*, March 5, 1995, E 15.

19. Quoted in Kenneth Jost, "Foreign Policy and Public Opinion," *CQ Researcher*, July 15, 1994, 617.

20. Quoted in Ibid.

21. David Briscoe, "Congressional Panel Grills Anchorman," Associated Press Wire, April 27, 1994.

22. Walter Lippmann, *Public Opinion* (New York: Free Press, 1965), 229.

Bibliography

BOOKS

Abel, Elie. *Leaking*. New York: Priority Press, 1987.

————. *The Missile Crisis*. New York: Bantam, 1966.

Adams, Valerie. *The Media and the Falklands Campaign*. New York: Macmillan, 1986.

Allen, W. B. *George Washington: A Collection*. Indianapolis: Liberty Classics, 1988.

Allison, Graham, and Gregory F. Treverton, eds. *Rethinking America's Security*. New York: W. W. Norton, 1992.

Arlen, Michael. *Living-Room War*. New York: Penguin, 1982.

Arnett, Peter. *Live from the Battlefield*. New York: Simon & Schuster, 1994.

Ash, Timothy Garton. *In Europe's Name*. New York: Random House, 1993.

Baker James A., III. *The Politics of Diplomacy*. New York: Putnam's, 1995.

Bennett, W. Lance, and David L. Paletz, eds. *Taken by Storm*. Chicago: University of Chicago Press, 1994.

Berry, Nicholas O. *Foreign Policy and the Press*. Westport, CT: Greenwood, 1990.

Beschloss, Michael R. *The Crisis Years*. New York: HarperCollins, 1991.

————, and Strobe Talbott. *At the Highest Levels*. Boston: Little, Brown, 1993.

Bradlee, Ben. *A Good Life*. New York: Simon & Schuster, 1995.

Braestrup, Peter. *Big Story*. Novato, CA: Presidio, 1994.

Brown, Charles H. *The Correspondents' War*. New York: Scribners, 1967.

Brzezinski, Zbigniew. *Out of Control*. New York: Macmillan, 1993.

Bulloch, John, and Harvey Morris. *No Friends But the Mountains*. New York: Oxford University Press, 1992.

Carter, Jimmy. *Keeping Faith.* New York: Bantam, 1982.

Cate, Curtis. *The Ides of August.* New York: M. Evans, 1978.

Catledge, Turner. *My Life and The Times.* New York: Harper & Row, 1971.

Clifford, Clark. *Counsel to the President.* New York: Random House, 1991.

Cockerell, Michael. *Live from Number 10.* London: Faber and Faber, 1988.

Cohen, Bernard C. *The Press and Foreign Policy.* Princeton: Princeton University Press, 1963.

————. *The Public's Impact on Foreign Policy.* Boston: Little, Brown, 1973.

Colby, William. *Honorable Men.* New York: Simon & Schuster, 1978.

Crowe, William J., Jr. *The Line of Fire.* New York: Simon and Schuster, 1993.

Deakin, James. *Straight Stuff.* New York: Morrow, 1984.

Dennis, Everette E., David Stebenne, John Pavlik, Mark Thalhimer, Craig LaMay, Dirk Smillie, Martha FitzSimon, Shirley Gazsi, and Seth Rachlin. *The Media at War.* New York: Gannett Foundation Media Center, 1991.

Dickie, John. *Inside the Foreign Office.* London: Chapmans, 1992.

DiNunzio, Mario R., ed. *Theodore Roosevelt: An American Mind.* New York: St. Martin's, 1994.

Dobson, John. *Reticent Expansionism.* Pittsburgh: Duquesne University Press, 1988.

Donovan, Robert J., and Ray Scherer. *Unsilent Revolution.* New York: Cambridge University Press, 1992.

Drew, Elizabeth. *On the Edge.* New York: Simon and Schuster, 1994.

Duffy, Michael, and Dan Goodgame. *Marching in Place.* New York: Simon & Schuster, 1992.

Dulles, Allen. *The Craft of Intelligence.* New York: Signet, 1965.

Eddy, Paul, Magnus Linklater, and the Sunday Times Insight Team. *The Falklands War.* London: Sphere Books, 1982.

Emery, Michael, and Edwin Emery. *The Press and America.* 7th ed. Englewood Cliffs, NJ: Prentice Hall, 1992.

Freedom Forum Media Studies Center Research Group, *The Media and Foreign Policy in the Post-Cold War World.* New York: Freedom Forum Media Studies Center, 1993.

Friedland, Lewis A. *Covering the World.* New York: Twentieth Century Fund, 1992.

Girardet, Edward R., ed. *Somalia, Rwanda, and Beyond: The Role of the International Media in Wars and Humanitarian Crises. Crosslines* Special Report 1. Dublin: *Crosslines Global Report* and the Italian Academy for Advanced Studies at Columbia University, 1995.

Glasgow University Media Group. *War and Peace News.* Milton Keynes, United Kingdom: Open University Press, 1985.

Gorbachev, Mikhail. *The August Coup.* New York: HarperCollins, 1991.

Graubard, Stephen R. *Mr. Bush's War.* New York: Hill and Wang, 1992.

Halberstam, David. *The Best and the Brightest.* New York: Random House, 1972.

Hallin, Daniel C. *The "Uncensored War."* Berkeley: University of California Press, 1989.

Hamilton, John Maxwell. *Entangling Alliances.* Washington: Seven Locks, 1990.

―――. *Main Street America and the Third World.* Washington: Seven Locks, 1986.

Harris, Kenneth. *Thatcher.* Boston: Little, Brown, 1988.

Harris, Robert. *Gotcha!: The Media, the Government and the Falklands Crisis.* London: Faber and Faber, 1983.

Hastings, Max, and Simon Jenkins. *The Battle for the Falklands.* New York: W. W. Norton, 1983.

Healey, Denis. *The Time of My Life.* New York: W. W. Norton, 1990.

Hilsman, Roger. *George Bush vs. Saddam Hussein.* Novato, CA: Lyford, 1992.

―――. *To Move a Nation.* Garden City, NY: Doubleday, 1967.

Hoopes, Townsend. *The Limits of Intervention.* New York: David McKay, 1969.

Jenkins, Peter. *Mrs. Thatcher's Revolution.* Cambridge, MA: Harvard University Press, 1988.

Johnson, Lyndon Baines. *The Vantage Point.* New York: Holt, Rinehart, and Winston, 1971.

Jordan, Hamilton. *Crisis: The Last Year of the Carter Presidency.* New York: Putnam, 1982.

Kagan, Donald. *On the Origins of War.* New York: Doubleday, 1995.

Kalb, Marvin. *The Nixon Memo.* Chicago: University of Chicago Press, 1994.

Karnow, Stanley. *Vietnam: A History.* New York: Viking, 1983.

Kearns, Doris. *Lyndon Johnson and the American Dream.* New York: Harper & Row, 1976.

Kennan, George F. *American Diplomacy.* New York: New American Library, 1952.

―――. *The Cloud of Danger.* Boston: Atlantic-Little, Brown, 1977.

―――. *Memoirs 1925–1950.* Boston: Atlantic-Little, Brown, 1967.

―――. *Memoirs 1950–1963.* Boston: Atlantic-Little, Brown, 1972.

―――. *Realities of American Foreign Policy.* New York: W. W. Norton, 1966.

Knightley, Phillip. *The First Casualty.* New York: Harcourt Brace Jovanovich, 1975.

Lederman, Jim. *Battle Lines.* New York: Henry Holt, 1992.

Leech, Margaret. *In the Days of McKinley.* New York: Harper and Brothers, 1959.

Lippmann, Walter. *Public Opinion.* New York: Free Press, 1965.

―――. *U.S. Foreign Policy.* Boston: Little, Brown, 1943.

MacArthur, John R. *Second Front.* New York: Hill and Wang, 1992.

Manheim, Jarol B. *Strategic Public Diplomacy and American Foreign Policy.* New York: Oxford University Press, 1994.

McCain, Thomas A., and Leonard Shyles, eds. *The 1,000 Hour War.* Westport, CT: Greenwood, 1994.

McFadden, Robert D., Joseph B. Treaster, and Maurice Carroll. *No Hiding Place.* New York: Times Books, 1981.

McGaffin, William, and Erwin Knoll. *Anything but the Truth.* New York: Putnam, 1968.

Mercer, Derrik, Geoff Mungham, and Kevin Williams. *The Fog of War.* London: Heinemann, 1987.

Miller, Merle. *Lyndon.* New York: G.P. Putnam's, 1980.

Milton, Joyce. *The Yellow Kids.* New York: Harper & Row, 1989.

Morris, Edmund. *The Rise of Theodore Roosevelt.* New York: Coward, McCann, and Geoghegan, 1979.

Morrison, David E., and Howard Tumber. *Journalists at War.* London: Sage, 1988.

Negrine, Ralph. *Politics and the Mass Media in Britain.* London: Routledge, 1989.

Nimmo, Dan, and James E. Combs. *Nightly Horrors.* Knoxville: University of Tennessee Press, 1985.

Oberdorfer, Don. *Tet.* New York: Avon, 1972.

Offner, John L. *An Unwanted War.* Chapel Hill: University of North Carolina Press, 1992.

O'Toole, G. J. A. *The Spanish War.* New York: W. W. Norton, 1984.

Owen, David. *Balkan Odyssey.* New York: Harcourt Brace, 1995.

Powell, Colin. *My American Journey.* New York: Random House, 1995.

Powell, Jody. *The Other Side of the Story.* New York: Morrow, 1984.

Pringle, Henry F. *Theodore Roosevelt.* New York: Harcourt, Brace, and World, 1956.

Public Papers of the Presidents of the United States: John F. Kennedy, 1961. Washington: Government Printing Office, 1962.

Ranelagh, John. *The Agency.* New York: Simon & Schuster, 1986.

Ranney, Austin. *Channels of Power.* New York: Basic Books, 1983.

Reeves, Richard. *President Kennedy.* New York: Simon & Schuster, 1993.

Reston, James. *The Artillery of the Press.* New York: Council on Foreign Relations/Harper & Row, 1967.

————. *Deadline.* New York: Random House, 1991.

Rielly, John E., ed. *American Public Opinion and U.S. Foreign Policy 1995.* Chicago: Chicago Council on Foreign Relations, 1995.

Rosenblum, Mort. *Who Stole the News?* New York: John Wiley, 1993.

Rozell, Mark J. *The Press and the Carter Presidency.* Boulder, CO: Westview, 1989.

Rubin, Barry. *Paved with Good Intentions.* New York: Oxford University Press, 1980.

Said, Edward. *Covering Islam.* New York: Pantheon, 1981.

Salinger, Pierre. *With Kennedy.* Garden City, NY: Doubleday, 1966.

Salisbury, Harrison E. *Without Fear or Favor.* New York: Times Books, 1980.

Schandler, Herbert Y. *The Unmaking of a President.* Princeton: Princeton University Press, 1977.

Schlesinger, Arthur M., Jr. *A Thousand Days*. Boston: Houghton Mifflin, 1965.

Serfaty, Simon, ed. *The Media and Foreign Policy*. New York: St. Martin's, 1991.

Shultz, George P. *Turmoil and Triumph*. New York: Scribners, 1993.

Silber, Laura, and Allan Little. *The Death of Yugoslavia*. London: Penguin/BBC, 1995.

Smith, Hedrick, ed. *The Media and the Gulf War*. Washington: Seven Locks, 1992.

————. *The Power Game*. New York: Random House, 1988.

Smith, Jean Edward. *George Bush's War*. New York: Henry Holt, 1992.

Smith, Perry M. *How CNN Fought the War*. New York: Birch Lane, 1991.

Sorensen, Theodore C. *Kennedy*. New York: Bantam, 1966.

————, ed. *"Let the Word Go Forth."* New York: Dell, 1991.

Steel, Ronald. *Walter Lippmann and the American Century*. Boston: Atlantic-Little, Brown, 1980.

Stephens, Mitchell. *A History of News*. New York: Viking, 1988.

Swanberg, W. A. *Citizen Hearst*. New York: Scribners, 1961.

Taylor, Philip M. *War and the Media*. Manchester, United Kingdom: Manchester University Press, 1992.

Tebbel, John. *The Life and Good Times of William Randolph Hearst*. New York: E. P. Dutton, 1952.

Thatcher, Margaret. *The Downing Street Years*. New York: HarperCollins, 1993.

————. *The Revival of Britain*. London: Aurum Press, 1989.

Thomas, Evan. *The Very Best Men*. New York: Simon & Schuster, 1995.

Tucker, Robert W., and David C. Hendrickson. *The Imperial Temptation*. New York: Council on Foreign Relations, 1992.

Turner, Kathleen J. *Lyndon Johnson's Dual War*. Chicago: University of Chicago Press, 1985.

Turner, Stansfield. *Terrorism and Democracy*. Boston: Houghton Mifflin, 1991.

Twentieth Century Fund Task Force on the Military and the Media. *Battle Lines*. New York: Priority Press, 1985.

Vance, Cyrus. *Hard Choices*. New York: Simon and Schuster, 1983.

Washington Post. *The Pursuit of the Presidency 1980*. New York: Berkley, 1980.

Westin, Av. *Newswatch*. New York: Simon & Schuster, 1982.

Westmoreland, William C. *A Soldier Reports*. Garden City, NY: Doubleday, 1976.

White, Theodore H. *America in Search of Itself*. New York: Harper & Row, 1982.

Wiener, Robert. *Live from Baghdad*. New York: Doubleday, 1992.

Wilkerson, Marcus M. *Public Opinion and the Spanish-American War*. New York: Russell and Russell, 1932.

Wisan, Joseph E. *The Cuban Crisis as Reflected in the New York Press*. New York: Columbia University Press, 1934.

Woodward, Bob. *The Commanders*. New York: Pocket Books, 1992.

————. *Veil*. New York: Simon & Schuster, 1987.

Wyatt, Clarence R. *Paper Soldiers*. New York: W. W. Norton, 1993.
Wyden, Peter. *Bay of Pigs*. New York: Simon & Schuster, 1979.
Yankelovich, Daniel and I. M. Destler, eds. *Beyond the Beltway*. New York: W. W. Norton, 1994.

ARTICLES, PAPERS, ETC.

Alter, Jonathan. "Unwilling Informants?" *Newsweek*, June 26, 1989, 29.
————. "When the World Shrugs." *Newsweek*, April 25, 1994, 34.
Altheide, David. "The Failure of Network News." *Washington Journalism Review*, May, 1981, 28.
American Assembly. "Final Report of the Eighty-Third American Assembly." In *Beyond the Beltway*, edited by Daniel Yankelovich and I. M. Destler. New York: W. W. Norton, 1994, 279.
Amos, Deborah. "Foreign Policy by Popular Outrage." *Nieman Reports*, Summer 1994, 74.
Anderson, Jack. "Assessing Carter's Caution in Crisis." *Washington Post*, January 7, 1980, B 12.
Apple, R. W. Jr. "Shelling Gives Clinton Chance to Change." *New York Times*, February 8, 1994, A 1.
Arlen, Michael J. "The Air: Tourists in Teheran; or, Cameras in Command." *The New Yorker*, January 21, 1980, 98.
Atkinson, Rick. "With Deliberate Force in Bosnia." *Washington Post National Weekly Edition*, November 27, 1995, 6.
Bailey, Charles W. "Foreign Policy and the Provincial Press." In *The Media and Foreign Policy*, edited by Simon Serfaty. New York: St. Martin's, 1991, 179.
Baker, Brent. "Decisions at the Speed of TV Satellites." *Vital Speeches*, July 15, 1992, 581.
Barnett, Steven. "Boundaries of Taste." *New Statesman & Society*, June 23, 1989, 43.
Beschloss, Michael R. "The Video Vise." *Washington Post*, May 2, 1993, C 1.
Boccardi, Louis D. "Redeploying a Global Journalistic Army." *Media Studies Journal* vol. 7, no. 4 (Fall 1993), 41.
Boyer, Peter. "Famine in Ethiopia." *Washington Journalism Review*, January 1985, 19.
Briscoe, David. "Congressional Panel Grills Anchorman." Associated Press Wire, April 27, 1994.
Brown, Les. "NBC News Defends Interview with Hostage as 'Public Service.'" *New York Times*, December 12, 1979, 4.
Carmody, Deirdre. "Number of U.S. Journalists in Iran Already Reduced." *New York Times*, April 18, 1980, A 11.

————. "Some News Groups Knew of 6 in Hiding." *New York Times*, January 31, 1980, A 10.

Cohen, Roger. "In Bosnia, the War that Can't Be Seen." *New York Times*, December 25, 1994, Sec. 4, 4.

Cronkite, Walter. "What Is There To Hide?" *Newsweek*, February 25, 1991, 43.

Daley, Steve. "Gulf War May Be Becoming More Like Vietnam Than Its Managers Realize." *Chicago Tribune*, January 27, 1991, 45.

DeParle, Jason. "Long Series of Military Decisions Led to Gulf War News Censorship." *New York Times*, May 5, 1991, 1.

Dobbs, Michael. "Foreign Policy by CNN." *Washington Post National Weekly Edition*, July 31, 1995, 24.

————. "The Year-End Report from Foggy Bottom." *Washington Post National Weekly Edition*, January 1, 1996, 18.

"Does Television Distort Public Opinion on Foreign Policy?" *CQ Researcher*, July 15, 1994, 617.

Dowd, Ann Reilly. "How Bush Decided." *Fortune*, February 11, 1991, 45.

Downie, Leonard, Jr. "How Britain Managed the News." *Washington Post*, August 20, 1982, B 2.

Eldon, Stewart. "From Quill Pen to Satellite." Occasional paper, Royal Institute of International Affairs (London), 1994.

"Elizabeth or Boadicea?" *The Economist*. May 1, 1982, 11.

Engelberg, Stephen. "Spy Agency Under Siege." *New York Times*, December 29, 1994, A 1.

Evans, Katherine Winton. "National Security and the Press: An Interview with CIA Chief William Casey." *Washington Journalism Review* (July 1986): 14.

Fitzwater, Marlin. "Real Time Communications and Diplomacy." Lecture delivered to Program in Presidential Rhetoric, 1994 Fall Lecture Series, Texas A&M University, September 29, 1994.

Frank, Reuven. "On Tiananmen Square, Echoes of Chicago in '68." *New York Times*, June 4, 1989, A 23.

Frankel, Max. "Beyond the Shroud." *New York Times Magazine*, March 19, 1995, 30.

————. "The Shroud." *New York Times Magazine*, November 27, 1994, 42.

Friedman, Thomas L. "Global Mandate." *New York Times*, March 5, 1995, E 15.

Gergen, David. "The President's Finest Hour." *U.S. News & World Report*, March 4, 1991, 64.

Goodman, Walter. "Images of Horror and Despair from the Balkans." *New York Times*, July 25, 1995, B 2.

————. "The Images that Haunt Washington." *New York Times*, May 5, 1991, H 33.

————. "Inspiring Compassion, If Not Action." *New York Times*, May 6, 1993, B 4.

——— . "Many Big News Stories to Tell, but the Biggest of All Is China." *New York Times*, June 5, 1989, B 2.

——— . "Re Somalia: How Much Did TV Shape Policy?" *New York Times*, December 8, 1992, C 16.

——— . "Silent Partner Emerging in Policy Councils: TV." *New York Times*, March 6, 1993, B 47.

Gordon, Andrew C. "Journalism and the Internet." *Media Studies Journal* vol. 9, no. 3 (Summer 1995), 173.

Gourevitch, Philip. "After the Genocide." *The New Yorker*, December 18, 1995, 78.

Gowing, Nik. "Behind the CNN Factor." *Washington Post*, July 31, 1994, C 1.

——— . "Real-Time Television Coverage of Armed Conflicts and Diplomatic Crises." Working Paper 94–1, Joan Shorenstein Barone Center, John F. Kennedy School of Government, Harvard University, June 1994.

Green, Bill. "Iran and the Press: First Questions." *Washington Post*, January 23, 1981, A 16.

Grossman, Lawrence. "A Television Plan for the Next War." *Nieman Reports*, Summer 1991, 27.

Gwertzman, Bernard. "Memo to the *Times* Foreign Staff." *Media Studies Journal* vol. 7 no. 4, (Fall 1993): 33.

Hadar, Leon. "Covering the New World Disorder." *Columbia Journalism Review*, July/August 1994, 26.

Hershman, Robert. "Crash Course for the Hostage Families." *Columbia Journalism Review*, March/April 1981, 25.

Hess, Stephen. "Our Foreign Failing." *Presstime*, February, 1996, 26.

Hill, Frederic B. "Media Diplomacy." *Washington Journalism Review*, May 1981, 23.

Hoffman, David. "Global Communications Network Was Pivotal in Defeat of Junta." *Washington Post*, August 23, 1991, A 27.

Hoge, James F., Jr. "The End of Predictability." *Media Studies Journal* vol. 7, no. 4 (Fall 1993), 1.

"Holy Message from the Front." *The Economist*, February 25, 1995, 42.

Isaacson, Walter. "The 'Senior Official.' " *Washington Journalism Review* November, 1992, 30.

Izyumov, Alexei. "Coup Unites Soviet Media." *The Quill*, January/February 1992, 27.

Jenkins, Simon. "When Soldiers Play Journalist and Journalists Play at Soldiers." *The Times* (London), May 10, 1982, 8.

Jost, Kenneth. "Foreign Policy and Public Opinion." *CQ Researcher*, July 15, 1994, 601.

Kennan, George F. "Somalia, Through a Glass Darkly." *New York Times*, September 30, 1993, A 23.

Knightley, Phillip. "The Falklands: How Brittania Ruled the News." *Columbia Journalism Review*, September/October 1982, 51.

Kurtz, Howard. "TV Viewers Join Military Critics of Media Spectacle on Beach." *Washington Post,* December 10, 1992, A 33.

Lamb, David. "Pentagon Hardball." *Washington Journalism Review,* April 1991, 33.

Lapham, Lewis H. "Trained Seals and Sitting Ducks." *Harper's Magazine,* May 1991, 10.

Lippmann, Walter. "'Defeat.'" *Newsweek,* March 11, 1968, 25.

MacNeil, Robert. "The Flickering Images that May Drive Presidents." *Media Studies Journal* vol. 9, no. 1 (Winter 1995), 121.

Mandelbaum, Michael. "Foreign Policy as Social Work." *Foreign Affairs* vol. 75, no. 1 (January/February 1996), 16.

Martin, John. "The Plan To Sell the War." ABC News program "20/20," January 17, 1992.

Matlock, Jack. "The Diplomat's View of the Press and Foreign Policy." *Media Studies Journal* vol. 7, no. 4 (Fall 1993), 49.

McDaniel, Ann, and Evan Thomas. "The Rewards of Leadership." *Newsweek,* March 11, 1991, 30.

"NBC Reporter Resigns Over Hostage Interview." *New York Times,* December 14, 1979, 6.

Nelson, Anne. "World News: Truth and Consequences." *Columbia Journalism Review,* January/February 1995, 4.

Oberdorfer, Don. "Now That It's Over." *Washington Journalism Review,* May 1981, 37.

O'Connor, John J. "TV News Faces Own Crisis in Iranian Situation." *New York Times,* December 20, 1979, C 26.

"Oh, What a Lovely War." *The Economist,* June 26, 1982, 63.

Parker, Richard. "The Future of Global Television News." Research Paper R-13, Joan Shorenstein Barone Center, John F. Kennedy School of Government, Harvard University, September 1994.

Peterzell, Jay. "The Government Shuts Up." *Columbia Journalism Review,* July/August 1982, 31.

Post, Tom. "Blood Bath." *Newsweek,* February 14, 1994, 20.

———. "For Shame." *Newsweek,* July 31, 1995, 21.

Ricchiardi, Sherry. "Covering Carnage in the Balkans." *Washington Journalism Review,* November 1992, 18.

Rosenstiel, Tom. "The Myth of CNN." *The New Republic,* August 22 and 29, 1994, 27.

Rowse, Arthur E. "Covering the Gulf War: The Guns of August." *Columbia Journalism Review,* March/April 1991, 25.

Ruffini, Gene. "Press Failed To Challenge the Rush to War." *Washington Journalism Review,* March 1991, 21.

Schanberg, Sydney H. "Censoring for Political Security." *Washington Journalism Review,* March 1991, 23.

Schechter, Danny. "South Africa: Where Did the Story Go?" *Africa Report*, March/April 1988, 27.

Schorr, Daniel. "Ten Days that Shook the White House." *Columbia Journalism Review*, July/August 1991, 21.

Seib, Charles B. "CIA's Media Connection." *Washington Post*, June 4, 1977, A 11.

————. "CIA and the Press: No 'Natural Affinity.' " *Washington Post*, January 6, 1978, A 13.

————. "CIA and Press 'Pollution' Abroad." *Washington Post*, December 10, 1976, A 21.

————. "The Confusing Coverage of the Submarine Story." *Washington Post*, March 27, 1975, A 23.

————. "Lessons from a Submerged CIA Story." *Washington Post*, October 29, 1977, A 13.

————. "News Business, Spy Business." *Washington Post*, January 30, 1976, A 23.

Seib, Philip. "Coverage Shapes Bosnia Policy." *Dallas Morning News*, February 14, 1994, A 23.

Shain, Yossi. "Multicultural Foreign Policy," *Foreign Policy* no. 100 (Fall 1995) 69.

Shales, Tom. "CBS's Unexpected China Coup." *Washington Post*, May 20, 1989, C 1.

————. "China: The Networks' Closing Chapter." *Washington Post*, June 21, 1989, G 1.

————. "Three Cheers in Berlin." *Washington Post*, November 13, 1989, B 1.

Sharkey, Jacqueline. "When Pictures Drive Foreign Policy." *American Journalism Review*, December 1993, 14.

Shevardnadze, Eduard. "The Tragedy of Gorbachev." *Newsweek*, September 9, 1991, 30.

Siegel, Ed. "TV Coverage Would Add New Immediacy to War." *Chicago Tribune*, December 13, 1990, 45.

Silverstein, Ken. "Follow the Leader." *American Journalism Review*, November 1993, 30.

"Situation, Mission, Execution." *The Economist*, December 24, 1994, 17.

Sonenshine, Tara. "The Revolution Has Been Televised." *Washington Post*, October 2, 1990, A 19.

Steel, Ronald. "The Domestic Core of Foreign Policy." *Atlantic Monthly*, June 1995, 85.

"The Soviet Coup and the Press." *Editor & Publisher*, August 24, 1991, 10.

Szulc, Tad. "Anti-Castro Units Trained To Fight at Florida Bases." *New York Times*, April 7, 1961, 1.

"Thatcher Attacks Media Coverage." *The Times* (London), May 7, 1982, 5.

Vanden Heuvel, Jon. "For the Media, a Brave (and Scary) New World." *Media Studies Journal* vol. 7, no. 4 (Fall 1993), 11.

"Voting for a Spectator's War." *The Economist*, May 1, 1982, 12.

Walker, Graham. "Reality in Real Time?" (unpublished paper).

"The War: Debate in a Vacuum." *Time*, March 15, 1968, 13.

Watson, Russell. "Russia's TV War." *Newsweek*, February 6, 1995, 30.

Weisman, Steven R. "U.S. Aides, Shunned in Iran, Complain of TV Diplomacy." *New York Times*, December 11, 1979, A 4.

Wicker, Tom. "'Marketing' the War." *New York Times*, May 8, 1991, A 23.

Wooten, Jim. "Parachuting into Madness." *Columbia Journalism Review*, November/December 1994, 46.

Yankelovich, Daniel and Immerwahr, John. "The Rules of Public Engagement." in *Beyond the Beltway*, edited by Daniel Yaukelovich and I. M. Destler. New York, W. W. Norton, 1994, 43.

Yardley, Jonathan. "In the Soviet Union, the Tube Test." *Washington Post*, August 26, 1991, C2.

Zoglin, Richard. "Live from the Middle East." *Time*, January 28, 1991, 69.

Index

ABOUT THE AUTHOR

PHILIP SEIB is Professor of Journalism at Southern Methodist University. He is a columnist for the *Dallas Morning News* and political analyst for WFAA Television, the ABC affiliate in Dallas. He is the author of eight other books, including *Campaigns and Conscience: The Ethics of Political Journalism* (Praeger, 1994).

CPSIA information can be obtained
at www.ICGtesting.com
Printed in the USA
FFOW02n1046150815
16012FF